DISNEYANA

DISNEYANA

CLASSIC COLLECTIBLES 1928–1958

ROBERT HEIDE AND **JOHN GILMAN**

A WELCOME BOOK

Disney
——
EDITIONS

NEW YORK

PAGE 2: A MADE IN JAPAN, HAND-PAINTED BISQUE TOOTHBRUSH HOLDER FEATURES MICKEY MOUSE AND MINNIE MOUSE SEATED ON A COUCH WITH PLUTO AT THEIR FEET. IMPORTED IN THE 1930S BY GEORGE BORGFELDT CORP. PAGE 3: FOUR-TUBE MICKEY MOUSE TABLE RADIO, WITH MICKEY PLAYING MUSICAL INSTRUMENTS ON ALL FOUR SIDES, IS MADE OF PRESSED WOOD SYROCO. MADE IN 1933 BY EMERSON RADIO AND PHONOGRAPH CO.

Principal photography by John Gilman. Photographs courtesy of Ted Hake, York, PA: page 52 (all), 53 (all), 57 (top), 60 (bottom right), 70 (bottom), 73 (bottom), 80 (bottom), 96 (top right), 101 (top right), 128 (bottom, far right), 131 (center), 136 (lower left, both), 137 (upper right, both), 162 (right), 185 (top, both), 190 (top), 192 (right). Photographs courtesy of Ivy Wharton: page 36 (all), 39, 40, 41 (bottom), and 43. Peter Pan dolls and figurines on page 189 are from the collection of Nancy Keller, New York City.

Produced by Welcome Enterprises, Inc.
588 Broadway, New York, New York 10012
Project Director: H. Clark Wakabayashi
Designer: Gregory Wakabayashi
Hyperion Editors: Christine Archibald, Lesley Krauss

Heide, Robert
        Disneyana : classic collectibles, 1928–1958 / by Robert Heide and John Gilman
        p. cm.
        Includes bibliographical references (p.).
        ISBN 0-7868-5376-X
        1. Walt Disney Productions--Collectibles. I. Gilman, John, 1941–. II. Title.
        NK808.H345 1994
        741.5' 09794' 93--dc20   94-13673
                                                                  CIP

PAPERBACK EDITION
Printed and bound in Japan by Toppan Printing Co., Inc.
10 9 8 7 6 5 4 3 2 1

Acknowledgments

For their help and support the authors thank:

Bob Miller at Hyperion; Wendy Lefkon and Jody Revenson at Disney Editions; Dave Smith and his staff at the Walt Disney Archives; Clark Wakabayashi, Gregory Wakabayashi, and Jacinta O'Halloran of Welcome Enterprises; Sara Baysinger; Kay Kamen's daughter June Gitlin, his grandson Bill Prensky, and his longtime assistant Ivy Wharton (nee Ivener).

Bill Wallace at the Worcester Historical Museum in Massachusetts; Bill Blackbeard, founder of the San Francisco Academy of Comic Art; Second Childhood in Greenwich Village; Fantasies Come True in Los Angeles; Oddtiques and the Sadagursky's Happy Days.

The Collectors: Mel Birnkrant, John Fawcett, Ward Kimball, Ed and Elaine Levin, Robert Lesser, Nipser Mackey, Henry Mazzeo, Kim and Julie McEuen, Stefan Sztybel, Phillip Raia, Elliot Sherman, Bernard C. Shine, Doug and Pat Wengel.

Ted Hake of Hake's Americana and Collectibles, P.O. Box 1444, York, PA 17405 www.hakes.com

Also by Robert Heide and John Gilman:

Mickey Mouse: The Evolution, The Legend, The Phenomenon!
The Mickey Mouse Watch: From the Beginning of Time
New Jersey: Art of the State
Home Front America
Greenwich Village: A Primo Guide to Eating, Drinking and Making Merry in True Bohemia
O' New Jersey—Day Tripping, Back Roads, Eateries and Funky Adventures
Popular Art Deco: Depression Era Style and Design
Box-Office Buckaroos: The Cowboy Hero from the Wild West Show to the Silver Screen
Starstruck: The Wonderful World of Movie Memorabilia
Cartoon Collectibles: 50 Years of Dime-Store Memorabilia
Cowboy Collectibles
Dime-Store Dream Parade: Popular Culture 1925–1955

CONTENTS

INTRODUCTION ◆ 7

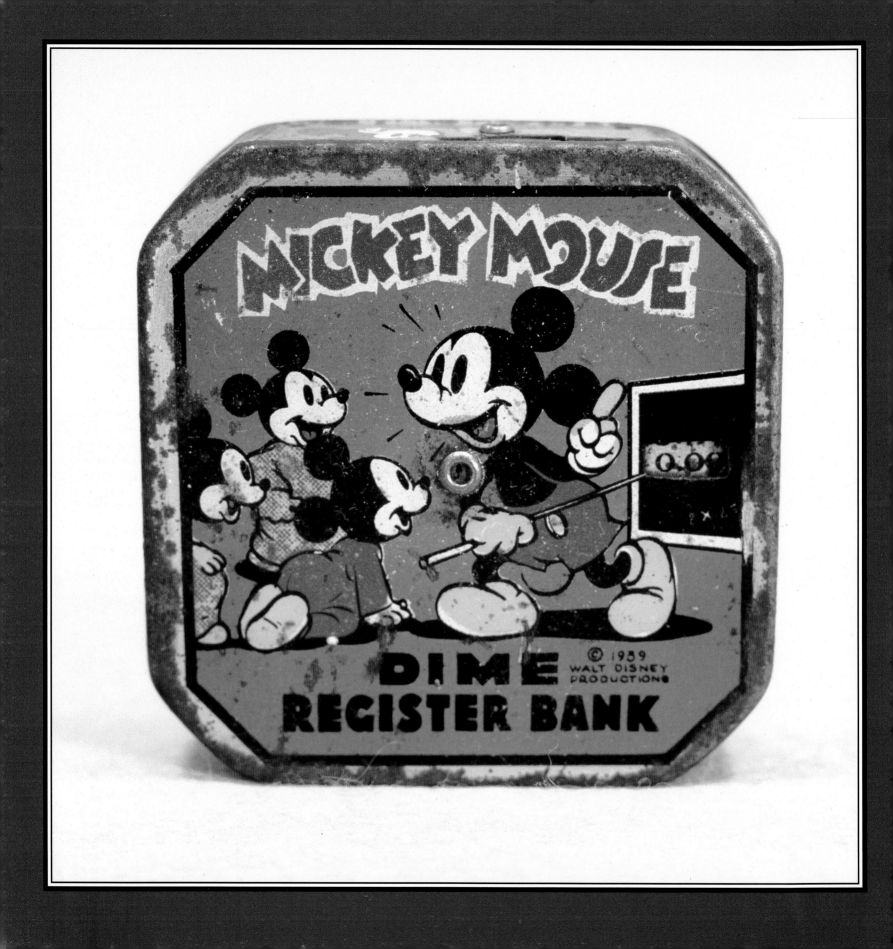

INTRODUCTION

The use of the term *Disneyana*, a play on *Americana*, as a catchword has come to be equated with the zealous collecting of the wide variety of Walt Disney character merchandise manufactured from the 1930s right up to the present era of new "instant" Disney collectibles. The vast array of mass-produced products includes those items that are promoted and distributed today at the theme parks, specialty Disney Stores, collector clubs, department stores, dime stores, variety stores, souvenir shops, and boutiques of all kinds. Certainly merchandise connected with *The Little Mermaid, Beauty and the Beast, Aladdin,* and *The Lion King* has joined the ranks of desirable new Disneyana collectibles—whether for future investment or simply for the purpose of collector enjoyment. It is clear from an examination of the yearly merchandise catalogues published during the 1930s and 1940s, and early 1950s by Kay Kamen, Disney's first licensing representative, that the ebullient Mickey Mouse himself and his quacking barnyard pal, Donald Duck, are the perennial leaders of the parade of the cheerful, ongoing Disney merchandising industry. These two familiar comic-cartoon characters have been represented on just about everything from knickknack kitsch, to pocketbooks, to boys' ties, to kitchenware, to back-to-school items, and food products for over sixty years.

This book on Disneyana is meant to turn the spotlight on what is now seen as the Golden Era, the late twenties through the fifties, decades when Disney merchandise was regarded only in terms of consumerism and not as rarities to be collected either as "new," twentieth century, antiques or investibles for future generations. Of course, one could point to the many Mickey Mouse fans among the millions during the Depression, the World War II years, or the Fabulous Fifties who held onto their Charlotte Clark–stuffed Mickey or Minnie Mouse, their favorite Pinocchio tin-litho windups, or painted Donald Duck or Mickey-Minnie Made-in-Japan bisque figurines that often doubled as toothbrush holders. Today collectors cringe when they

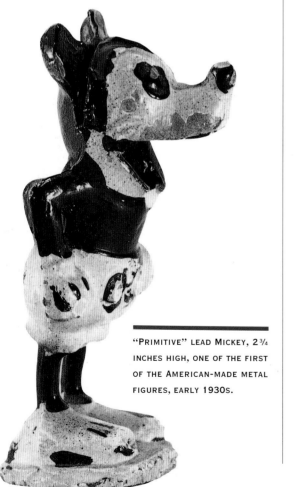

"PRIMITIVE" LEAD MICKEY, 2¾ INCHES HIGH, ONE OF THE FIRST OF THE AMERICAN-MADE METAL FIGURES, EARLY 1930S.

think of the great numbers of these mass-produced items that were simply thrown away or given to the junkman with no thought for the heritage of the future. Certain enthusiastic mothers and thrift-minded fathers of the Depression era kept a Mickey Mouse toy chest in the family attic filled with their children's special toys that might include a now rare Mickey Mouse or Donald Duck or other Disney character—a great boon in the field of Disneyana.

There are as well accounts of eccentric parents who hoarded their children's Christmas toys in sealed cardboard boxes, storing them in closets or attics, out of sight, out of mind. The thought was that the toys would not become scratched or broken if the children were denied access after the holiday season was over. Hollywood star Joan Crawford followed this practice with her adopted children, sometimes packing their toys and gifts in boxes or giving them away to a charity. This hoarding, not as uncommon as one might think, particularly during the Depression and World War II years, is still carried on by some collectors who persist in their parents' ways and never bother to display their collections on shelves or in cabinets.

Collectors today are also thankful for those merchants who took to storing their unsold toys in the basements of their stores

or moved them into warehouses. Many of today's fiercely determined collectors recall being deprived of toys when they were children, and readily admit to having become tenacious and extremely competitive in their ongoing search for undiscovered Mickey Mouse treasures. The hunt for rarity drives these collectors onward; and this is always the key to pricing. At the same time, bona fide Disneyophiles detest price guides, as they often price items either too high or too low, and take the fun out of the bargaining process and the joy out of making what might amount to an "archeological" discovery. Some guides published by collectors deliberately misquote prices so that the publisher/collectors can make better deals for themselves in the marketplace. Such practices occur in the competitive world of collecting: Some prices are pushed up only because a collector-turned-dealer may not want to sell his prize items, instead thinking of them as display pieces or come-ons to sell cheaper, more readily available wares.

Most of the early licensed Disney character merchandise was sold by businesses such as the George Borgfeldt Company of New York, which imported millions of Made-in-Japan Disney character bisque figurines; the Ingersoll-Waterbury Clock Company of Waterbury, Connecticut, which

manufactured the Mickey Mouse watches and other timepieces; or the Lionel Corporation of Irvington, New Jersey, which produced the popular Mickey Mouse handcar, featuring an up-and-down moving Mickey and Minnie. The mass marketing of these original toys has provided ample supplies for Disneyana collectors. Prices have risen dramatically on many items over the years due to the increasing numbers of collectors in the field who are spurred on by the vast amounts of merchandise in the specialty dealer mail-order collectibles catalogues, Mouse collector-club newsletters, and "Mickey for Sale" and "Disneyana Wanted" advertisements in periodicals catering to collectors. Mickey and his friends are also constantly on display at antique shows, flea markets, toy sales, and at

art auction houses. Specifically, items that originally had a limited production run, such as a Mickey Mouse radio, phonograph, playroom desk, or child's sled; fine, German tin windups; or French porcelain plates, command the higher prices at upscale antique shows. Antiquarian book fairs, poster shows, and auctions fetch the highest prices for original studio drawings, painted animation celluloids (cels) from the feature films and cartoons, posters, lobby cards, film books, movie campaign folios, and other promotional material that was originally produced to publicize a Disney picture. Today Mickey Mouse and his friends as collectibles are acknowledged by publications like *Life*, *Fortune*, *Business Week*, and other periodicals as very good "futures" investment. Added to the investment angle, collecting Disneyana can be an exciting hobby that is just plain good fun. To many the nostalgia of days gone by is appealing, while to others it may be the artfulness of the collectible itself that is enjoyable.

Ward Kimball, a Disney animator, saved some of his Disney toys when he worked at the studio in the thirties, forties, and fifties, but laments

throwing a great deal of it into the trash can. "During the 1930s when Kay Kamen was handling the Disney merchandising business, he would occasionally stop by the animation building to distribute some samples of the latest Mickey Mouse toy creations to us animators," Ward said. "Sometimes I would give these Mickey offerings to neighborhood kids, but most of the time, believe it or not, I dumped these

'future collectibles' right into the wastepaper basket." Ward did not realize the full impact of this early "tragic trashing" until the late sixties when he was shocked at the $100-plus price tag on an original 1933 Mickey Mouse watch he discovered at the Pasadena flea market. Kimball's first purchases back in 1935, discounted in the Disney gift shop for employees, included a Lionel Mickey and Minnie handcar for 75¢ and a Mickey Mouse Circus Train set for $1.50. Reflecting his hobby of collecting real, working steam locomotives and railroad cars, which are housed on his property, these toy trains whetted his appetite. Today he is regarded as a serious Disneyana collector who haunts flea markets and toy shows and continues to buy, though at appreciably higher prices. He cannot help being amused by the idea of Disney memorabilia now being perceived as "high art." In his day, the creation of a film may have sometimes been labeled "art," but the merchandise was primarily intended for popular consumption to be

ABOVE: IMPORTED FRENCH CANDY TIN, 1930S. BELOW: MICKEY MOUSE AND MINNIE MOUSE AUTOMOTIVE RADIATOR CAPS OF PAINTED CHROMIUM METAL WERE MADE IN ENGLAND IN 1934 BY THE DESMO CORPORATION.

used at play and eventually discarded.

Ward Kimball today laments the moneymindedness that surrounds the collecting of Disney memorabilia. "Nowadays people going to a Disneyana convention where these things are sold sleep all night outdoors just to keep their place in line so they can be the first to get in to get the jump on everyone else. It's fantastic! I saw a cel that I thought was not even a particularly good one—and selling for $150,000 too! Imagine! Everyone is so concerned with the value of this and that today. Can't they just enjoy it for what it is?" A bona fide original himself, and recognized as a great Disney artist and animator from the Golden Age, Kimball says he turns down offers from

avid collectors who want to buy pieces of his collection all the time. "They offer me top dollar for some of my collectibles; but that's not what it's all about in my mind." Ward Kimball is the man who drew Jiminy Cricket, and like the sassy cricket, he is a man of conscience and concern.

The 1960s Revival

The sixties counterculture hippies began wearing original 1930s Ingersoll Mickey Mouse wristwatches in jest and as a sort of "new-old" status symbol protest prank in the face of the older establishment who regarded Mickey on a watch as tacky. However, in the wake of the youth revolution, astronauts Walter Schirra and Gene Cernan wore their Mickey Mouse watches proudly aboard the Apollo spacecrafts in 1968 and 1969. Ethel Kennedy, Carol Burnett, Sammy Davis Jr., Tiny Tim, and Johnny Carson were among the first celebrities sporting both brand new and 1930s original Mickey Mouse watches as "now" statements in the pop culture of the late sixties.

Pop artists like Claes

Oldenburg, Roy Lichtenstein, Andy Warhol, Ray Johnson, and John Fawcett used Mickey Mouse and other cartoon characters out of the Disney menageries as subjects for their Pop Art, which then created a breakthrough movement in the art world. Pop Art came to represent the ordinary things that people lived with and utilized, as opposed to the spontaneous drippings and broad paint strokes used by abstract expressionists like Jackson Pollack or Franz Kline from the previous generation. Before long, real, everyday artifacts like Coca-Cola advertising signs, Royal Crown soda-pop bottles, A&P coffee tins, green Lucky Strike cigarette packages, Log Cabin syrup tins in the shape of log cabins, Oxydol or Gold Dust soap powder boxes, and other mass-market products, including Knickerbocker Mickey Mouse dolls, were sought after by dealers who sold to a new group of eager collectors. New pop-culture collectibles could be bought cheaply in this period at Salvation Army, Goodwill thrift stores, and other used-goods outlets. The cold, sharp, hip awareness developed by the sixties Pop Art revolution told the world

to put aside its outmoded Victoriana and take a fanciful look at what was inherent, striking, or appealing in fresh, everyday twentieth-century design. Atop this treasure heap of yesterdays "junque" (circa 1930) were a jubilant Mickey Mouse and his friends from the five-and-dime. Somehow, in the 1960s, they had *arrived*, as if

it were a second coming.

Designer Kenny Kneitel, the grandson of *Out of the Inkwell* cartoonist Max Fleischer, operated his antique boutique Fandango on East 52nd Street in Manhattan from 1966 to 1969. Kneitel filled his store from the floor space to the walls to the ceil-

ing with such new boutique items as Captain Midnight Ovaltine shake-up mugs, Planters Peanuts tins, Campbell Soup kids drinking tumblers, and other "instant" collectibles. Retro-clothing and nostalgia collectibles, including Big Little Books and Catalin radios, were featured as desirable antiques that were not then even fifty years old. Maurice Sendak, author and premier illustrator of artful children's books made his first purchases of Mickey Mouse memorabilia at Fandango. Kneitel said recently, "It was a time when even wax and other artificial foods from commercial restaurant and department store displays were being recognized as objects of legitimate design and beauty." Michael Malce's Tunnel of Love in Greenwich Village featured Disney items from the thirties and Serendipity 3 on East 60th Street and movie costume maven Gene London's specialty toy shop in Chelsea offered a mix of antiquarian and new boutique merchandise highlighted by a smiling Mickey Mouse.

The Mickey Mouse image that was preferred by the legions of beginning collectors and beatniks of the sixties was not the

ABOVE LEFT: MICKEY MOUSE
BIRTHDAY GREETING CARD FROM
HALL BROTHERS, KANSAS CITY,
MO., AND NEW YORK, 1934.
ABOVE RIGHT: BUTTON-NOSE
MICKEY MOUSE BIRTHDAY
GREETING CARD (OPENED).

more rounded, pink-faced Mickey Mouse so prominent in the forties and fifties, but the Depression-era rodentlike, white-faced, mischievous imp who wore only red shorts held up by two big oval buttons, yellow clown-size shoes, and thick four-fingered gloves. He had black balloon ears, a black stub of a nose, and a long, skinny tail.

The more astute collectors of the sixties and seventies, many of whom are still collecting today, say they particularly seek out the Mickey who gnashes his big teeth in a growling grin as he does in the Dean Rag dolls from England or some of the German tin windups or Made-in-Japan bisque figurines. The more ratlike the mouse image, with an elongated snout and pointed nose, the better.

Most post-Depression conceptions of Mickey or Minnie Mouse smiles, it should be noted, are toothless, usually showing only a red heart-shaped tongue against a black background. The other elements that make up the early, youthful image of Mickey Mouse, including two black oval eyes with a white pie-wedge indentation and stovepipe legs and arms, give the impression of a troublesome primitive. Artists who reinterpret Mickey Mouse for Pop Art canvases or lithos today still prefer to use the more rodentlike character—the same one the collectors cherish; and even in today's new clothing from Mickey & Co., it is the retrostyle mouse that comes into play.

In terms of graphics, this early Mickey Mouse image is seen as more artistic and interesting. Up to the late sixties, and especially in the late forties, fifties, and sixties, a zoot suit, straw hat, long mouse pants, or a shirt and tie—even a protruding middle-aged stomach—had Mickey looking like a Broadway or Hollywood rat pack character that had eaten one too many pieces of Lindy's cheesecake. Disneyana collector Mel Birnkrant has said, "The mistake of the later Mickey was in Disney's attempt to make him seem 'more real,' to make each feature and each movement become more lifelike. It was an attempt at improving what was already, in 1930, a perfect image. And in that attempt, the perfection was lost."

It was Walt Disney's purpose to humanize his cartoon characters over the years, and Ward Kimball remembers that the early Mickey came to be regarded as somewhat of a misfit at the Disney Studios. Disney felt Mickey ought to grow up and become more adult in his manner and appearance as time moved on. Perhaps as Walt was maturing he felt Mickey should grow older along with him.

The 1930s Donald Duck, with his extra long bill, is also seen as more interesting to sophisticated collectors than the later short-billed squat duck character of the forties and fifties. This trend back to the original mouse image was noted in a September

1968 issue of *Life* magazine, which celebrated Mickey's fortieth birthday and featured Mickey Mouse memorabilia from the Depression era focusing in on leading collectors like Ernest Trova, Robert Lesser, and Mel Birnkrant. *Life* reported that the Timex Corporation had sold out its fortieth-birthday Mickey watch in just a month. Artist-collector John Fawcett was photographed with his Disneyana in a special nostalgia Christmas issue of *Newsweek* in 1970, the same year the annual report of Walt Disney Productions made note of a growing interest in what they called the "camp" Mickey Mouse of 1930s vintage.

When flower children began sporting Mickey Mouse watches during the 1967 "summer of love" in San Francisco, a Mickey fashion trend really began to take hold across the country. Sales for new Mickey character watches tripled in three years, and in a six-month period in 1970 they accounted for over $7 million in sales. Mickey Mouse on a T-shirt or sweatshirt became the "in" counterculture wearables to be worn with tie-dyed bell-bottom trousers and Indian moccasins. *Business Week* reported in their 1975 "Business Investment Outlook" that Disneyana was becoming a standout antiques investment, showing a 50 percent jump in that year. Windup Mickey Mouse toys were suddenly

deemed "investibles" by Wall Street.

Lincoln Center honored the Disney Studios on its 50th anniversary during the summer of 1973, and the mouse that Walt Disney said had started it all was honored when he turned fifty on November 18, 1978, by the city of New York and at the Museum of Modern Art. On hand to look at the early black-and-white cartoons at that event was master of ceremonies Ward Kimball and other luminaries. Kimball remembers going cross-country on a Disney train on the 50th anniversary and at stops in towns all over America he and a costumed Mickey would wave at the crowds. On this tour Mickey was played by a young woman which Ward Kimball felt was a very funny idea. In 1977 a grinning litho-on-tin German windup of Mickey Mouse, a toothsome rodent, cranking away on a hurdy-gurdy while a tiny Minnie twirled atop, fetched the then-record price for a Mickey toy of $3,105 at Sotheby's in London. Rita Reif, the author of a syndicated antiques column appearing in the *New York Times* and an insightful reporter on Mickey Mouse collectibles, made the pronouncement that Mickey had become the year's "star" of the auction market. The runners-up included a $200,000 125-year-old Heriz rug and a $220,000 Fabergé egg. "Mickey has arrived in the world of bona

fide antiques," said Ms. Reif, whose book, *The New York Times World Guide to Antiques Shopping*, featured a picture of a vintage Knickerbocker Mickey Mouse doll on its cover.

The 1970s is generally regarded as the nostalgia decade. Revivals of the 1930s Ginger Rogers and Fred Astaire movies,

TOP: MICKEY MOUSE PINBACK BUTTON FROM THE 1973 LINCOLN CENTER FESTIVITIES IN NEW YORK, CELEBRATING THE FIFTIETH ANNIVERSARY OF THE FOUNDING OF WALT DISNEY STUDIOS. ABOVE: PINBACK BUTTON ISSUED FOR MICKEY'S FIFTIETH BIRTHDAY, 1978.

rereleased in bright reprocessed prints, and Busby Berkeley films like *42nd Street, Footlight Parade, Dames,* and the *Gold Digger* series of 1933, 1935, and 1937, and *Wonder Bar* were all the rage. *No, No Nanette,* starring Ruby Keeler and Patsy Kelly and directed by Berkeley himself, opened on Broadway on January 19, 1970, becoming a smash revival that began another "new-old" trend on Broadway. Stephen Sondheim's *Follies,* another highly stylized Broadway musical in the nostalgic mood, starring Alexis Smith and Dorothy Collins, received rave reviews when it opened in April of the same year. This nostalgia for Depression-era Broadway continued right into the 1980s, with revivals of *42nd Street* and Cole Porter's *Anything Goes.*

In the 1990s it was *Crazy for You, Jelly's Last Jam,* and *Annie Warbucks* that took us back to those classic good old days of song and tap. There was a startling change in auction prices for Disneyana in the 1990s as well. The Mickey Mouse hurdy-gurdy that sold for $3,105 in 1977 sold at auction in Byfield, Massachusetts, in 1993 for $18,700, a record-breaking price for this rare animated toy. What was regarded in the decade of the seventies as nostalgia trivia, sentimentalia, or campy is now thought of as classics of the twentieth century.

This pronounced shift in thinking certainly affected the collecting of Disneyana of the thirties, forties, and fifties. Some dealers and inexperienced collectors still confuse the 1950s Mickey or Donald with their 1930s counterparts. However, most items from the pre–World War II period are marked Walt Disney Enterprises, Walter E. Disney, or just W.E.D. By 1940, merchandise was stamped Walt Disney Productions or W.D.P. Pre–World War II items are still considered the classics most sought after, and these are the ones that usually fetch the higher prices in the collectors' marketplace.

The character merchandise produced in the early 1930s is dominated by Mickey Mouse, Minnie Mouse, and that oddball couple Horace Horsecollar and Clarabelle Cow, who went out on country picnics and seashore trips with the mouse couple and their "nephews" Morty and Ferdy. Sometimes even Peg Leg Pete, Pluto, or Goofy would come along on these romps. Donald Duck along with nephews Huey, Dewey, and Louie, and sometimes girlfriend Daisy Duck, were another family that were popular sellers in the 1930s. In 1934, when Donald Duck appeared in his first movie, *The Wise Little Hen,* the obstreperous quacker immediately became a second lead to Mickey and Minnie in the merchandising marketplace, followed by Pluto and

Goofy. Three Little Pigs and Big Bad Wolf character merchandise first appeared in 1933 following the hit cartoon *Three Little Pigs.*

Throughout the decade the Pigs, the Wolf, and *his* three nephews enjoyed great popularity in the dime stores and other toy outlets, well beyond the other Silly Symphony roster of characters, which included Clara Cluck, the Wise Little Hen, the Funny Little Bunnies, Peter Pig, Peter and Polly Penguin, Little Red Riding Hood, Tillie Tiger, the Flying Mouse, the Robber Kittens, the Three Orphan Kittens, Bucky Bug, Toby Tortoise, Max Hare, the Ugly Duckling, Elmer Elephant, Ferdinand the Bull, and Little Hiawatha. Today some of the more obscure Silly Symphony characters, which were often licensed only for a short period during the time of the initial release of the cartoon, have become highly desirable as rarities. Such an example would be a Knickerbocker Red Riding Hood, a Robber Kitten doll, a bisque Toby Tortoise, or a Miss Cottontail figurine.

By 1938, prior to the release of the animated feature film *Snow White and the Seven Dwarfs,* the film's characters had appeared on every conceivable kind of product. This continued right into the 1940s and was followed by the new 1940 merchandise featuring Pinocchio and his conscience sidekick Jiminy Cricket and *their* friends Figaro the Cat; Cleo the Goldfish; the Blue Fairy; Geppetto; Stromboli; J. Worthington Foulfellow; Gideon the Cat; Monstro the Whale; Lampwick, the bad boy of Pleasure Island; and a Donkey. The 1940s also introduced what is now regarded as top-notch Disneyana from *Dumbo, Bambi, Saludos Amigos, The Three Caballeros* (José Carioca, the parrot; Panchito, the rooster; and Donald Duck), and *Fantasia*. During the World War II years, Donald Duck seemed to take a lead in popularity over Mickey Mouse. It was Donald who could really spew vitriol and drop bombs onto a common enemy. However, Mickey would regain his lost lead when the Mickey Mouse Club, starring Mickey Mouse and the Mouseketeers, premiered on television in 1955 and took America by storm. Collectible merchandise was also produced in the 1950s to coincide with the animated feature films *Cinderella* (1950); *Alice in Wonderland* (1951); *Peter Pan* (1953); *Lady and the Tramp* (1955); and *Sleeping Beauty* (1959).

It has been theorized that Donald Duck was permitted to express rageful fits of anger, while Mickey, under Walt Disney's watchful eye, was increasingly forced into the role of a beatific good little boy mouse. Ultimately he was dressed up in a top-hat with suit and tails to become the goodwill ambassador for Disneyland, Walt Disney World, and the other theme parks. It seemed Disney and America wanted Mickey to become just a happy icon, no

NEON SIGN ATOP THE DISNEY STUDIOS, 2719 HYPERION AVENUE, HOLLYWOOD, CALIF., MID-1930S.

matter what was going on out there in the real world.

In 1970, the Disney Studios appointed Dave Smith as their chief archivist, to organize the vast collection of materials they had retained. Over the years much of this dead storage either had been given away, lost, destroyed, or had mysteriously disappeared. The Walt Disney Archives today, located on the Disney Studios lot in Burbank, California, contains cels, original animation art, character sketches, movie posters, promotional flyers, Disney Big Little Books in every language, comic books and original strip art, labels for Donald Duck, Mickey Mouse, or Snow White products, and a good sampling of mint condition merchandise such as the 1934 Mickey Mouse Velocipede made by the Colson Company of Elyria, Ohio. Rare cartoon character ceramic figurines from *Pinocchio* and *Fantasia* are displayed in recessed light boxes in the Archives offices and its lobbies.

Collecting Disneyana has now become a global affair, with an infinite variety of collectible categories to satisfy almost anyone. This book is not meant to be an "everything" or "anything" catalogue; nor is it meant to function as a quick "current" price barometer of the Disneyana marketplace. Instead, we have chosen to highlight some of the most prized pieces, along with those regarded as having top quality in design and others that are just plain spirited and fun to collect and have around the house.

ONE

A MICKEY MOUSE-EUM IN DOWNTOWN NEWARK, NEW JERSEY

One of the world's leading collectors of Disneyana, and in particular the character merchandise of Mickey Mouse, is Mel Birnkrant, who began collecting early Mickey objects in the mid-1960s. During the Christmas season of 1973, Birnkrant installed a portion of his vast collection in a Mickey Mouse-eum at L. Bamberger's department store in downtown Newark, New Jersey. The store wanted to celebrate Mickey's 45th birthday. An account of this event appeared in the *New York Times* on November 18, headlined MICKEY MOUSE COMES TO NEWARK. Full-page advertisements appeared in *The Newark Star Ledger* and *The Asbury Park Press*, two of New Jersey's leading papers, heralding this special exhibit sponsored by Eastern Airlines and Hertz Rent-A-Car.

What was unique and significant about this early seventies store exhibition was that Disney merchandise items that originally had been sold in L. Bamberger's and other leading department stores in the Depression–World War II era—the dolls, games, toys, books, watches, clocks, radios, figurines, Christmas tree lights, and ornaments—were now being presented almost as if they were *art* for the very first time. If you rode the escalator to the fifth floor of Newark's great department store, the first thing you would notice were two king-sized handmade wooden Mickey-Minnie armchairs that offered hectic shoppers a cheerful rest. The installation, with its tidy, colorful, and well-lit glassfront display boxes built directly into the walls, behind which were artful arrangements of a first-rate Disneyana collection, was a sight to behold for children and adults alike. A British "Mickey Mouse" gas mask in one of these display boxes gazed ominously out into the room as a relic worn by English children to protect them from German

OPPOSITE: LIFE-SIZED PAINTED AND HAND-CARVED WOOD FRENCH CAROUSEL FIGURES OF MICKEY AND MINNIE ADORN THE ENTRANCE TO THE MOUSE-EUM AT L. BAMBERGER'S DEPARTMENT STORE IN DOWNTOWN NEWARK, N.J. BELOW: CARDBOARD DISPLAY SIGN FROM L. BAMBERGER'S, FOR A SPECIAL CHRISTMAS IN 1973.

HI ! VISIT
THE MICKEY MOUSE-EUM
FIFTH FLOOR
AND
THE MICKEY MOUSE THEATRE
FOURTH FLOOR

poison gas during World War II. Across the foyer from the Mouse-eum was a floor-to-ceiling photo mural of an audience of children at a 1930s Mickey Mouse Club movie-matinee, all of them wearing paper giveaway Mickey or Minnie face masks with laughing expressions. These paper masks manufactured by the Einson-Freeman Company were just the opposite in feeling of the 1940s canvas and rubber gas-mask contraptions that were called "Mickey Mouse" in order to persuade British children to put them on.

Within the exhibit were the mini-Mouse-Oleums containing dense arrangements of hundreds of hand-painted Made-in-Japan bisque figurines of Mickey Mouse and Minnie, Pluto, Donald Duck,

Clarabelle, Goofy, Horace Horsecollar, Snow White and the Seven Dwarfs, Elmer Elephant, the Three Little Pigs (Fifer, Fiddler, and Practical), the menacing Big Bad Wolf, Little Red Riding Hood, Pinocchio and his good and ill-begotten friends Geppetto, Jiminy Cricket, Figaro the Cat, Cleo the Goldfish, J. Worthington Foulfellow (aka Honest John), Gideon, Stromboli, and Monstro the Whale. Standing on elevated white platforms, these creatures evoked in the adult spectator a powerful nostalgia for childhood times gone by. Children visiting L. Bamberger's giggled and stared in wonder, some yelling "Mickey!" at the familiar rodent.

Disneyana collectors from Manhattan, who had heard of the L. Bamberger show, traveled to Newark's downtown shopping area, which had still remained active in the middle of a city blighted by race riots in 1967. And so it was that a cheerful Mickey Mouse and his friends were selected to bring a touch of Holiday cheer into the general despair, just as they had when they first appeared at dime stores and department stores during the Great Depression.

Early seventies pioneer Disneyana collectors who went to this exhibit were astounded at the assemblage. In a state of wonder they made note of some of the great variety of objects like the giant, gleaming red-and-blue neon clock in which Mickey did a complete somersault every minute while his hands pointed out the time, giant display figures of Clarabelle the Cow and Horace Horsecollar manufactured by the Old King Cole Company, rare and unusual human-sized Mickey and Minnie Mouse merry-go-round figures in wood, hand-carved and painted in France, an Austrian bronze Mickey Mouse orchestra, which included ten tiny painted figurines with musical instruments, and other pieces they might not have previously noticed at flea markets, auctions, or antique shops. Now they had a sense of what to look for out there to add to their own growing collections.

One of the items on display was the Lionel Mickey Mouse circus train set, as was the famous Mickey Mouse handcar that had saved the Lionel Corporation from bankruptcy in 1934. These were originally manufactured in the toy train factory in Irvington, a suburban town bordering Newark. Some collectors felt that there might still be a warehouse in the area somewhere with cartons of these Mickey–Minnie Mouse or Donald Duck–Pluto handcars; and they even walked obsessively up and down the streets of Newark and Irvington in hope of the possibility of finding a stockpile.

At Bamberger's, one flight down from the Mouse-eum, was a movie theater showing early black and white Mickey Mouse cartoon shorts to delighted children. The toy department had giant red, white, and green displays of the old-style Mickey, the rodent in Santa outfit and holding a big Christmas bell. Santa Claus himself, sitting on a throne, listened to requests from tots for, yes, Mickey Mouse, Minnie Mouse, and Donald Duck seventies dolls, plastic windups, and storybooks.

LEFT: OCTAGONAL NEON INDUSTRIAL-STYLE CLOCK FEATURING AN ANIMATED "TURN-ABOUT" SOMERSAULTING MICKEY MOUSE. THE MOUSE-EUM EXHIBIT, L. BAMBERGER'S. BELOW: MADE IN JAPAN BISQUE FIGURINES AND TOOTHBRUSH HOLDERS, FEATURING AN ARRAY OF WALT DISNEY CARTOON CHARACTERS, INCLUDING: SNOW WHITE AND ALL SEVEN DWARFS, ELMER THE ELEPHANT, DONALD DUCK, MICKEY AND MINNIE MOUSE, FERDINAND THE BULL, THE THREE LITTLE PIGS, THE BIG BAD WOLF, AND CHARACTERS FROM *PINOCCHIO*. THE MOUSE-EUM EXHIBIT, L. BAMBERGER'S.

Art Deco Disneyana: The French Mickey Mouse Bank

The Mouse-eum at L. Bamberger's is always vividly remembered by those avid Disney collectors who attended at a time of innocence and discovery in the newly awakening world of Disneyana. This Birnkrant Mouse-eum offered a chance to view what was even then considered a rare Mickey Mouse icon, a cast-iron bank Birnkrant reportedly discovered in a Paris flea market. Some painted aluminum versions of this iron ratlike Mickey turn up today with the imprint "License Exclusive" engraved on the ears or the word "Déposé" across Mickey's back, but even these are scarce and sell into the four figures. This ratty Mickey, displayed under a thick Plexiglas cover on a white Doric column, a bright beam of light shining down, looked like some strange artifact dug up from a lost civilization that might have existed prior to the technological age. The French bank, which is about the same size as a real rat, was the centerpiece of the entire exhibit and caused a great deal of excitement.

The well-known artist and Disneyana collector John S. Fawcett, in a magazine article he wrote for *Collectors' Showcase*, called this particular bank a magnificent piece of geometric Art Deco sculpture and the ultimate Mickey Mouse image and collectible. Mr. Fawcett is the owner of several aluminum and iron banks and also has one in brass weighing in at five pounds. He claims it is the only one made of this material known to exist. No collector or dealer up to this point has been able to determine which French company produced these figural banks, and some confusion exists as to why they were made in three different metals. One theory is that a schoolchildren's molding set existed, but no proof of such a set has been found.

MUSEUM EXHIBITS
AND DISNEY AT AUCTION

Several official museum tributes honoring Disney and Mickey Mouse followed the exhibit at L. Bamberger's in Newark, New Jersey. The Bowers Museum in Santa Ana, California, mounted an exhibition in 1978 dedicated to the more serious collector whose "foresight in collecting ensured the preservation of Mickey Mouse art and memorabilia." On exhibit were eighty examples of original Disney Studio art, cels and movie posters, books and other printed ephemera, as well as figurines, toys and dolls, watches and clocks, and over one hundred other pieces of Disneyana.

1978 was the year the world celebrated Mickey Mouse's fiftieth birthday. A film tribute was held at the Museum of Modern Art in New York, and an exhibition at the Library of Congress in Washington, D.C., entitled "50 Years of Animation—Building a Better Mouse" showcased 120 rare and previously unseen examples of Mickey Mouse memorabilia and Disneyana. Culled from various collections within the nation's greatest library were unpublished Disney sheet music; numerous first editions of mint condition Big Little Books featuring the Mouse, rare Mickey comics, Pop-Up and Waddle Books, a map of Mickey and Donald going to the 1939 Treasure Island World's Fair in San Francisco, original drawings, cels, posters, and first run original stills from the cartoons.

The Whitney Museum of American Art in New York mounted a fine exhibit of over 1,500 drawings, cels, and original backgrounds in 1981. One hundred and fifteen Disney films were shown throughout the exhibition, which was attended by 500,000 visitors. Various elements of the cinema—movement rhythm, illusion, shadow, light, darkness, and projection—were utilized in the installation to convey the processes of animation. Other material on display included sketchbooks, character sketches, scale models, layouts, test reel, cels, and film, all set up in an atmospheric movie theater created through the illusion of silver light beaming onto dark walls.

The Whitney continued its exploration of animation art with a 1983 exhibit illustrating the influence such cartoonists as Walt Disney, Al Capp, Milton Caniff, Walt Kelly, and others had on Pop artists like Andy Warhol, Claes Oldenburg, Jasper Johns, Roy Lichtenstein, and Robert Rauschenberg. This exhibit highlighted a never-before-seen 1950 Hopi Indian Mickey Mouse doll with a decidedly primitive look.

Department store Mickey Mouse exhibits continue: A recent Bloomingdale's holiday window display offered delightful animated figures of Mickey, Minnie, Donald

OPPOSITE: MICKEY MOUSE WOODEN PULL-TOY FROM FISHER PRICE TOYS, NEW YORK, C. 1946.

Duck, the mouse nephews, and Uncle Scrooge. A "den" on the second floor of the New York store was dedicated to Disney and advertising giveaways, and signs proclaimed: "The little characters positively cavort on everything from Mickey Mouse T-shirts to very, very Goofy boxer shorts. And stuffed Donald Ducks, Minnie Mouses and friends await your pleasure."

"Lunch Box Heroes" was the title of an exhibition at the Worcester Historical Museum in Worcester, Massachusetts, from October 1992 through January 1993. The museum's director, William Wallace, highlighted Mickey Mouse alongside The Lone Ranger and Hopalong Cassidy. The exhibit emphasized Mickey Mouse collectibles as they were used in the home during the Depression. Whole room settings were featured with Mickey Mouse as the central character on everything: linoleum, furniture, radios, film projectors, and dining-room place settings. Also shown were vintage Mickey wearables, such as sweaters, knickers, pinafores, belts, shoes, ties, and jewelry. At the museum's workshop program Bill Justice reminisced about working as a Disney animator for over forty years, and children of all ages were invited to the Mouse Club Morning, a re-creation of a 1930s Saturday Matinee Mickey Mouse

WHITNEY MUSEUM OF AMERICAN ART
June 24 – September 6, 1981
©WALT DISNEY PRODUCTIONS

T-SHIRT FROM THE WHITNEY MUSEUM OF AMERICAN ART "DISNEY ANIMATIONS AND ANIMATORS" SHOW, JUNE 24–SEPTEMBER 6, 1981.

Club Meeting. Mickey Mouse cartoons, prizes, and a Mickey Mouse band rounded out the general good fun. One of the souvenirs from this exhibit was a Day-Glo plastic lunch box filled with new Pop-culture collectibles, including a Roger Rabbit trading card, a rack of Italian Chip n' Dale trading cards from Panini, a package of Little Mermaid printed tissues, a Donald Duck notepad, and a Donald Duck pencil.

Mickey Mouse at the auction block has been a growing affair since 1972, when Kay Kamen's daughter June Gitlin consigned her Disney collection to Sotheby's in Los Angeles. Some of the items were a collection of Kamen's own merchandise catalogs and included samples of early print material and other ephemera from the Kamen estate. Mrs. Gitlin regarded these pieces nostalgically; at that time she had no notion

that there would be such great interest from collectors. She and Kamen's grandson Bill Prensky did not anticipate the hefty prices realized from this auction. But they did begin to understand why Kay Kamen was becoming a legendary aspect of the Disneyana phenomenon which was, by then, growing in leaps and bounds.

Another such auction was held in New York at Phillips Son & Neale, Inc., on October 5, 1981, entitled "Disneyana." Animation cels, original art, books and comics, watches and toys, most from the estate of Al Taliaferro, a Disney animator who specialized in Donald Duck, brought in top prices. International dealers suddenly interested in Disneyana bid fast and furiously for the rare Donald Duck movie posters. A one-sheet poster for *Donald's Tire Trouble* (1943) brought $1,100. Donald in a vivid one-sheet for a cartoon called *A Good Time for a Dime* (1941) sold for $750. A poster featuring Donald and Mickey in *Orphan's Benefit* sold for $1,100, and a beautiful, multihued poster of *Father Noah's Ark* brought $2,700. An animation cel of Donald Duck from *The Band Concert* went for $2,750. A successful bid of just $10 netted one participant at the auction a Donald Duck eggcup made by T. W. Hands Fireworks Company of Canada, in the original box; a Donald Duck Popcorn can, unopened, distributed by Popcorn, Inc., Carnovon, Iowa; two bottle caps from Donald Duck Cola; and a bottle of Donald Duck Grapefruit Juice, unopened, distributed by the Citrus World Corporation, Florida. Oh, Happy Duckiana!

A rare German lithographed movie poster from 1931, which had been exhibited at the Bowers Museum in Santa Ana in 1978, surfaced at a Guernsey auction house sale in New York in 1985 and sold at an undisclosed price (it had been estimated at $6,000 to $8,000) to collector Mel Birnkrant. French and Danish posters of many Disney re-releases were also on sale at this auction.

The December 1984 Christie's East auction of John Basmajian's Walt Disney animation art established quite respectable sales, giving further credibility to what was called "patinated" animation art. One buy at this auction was twenty-two pieces of *Snow White* art that sold for $52,000. Also in 1984, at Phillips Son & Neale, Inc., an original oil painting by Carl Barks featuring Donald Duck sold for $8,500, and an original pencil sketch of a long-billed squat Donald Duck drawn by a Disney artist for *The Wise Little Hen* (1934) sold for $2,600. In 1985 at a Christie's East auction a cel of Mickey Mouse and his band in *The Band Concert* sold for $24,000. Alexander Acevedo, a dealer in original Disney Studio art, has been very

successful with his annual Disney-Art Festivals held at the Alexander Gallery in New York. He estimates that a cel setup from *Pinocchio*, featuring a watercolor background of the townscape, could go for $50,000 or more at auction. A cel of the Wicked Witch from *Snow White* set a then-record when it sold for $28,000 in 1986 at Christie's East. Acevedo said, "Collectors are spending increasingly serious, five-figure sums on animation art, and the market is highly competitive. The most valuable pieces are animation cels picturing major Disney characters from the 1930s and early 1940s—the Golden Age of Disney films."

On Sunday, January 17, 1988, Rita Reif announced in a feature article in the *New York Times* that the most comprehensive collection ever assembled of comic character toys from the collection of Robert Lesser, including his remarkable Disneyana pieces, was up for sale at the Alexander Gallery. Early, and rare, German and Spanish litho-on-tin windup Mickey and Minnie Mouse toys as well as celluloids, bisque figurines, Charlotte Clark dolls, animated watches and clocks, and bubble gum cards were among the 4,000-plus items. In addition to the Disney artifacts there were toys featuring Popeye, Little Orphan Annie, Maggie and Jiggs, Hi-Way Henry, Little

King, The Yellow Kid, The Katzenjammer Kids, Felix the Cat, Betty Boop, and others. The asking price for the entire collection, which included a French hand-painted iron Mickey Mouse still bank, was $1,150,000.

The collection, practically in its entirety, was purchased by Phillip Samuels. In her Sunday *New York Times* "Antiques" column of July 23, 1989, Rita Reif reported from Clayton, Missouri, on the newly opened Samuels Museum of Comic Toys. Mickey Mouse was the main attraction there, according to the article, upstaging in number other toys in the likenesses of Krazy Kat, Popeye, Felix the Cat, Betty Boop, and Mickey's old sidekick Donald Duck. At the Samuels Museum installation viewers gazed at many of the fabulous toys originally brought together by collector Robert Lesser.

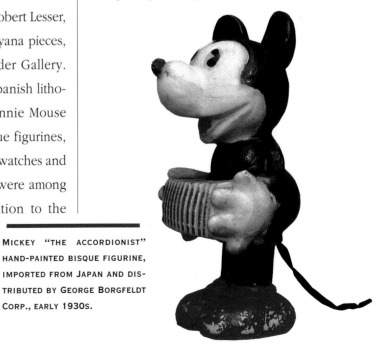

MICKEY "THE ACCORDIONIST" HAND-PAINTED BISQUE FIGURINE, IMPORTED FROM JAPAN AND DISTRIBUTED BY GEORGE BORGFELDT CORP., EARLY 1930S.

Reif also noted that Samuels had been buying everything of any quality in sight at high prices, and that he himself again pushed prices up higher and higher in the comic character toy market. The article quotes Eric Alberta, head of collectibles sales at Christie's East in New York City: "In a very short time Phillip Samuels amassed the best comic-character toy collection anywhere in the world."

The Samuels Museum of Comic Toys did not last long. A year later on October 30, 1990, at Christie's East, the deaccessioning started: A rare German tin-litho Mickey Mouse tap dancer from Samuels's collection sold for $17,600; a celluloid Mickey and Minnie astride a white elephant sold for $7,150; and a Waddle Book sold for $9,550. In October of 1991, the Bernard Shine Gallery in Los Angeles grossed over $150,000 in a Disneyana auction comprised mostly of vintage Disney items consigned by Philip Samuels of St. Louis. Samuels, Acevedo, and a few other high-powered dealers now see gold in a tin or celluloid windup that might have once sold for a nickel, a dime, a quarter or, maybe, one dollar. A collector feeding frenzy has been happening in the last decade of this century, and it seems that the art investment marketeers are moving in full speed ahead.

One auction, apparently missed by the above-mentioned moguls, and just the thing for the frugal collector dazed by the high prices being realized for the special pieces and original art, was held at Christie's East on March 3, 1987. Advertised as a "doll" auction, it included a small collection of Disney storybooks; records; songbooks; sheet music; games; puzzles; coloring books; calendars; product-related material; boxed greeting cards; Disney textiles and garments, including bolts of printed cotton, handkerchiefs, a Mickey Mouse Club cap, a pair of felt shoes in the form of Flower, the Skunk; copies of the 1933 Mickey Mouse magazine; watches; silver baby rattles; ceramic and glass items from Vernon Kilns; and an even dozen stuffed dolls, including felt Bambi, Pluto, and Donald dolls; a velveteen Mickey Mouse with corduroy trousers and shoes; four corduroy "Widgets"; a plush dog from *101 Dalmatians*; and two felt and velveteen lambs from *So Dear To My Heart*—all from the estate of Kay Kamen's assistant, Ruth Ivener. Miss Ivener, who had been with Kamen from the very beginning through the time he was dubbed the "King of Character Merchandise," was killed by a speeding New York City cab in 1986. Her sister, Ivy, also a former employee of Kamen's, realized a grand total of $6,360 from the sale of the collection.

Records continued to be set at auction. Christie's East sold a celluloid toy of Mickey riding atop Pluto in December 1988, for $6,600, a set of *Snow White* Seven Dwarfs composition dolls from Knickerbocker for $950, and an Ideal 18½-inch Pinocchio composition doll for $950. Also in 1988, at this same auction house, a cel from *The Mad Doctor* (1933) sold for $63,800! In the summer of 1991, Christie's East and Sotheby's held collectibles sales that included cels and rare Disneyana, realizing a combined total of over $2 million.

Steven Spielberg, a major animation art collector, writing in a recent Christie's animation art catalog, said "In recent years, those of us who love animation have seen its renaissance throughout the world. That is a tribute to those creative talents who have painstakingly sketched and painted the original cels, bringing stories and characters to life. It is also a tribute to the audiences and collectors who have again recognized and appreciated the artistry of classic animation. This is an art form that deserves to be nurtured and preserved. It represents the ever-expanding frontier of the imagination."

Other recent auctions around the country have seen rising prices not only for cels but for collectibles as well. Bernard C. Shine's Los Angeles auction in October of

1991 saw a French Mickey Mouse tea set going for $4,620, a ceramic Donald Duck cookie jar going for $2,518, and a Vernon Kilns ceramic stork (from *Dumbo*) selling for $2,640. Rick Opfer of Timonium, Maryland, realized $4,235 in a 1992 auction for a Mickey Mouse circus celluloid pull-toy from Nifty/Borgfeldt, and $1,512 for a celluloid Mickey Mouse on a rocking horse. In August 1993 James D. Julia of Byfield, Massachusetts, auctioned the exalted Disney collection of Californian Michael Del Castello. A German Mickey Mouse slate dancer (1931), estimated at $15,000, brought in $29,150; the Mickey Mouse hurdy-gurdy realized $18,700. (Note: the twirling Minnie atop this toy is often missing and may be a reproduction, though not in the case of this most recent sale.) An Isla of Spain Mickey and Felix brought $11,000, and a Mickey Mouse whirligig sold for $5,500. Two last-minute bargains at this auction were the Mickey Mouse plaster lamp by Soreng-Manegold for $1,760, and a Geuder, Paeschke & Frey Mickey Mouse lunch box that sold for $3,025.

Ted Hake's Americana and Collectibles of York, Pennsylvania, held a telephone call-in and catalogue mail-bid auction on February 1 and 2, 1994, offering a variety of over three thousand collectibles. They ranged from Civil War campaign commem-oratives and 1930s and 1940s tin and celluloid advertising buttons to Wild West cowboy collectibles like Wheaties Lone Ranger sendaway premiums and tin-litho lunchboxes emblazoned with box-office icons Tom Mix, Gene Autry, Roy Rogers, and Hopalong Cassidy. Prices realized for some of the Disneyana at this auction include $950 for a Donald Duck bisque (a scarce figure with a mandolin); $1,236 for an Ingersoll #1 Mickey Mouse wristwatch with die-cut silvered-brass Mickeys that grasp the watch's leather strap (a price that reflected the timepiece's rare wire lug case); $619 for a glazed ceramic Pinocchio figurine by Goebel, which had been estimated at from $400 to $700; $400 for a Dumbo Goebel; $300 for a 1937 Mickey Mouse Cookies box (color lithograph cardboard and without the cookies); $288 for a Made-in-Japan glazed china Mickey Mouse ashtray; and $250 for a matching Minnie Mouse ashtray. Two movie posters of *Saludos Amigos* and *The Three Caballeros* were a bargain at $397 each. These World War II–era RKO Radio Pictures "window cards" are color lithographed on stiff cardboard, measuring 14" x 22". Treasure-trove auctions like this one are held several times a year by Hake's Americana and Collectibles, and are prime sources for nostalgia collectibles and Disneyana.

PORTION OF THREE-SHEET MOVIE POSTER FOR *HOLLYWOOD PARTY*, A 1934 MGM VARIETY PICTURE FEATURING DISNEY'S MICKEY MOUSE TAP-DANCING FOR LAUREL AND HARDY.

THREE

MICKEY MOUSE: THE ORIGIN

When the sound-synchronized animated short film entitled *Steamboat Willie* opened at the Colony Theater on November 18, 1928, in New York City, movie audiences were delighted by the happy cartoon character mouse. Dressed in boys' shorts and big clown shoes, Mickey squeaked and whistled his way into the hearts of viewers. Walt Disney had worked closely on this new mouse character with animator Ub Iwerks and was astounded by the reception of *Steamboat Willie*. Iwerks, who contributed extensively to the original design of Mickey and who drew the mouse rather than Disney himself, was given the go-ahead by his boss to continue developing more of these cowbell-music-into-mayhem shorts.

In 1922 a twenty-year-old Walter Elias Disney formed Laugh-O-Gram Films in Kansas City with his best friend Ub Iwerks.

Together these two geniuses created animated silent shorts of fairy tales like *Jack and the Beanstalk*, *Goldilocks*, *Little Red Riding Hood*, and others taken from old-time storybooks. This early experimentation with animated fairy tales did not catch on and soon drove Laugh-O-Gram and its self-starters into bankruptcy. In 1923, Walt decided to take the train to Hollywood in search of greener pastures and greater cash flow. Walt Disney soon was transfixed by the idea of combining live actors with animated cartoon characters, and the result of this interest was the Alice comedies, which featured a real girl named Virginia Davis, brought from Kansas City.

With brother Roy O. Disney acting as business manager, fifty-six Alice comedies were produced. In 1927, Disney had become focused

ABOVE: MICKEY MOUSE AS THE CAPTAIN IN *STEAMBOAT WILLIE*, THE FIRST SYNCHRONIZED SOUND CARTOON, 1928. OPPOSITE: MICKEY MOUSE 16MM MOVIE PROJECTOR, MODEL E-18, MANUFACTURED IN 1935 BY THE KEYSTONE MFG. CO., BOSTON, MASS.; SHOWN HERE WITH MICKEY MOUSE CINE-ART PROJECTOR FILMS AND THE ORIGINAL BOX FOR THE PROJECTOR.

on the creation of a character he called Oswald the Lucky Rabbit. In the tradition of the black-and-white cartoons of the day, Oswald had a white face and a black body. Except for his long rabbit ears and bushy tail, we can see from today's perspective that he has a noticeable resemblance to his later incarnation— Mickey Mouse!

The clown shoes, four-fingered gloved hands, and shorts with buttons certainly were taken over by Mickey. At one point, to add further to the mixed-up jumble of Mickey's identity, schoolchildren who were questioned in a poll during the Depression said they were not really certain whether Mickey was a mouse, a dog, or a cat. Otto Messmer's *Felix the Cat* was often confused with Mickey in the late twenties and early thirties.

Oswald the Lucky Rabbit cartoon shorts became very successful for Disney and his distributor, Universal Pictures. While laboring over twenty-six of these bunny shorts, Disney decided he should go to New York and request more advance money to meet his cost of production. When he arrived he was not only turned

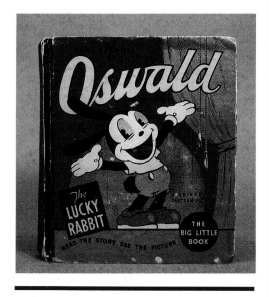

OSWALD THE LUCKY RABBIT: "READ THE STORY—SEE THE PICTURE." BIG LITTLE BOOK, WHITMAN, 1934.

down flat but was informed that because of the existence of a mini-clause in his contract, he did not own the rights to Oswald. Disney was stunned. Angry and depressed, he took the next train home to California with his wife Lillian. Legend has it that it was on this train heading west that Disney, doodling with a pencil and pad, came up with the idea for a new character called Mortimer Mouse. Apparently, Mrs. Disney christened the character with the name "Mickey" because it had more syntax, and because she thought it more appropriate for a cartoon imp. Thus the cartoon abstraction Mickey Mouse was born.

In 1928, Disney first sat down with Ub Iwerks at the drawing board to detail the image for Mickey. Tousled hair was added to the mouse so that he might resemble Charles Lindbergh, the celebrated aviator who in 1927 crossed the Atlantic in a single-engine plane. *Plane Crazy*, the very first Mickey Mouse cartoon, was animated entirely by Ub Iwerks. Next on the assembly line was *The Gallopin' Gaucho*. Just

before scheduling the release of these two silent shorts, Walt Disney traveled again to New York. It was in a movie theater in Times Square that he both saw and heard Al Jolson in black face wailing "My Mammy" in the sound feature film *The Jazz Singer*. As Disney observed the sense of wonder on the faces in the audience that night, as well as the technical proficiency of the new synchronization sound process, he knew at that moment that his new cartoon had to have sound added.

Steamboat Willie is usually thought of as the very first talkie cartoon, because it had a more sophisticated unity of sound, music, and action than had been previously produced. But the Fleischer brothers had actually made their own experimental sound cartoons before this time. Furthermore, just before *Steamboat Willie's* November 18, 1928, premiere, a Paul Terry sound cartoon called *Suppertime*, based on an Aesop's fable, was offered at movie houses. The impact of Mickey Mouse, however, a new cartoon star sensation, swept all others under the rug.

Steamboat Willie established Walt Disney and Mickey Mouse, and the small team never looked back. As the America of the 1930s entered a great Depression filled with bread lines, soup kitchens, and scores of makeshift outdoor live-in shelters, a rapscallion of a creature, who seemed to take on any punishment and survive it all with a big toothy smile, almost replaced the great silent tramp Charles Chaplin in popularity. Disney admitted to everyone that Chaplin had had a profound influence on the early style of Mickey. The success of *Steamboat Willie*, *Plane Crazy*, and *The Gallopin' Gaucho*—the last two with added sound—had the whole world talking about Mickey Mouse. Disney was amazed; and this time around Mickey was all his. Even Oswald disappeared in the dust.

FOR 16MM PROJECTORS

LEFT: Movie-star Mickey on the cover of a respectable book of film criticism, *Movies for the Millions* by Gilbert Seldes, with a foreword by Charles Chaplin. B. T. Batsford, London, 1937. **ABOVE RIGHT:** Mickey Mouse safety film for 16mm Mickey Mouse movie projector, Keystone Mfg. Co., Boston, Mass., 1934. **BELOW RIGHT:** The first Mickey Mouse movie poster, 40 x 26 inches, 1929.

FOUR

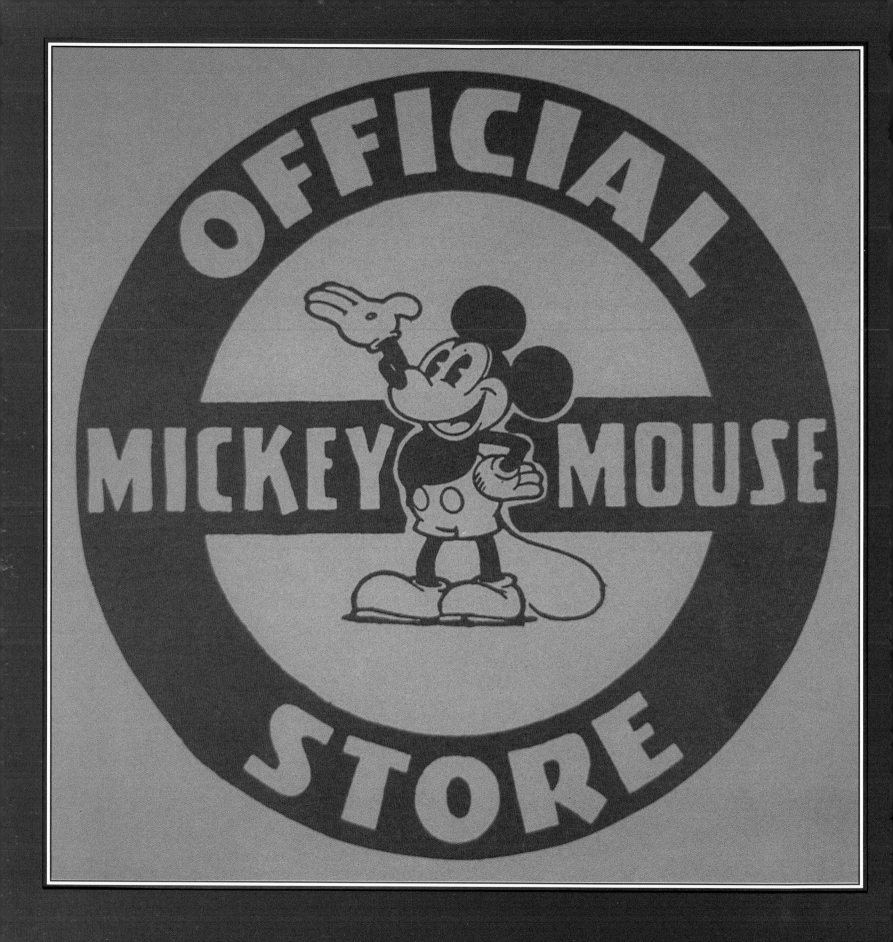

MICKEY MOUSE AT THE
SATURDAY MOVIE MATINEE

arry W. Woodin, a manager of the Fox Dome Theater in Ocean Park, California, began the first Mickey Mouse Club for children's Saturday movie matinees. Walt Disney was keenly interested in this concept, as he saw the clubs as an outlet for merchandising, reasoning as well that they would help inspire more and more children to go to see Mickey cartoons. Through 1929 there had been fifteen Mickey cartoon shorts released to movie theaters nationwide, and the fame of Mickey Mouse continued to build. Woodin was subsequently hired by Disney as a general manager to organize the kiddie-matinee activities. Mickey Mouse Club bulletins were printed up and sent to theater managers, instructing them on how to develop clubs in their own hometowns. This included a focus on local business and tradesmen who participated through advertisements in the club bulletins. Soon

bakeries offered children free Mickey Mouse birthday cakes; dairies offered ice cream to contest winners; banks gave away Mickey savings banks; and department stores gave out free Mickey Mouse toys to help promote sales for their more expensive toys. By 1930, Mickey Mouse Clubs were established in England, Canada, and other countries as well. Great Britain's Odeon Theater chain alone boasted 160 clubs with 110,000 members. By 1932, the Mickey Mouse Clubs had one million members worldwide.

On Saturday afternoons Mickey Mouse Clubs taught children how to follow the rules and become good boys and girls. Attending Sunday school, doing homework, respecting parents, helping old men or women to cross a street, honesty

ABOVE: PROMOTIONAL GIVE-AWAY PINBACK BUTTON FROM THE ORIGINAL MICKEY MOUSE CLUB, 1928–1930. OPPOSITE: OFFICIAL MICKEY MOUSE CLUB STORE WINDOW CARD.

and honor, were the orders of the day for kids of the Depression era. Calling out in unison, the matinee boys and girls would declare: "Mickey Mice do not swear, smoke, cheat, or lie!"

Mickey Mouse also instructed kids on how to brush their teeth, wash behind their ears, and to make their own beds. After a program that included games, contests, and tap dancing, children would sing:

Happy kids are we!

Eenie! Ickie!

Minnie! Mickey!

M-O-U-S-E!

This basic formula continued with the stamp of Disney's approval until 1935, and unofficially throughout the war years, when children were told by Mickey and his

friends to plant Victory Gardens and to collect old toys for the scrap heap. In the 1950s, the club was revived for television featuring the Mouseketeers. It is conceivable today that some of those same youngsters, as adults, are searching for and collecting Mickey Mouse memorabilia from the club tie-ins. Ephemera from the club days of the 1930s includes the 8½" x 8½" orange-and-black store window signs given to shopkeepers that read "Official Mickey Mouse Store," Mickey Mouse birthday cards, club membership cards, paper masks of Mickey and Minnie, the official club bulletin, the club newsletter, and the Mickey Mouse magazine. Original Mickey Mouse Club pinback buttons are also prized by collectors as mementos of more innocent days gone by.

Among Mickey's many admirers and

fans in the early 1930s were famous tots like the Dionne Quintuplets, Shirley Temple, and Jane Withers—all of whom had doll collections, which naturally included cloth Charlotte Clark Mickeys and Minnies. Franklin and Eleanor Roosevelt often showed Mickey Mouse cartoons at the White House for their guests, and Queen Mary of England delighted visitors by screening "a Mickey Mouse." Mary Pickford, Ruby Keeler, Toby Wing, and other movie stars became stalwart fans of Mickey Mouse, whose creator received a special Academy Award in 1932.

The first Silly Symphony, *Flowers and Trees*, which was in Technicolor and premiered at Grauman's Chinese Theater with Irving Thalberg's movie version of Eugene O'Neill's *Strange Interlude*, also won an Oscar for Disney that same year. Title billing for the Silly Symphonies read "Mickey Mouse Presents a Walt Disney Silly Symphony"—presenting Mickey in effect as a producer. Walt thought that Mickey's worldwide fame could act as a selling point for the more lyrical Symphonies, all of which were made in color after the success of *Flowers and Trees*. Mickey Mouse never appeared in a Silly Symphony because his cartoon image was seen by Disney as unique unto itself.

Walt never liked the idea of Mickey becoming too arty or highbrow and felt Mickey should maintain an affinity with the common man who lived a workaday existence, or who was struggling to survive in the Depression. This point is brilliantly made in the classic 1941 Preston Sturges film *Sullivan's Travels* when a group of miserable, beaten-down prisoners are shown a Mickey Mouse cartoon and burst into gales of laughter. The character of Sullivan (played by Joel McCrea) realizes that laughter is the only cure for despair, and through tears of joy he finally sees a way out. Through Mickey he gains the strength to fight back, eventually returning to his former identity—a film producer—and making hilarious comedies instead of portentous dramas.

RUTH IVENER
Kansas City, Mo.

FIVE

WALT DISNEY MEETS KAY KAMEN IN PRODUCTVILLE

In the years of the Great Depression—approximately 1929 to 1939—no other success story measures up quite like that of Mickey Mouse. When the stock market crashed in October 1929, he was only a year old, and already the leading attraction on movie marquees all across America. With eleven Mickey Mouse shorts and *The Skeleton Dance*, the Silly Symphony short drawing in record crowds, Disney was sitting on top of the world. Mickey Mouse Clubs were established in small towns and cities, and the brothers Roy and Walt began receiving a great number of requests for merchandise licenses. By the early 1930s unlicensed Disney merchandise began to appear, much of it produced in Germany, France, England, Czechoslovakia, Italy, and Spain.

Walt and Roy became focused on the financial advantages of licensing their creation. Walt's firsthand experience with char- acter merchandising went back to 1927–28, when he was cheated out of the profits he felt were due him as the creator of Oswald the Lucky Rabbit. Since Universal owned the copyright, it was they who received the royalties from the Lucky Rabbit Milk Chocolate Frappe candybars, celluloid baby rattles, stuffed Oswald dolls, and other Oswald merchandise. Early Oswald merchandise is rare. Advertisements, counter- cards, or store window stickers connected to the chocolate bar ad campaign have been found, and there are Oswald pinback buttons, toy stencil sets, and embroidered pillowcovers. Walter E. Disney's Oswald the Lucky Rabbit, a Universal cartoon character, also inspired Big Little Book stories. Indeed, Oswald is now thought of as the earliest pre-Mickey Disneyana.

The success Universal Pictures and Charles Mintz had with Oswald gave Disney the idea of using widespread mer- chandising as a means of creating a larger audience for the Mickey Mouse cartoons. Roy Disney, committed to supplying his brother with the funds he needed to oper- ate a busy studio, knew that the merchan- dising of Mickey Mouse could be a major financial contribution. In December 1929, Walt, the visionary and artist, and Roy, the conservative and astute businessman, turned Walt Disney Productions into four

OPPOSITE, CLOCKWISE FROM TOP LEFT: THE CREATOR AND THE MERCHANDISER HAPPILY POSE TOGETHER IN HOLLYWOOD, CALIF., IN 1933. WALTER ELIAS DISNEY (LEFT) AND HERMAN "KAY" KAMEN (RIGHT), WHO WAS CITED BY TOY MANUFACTURERS AS "THE KING OF CHARACTER MERCHANDISE." TWO SIZES OF MICKEY MOUSE AND MINNIE MOUSE LAMINATED PAPIER-MÂCHÉ STORE DISPLAY FIGURES, ACCOMPANIED BY A SMALL HORACE HORSECOLLAR AND PLUTO THE PUP, ON THE PORCH OF A BACKYARD PLAYHOUSE. FIGURES MANU- FACTURED BY THE OLD KING COLE CO., C. 1933. PERSONALIZED SHEET OF MICKEY MOUSE WRITING STA- TIONERY FOR RUTH IVENER, KAY KAMEN'S VICE-PRESI- DENT, FROM THE LEO HART COMPANY OF ROCHESTER, N.Y., C. 1934. CHILD'S PLAYHOUSE INTERIOR FEATURING MICKEY MOUSE PLAYTHINGS, INCLUDING TWO LARGE CHARLOTTE CLARK PLUSH DOLLS, PHOTO C. 1933.

subcorporations: a production company, a film recording company, a real estate holding company, and a licensing and merchandising company—the latter known as Walt Disney Enterprises. Roy Disney drafted the first formal contract for the merchandising of Mickey Mouse, which was signed by Walt Disney and the George Borgfeldt Company on February 3, 1930. Borgfeldt & Co. was an established toy and novelty firm, then located in the heart of New York City's international toy district. The company also had offices in a number of foreign countries, and they licensed other manufacturers in America and abroad, also subcontracting for supplies themselves.

Borgfeldt's imported and American products were distributed widely through the toy trade all over the United States. With their exclusive licensing and full distribution rights for the Disney characters, Borgfeldt & Co. flooded the dime stores, department stores, and gift shops with bisque and porcelain figurines of Mickey Mouse, made in Japan, as well as fine porcelain tea sets, made in Germany and Czechoslovakia. The very first Mickey Mouse sublicensing rights were granted to a Swiss company called Waldburger, Tanner & Company, which produced a handsome boxed set of Mickey Mouse and Minnie Mouse handkerchiefs.

The Nifty Toy Company created a variety of early toys distributed by Borgfeldt, featuring a Mickey Mouse that tumbled, jumped, danced, squeaked, and clicked, made from lithographed tin, wood, cardboard, and rubber. Other early Borgfeldt toys included a metal sparkler with a Mickey Mouse head, a seven-inch tin-litho Mickey animated drummer, a thirteen-inch metal Mickey and Minnie drum, a Mickey Mouse shooting game, a felt Mickey Mouse hand doll, a rubber sport ball, and tin-litho spinning tops. The first licensed Mickey Mouse character merchandise was often made from the cheapest available material, such as celluloid or tin.

With the studio established in Hollywood, Walt and brother Roy were determined to reach out to new horizons. They signed their first publishing contract with King Features in January 1930 for the Mickey Mouse comic strip. It began newspaper syndication January 13, 1930 (although the actual contract was not signed until January 24, 1930), in a single-strip series drawn by Ub Iwerks, who was later replaced by Disney artist Floyd Gottfredson. A free "autographed" photograph of Mickey Mouse was the first giveaway offered as a promotion and sent to thousands of kids who requested it by mail. Iwerks also designed an eight-inch double

cardboard disk with eight different drawings of Mickey for another mail giveaway. An animated cartoon itself when the spinning disk, with the aid of a straight pin, was seen in the mirror delighted youngsters who saw a reflected Mickey skipping, hopping, and jumping. These now rare promotional pieces and the few early comic strips Iwerks drew are sought after by collectors because they bear the imprint of Disney's first collaborator.

By 1930 Mickey Mouse cartoons were enjoyed all over the globe. In order to supply the increasing demand for Mickey Mouse merchandise and to protect their merchandising interests in Europe, the Disneys selected William Banks Levy, the manager of the Powers Cinephone in London, which in 1930 was handling Mickey Mouse film distribution, to license manufacturers in England, France, Germany, Italy, and other countries. Levy was given licensing and sublicensing rights similar to those held by Borgfeldt, and there was some confusion about their territories, which often overlapped. This apparent conflict often had both companies ordering the same merchandise from the same suppliers, resulting in similar or identical toys for both the European and American marketplace. One of the key reasons Disney chose Levy was that he had already lined up dozens of licensees, and the demand for Mickey Mouse toys in England was immense.

The first licensed English product was a cellophane filmstrip mounted under glass to be sold with a toy lantern projector, made by Johnsons of Hendon, Ltd. Also from England were the eight sizes of Mickey and Minnie dolls produced by the Dean's Rag Book Company, Ltd., London. Some of these toothy rodent-like Mickey or Minnie dolls were jointed with limbs so that their bodies could be twisted into different positions. Other Dean Rag dolls offered include the fantastic "Jazzer," which attached to a record player and danced as the record spun around; Mickey Mouse and Minnie Mouse "dancer" dolls, toy dolls that moved about together; a Mickey "skater" on wheels; a "Li-Vo" Mickey puppet controlled through an opening in the back; and a velveteen handpuppet, which was a Mickey Mouse "glove" toy.

Though Borgfeldt & Co. was the chief American producer and distributor of Mickey Mouse character merchandise in the United States, Disney was not altogether happy with the quality and design of the

toys, games, figurines, and dolls. Mickey Mouse cartoons were often billed right next to the regular features on movie marquees and were certainly gaining all the time in popularity. But nickel, dime, and quarter

J. GUIDUCCI, A DISNEY STUDIO EMPLOYEE, AND WALT DISNEY POSE WITH GIANT-SIZED PLUSH MICKEY MOUSE AND MINNIE MOUSE CHARLOTTE CLARK DOLLS, 1933.

admissions were not adding up to the dollars Disney needed in order to expand his organization. Film distributors demanded

promotional ideas to tie in the cartoons to the Mickey Mouse Clubs and to their local merchants and retailers. During the Depression, when all sales were falling, more manufacturers were taking a good hard look at their products following a poor Christmas season and turning to the sales power of Mickey Mouse and his friends. Disney realized that the future of the studio could become secure only if enough revenue was generated by the character merchandising division.

Walt Disney did not encourage individuality in his artists and staff members, feeling that everyone should contribute as much as they could to the overall product. He also knew that they might jump ship and start their own companies. He made an exception when he tapped Herman "Kay" Kamen to be his licensing representative in the all-important character merchandising division of Walt Disney Productions.

Kay Kamen was an advertising and promotion specialist from Kansas City, known as a gentleman in the grand tradition of the old school. Kamen was polished and charming, forthright and self-taught, tailored and impeccably groomed, a man with a large and imposing frame who sported a part-down-the-middle Vaselined hairstyle. A mischievous punster who always told good jokes, Kamen was known to speak in an almost imperceptible voice, which forced his listeners to lean in close for a punch line.

Kamen used his sales techniques to perfection in the sellers' game and his customers returned over and over for marketing advice. The methods he utilized for retail sales, involving the retailer and the consumer alike in huge overall sales campaigns, had gained him a respected reputation among many retailers, particularly those who were involved in producing and selling children's clothing. Kamen's brand of showy salesmanship combined with his luxurious personal lifestyle and elegant eastern manner helped to seduce many a client into closing on a deal.

Herman Samuel Kamen, born on January 27, 1892, in Baltimore, Maryland, literally invented the happy supersales character known as "Kay Kamen," and he relished his self-made role.

Though the showman in Disney appreciated Kamen's style, it was primarily Kamen's proven abilities in merchandising along with his conservative midwestern views on life and money that coincided with Walt's own philosophy of "putting every penny back into the pot." Walt Disney once spoke on this subject, stating:

WALT DISNEY, POISED IN THE CENTER WITH PEN IN HAND, SIGNS AN EXCLUSIVE MERCHANDISE LICENSING CONTRACT WITH KAY KAMEN, (LEANING OVER DISNEY'S SHOULDER). ROY DISNEY IS AT FAR RIGHT, 1933.

Money is something I understand only vaguely, and think about only when I don't have enough to finance my current enthusiasm, whatever it may be. All I know about money is that I have to have it to do things. I don't want to bank my dividends. I'd rather keep that money working. When I make a profit, I don't squander it or hide it away; I immediately plow it back into a fresh project. I have little respect for money as such, regard it merely as a medium for financing new ideas. I neither wish nor intend to amass a personal fortune. Money—or rather the lack of it to carry out my ideas— may worry me, but it does not excite me. Ideas excite me.

The Walt Disney–Kay Kamen alliance was to make the cartoon image of Mickey Mouse into a first-rate product that was to be bought, they hoped, by everyone. This in turn could provide the funds Disney needed to continue creating animated movies.

Kamen had already developed a nationally known reputation in merchandise promotion when he joined Disney in 1932. His satisfied clients of the early Depression era included the Nelly Don Company, manufacturers of the ubiquitous floral cotton-print house dresses worn by millions of women throughout the Midwest, and Hal Roach's Our Gang, Hollywood's most successful comedy series. Product and toy endorsements for the Our Gang series, in production from

1922 to 1944, ranged from lunchboxes and balloons to clothing and roller-skates—all featuring Farina, Buckwheat, and the rest of the gang, which included a pit bull terrier named Pete. These Gang characters appeared on a set of plates, on mugs and bowls, on a tipple-topple game, as paper dolls, bisque figurines, calendars, on safety-first buttons, on children's playroom furniture, on wooden stilts, as chalk figures in a paint set, in a die-cut cardboard coloring set, on notepads and school tablets, in storybooks, as a Big Little Book, and as Bakelite pencil sharpeners. Doing radio endorsements for Bab-O and posing for Kellogg Company giveaways and advertisements kept the Gang so busy they could

hardly eat their Spanky Candy or chew away on a stick of Our Gang Gum.

With a partner named Streeter Blair, Kamen formed the Boy's Outfitter, first in Omaha and later in Kansas City, specializing in display promotion for boys' clothing.

It was from his Kansas City office that Kamen instituted his most successful pre-Disney promotional campaign, one that featured an all-American-boy comic character named Tim, his chums, and Tim's Pup, who had one black eye and large floppy ears. The Tim character was noted as the "champion pie-eater of the world." Tim was also the editor of *Knicker's* magazine, which described his various inventions, including a new patent telescope ice cream cone. "Tim's Official Handbook and Secret Code for Tim's Pie Eaters," a promotional booklet, carried the warning: *The Pie Eaters Club is*

GUM-BACKED COLOR LITHO-GRAPHED PAPER SEAL FOR CLOTH-ING, WALT DISNEY ENTERPRISES, KAY KAMEN INC., SOLE REPRE-SENTATIVE, NEW YORK, C. 1935.

a secret organization. Do not tell any of its secrets or let any one who is not a pie eater see this book.

There were two rules for membership: (1.) If one pie eater is in trouble another pie eater should help him. (2.) All pie eaters should be friends. By signing up and becoming a member of the Knickers, a boy and his buddies got a free monthly magazine, the free secret code booklet, and periodic adventure story handbooks outlining Tim's plans to "end all War!" While kids were having a good time in Tim's Club, parents received notices in the mail about the "mighty good boys clothes" available in all the Official Tim's Stores across the country, reminding them that after their boys' birthdays they would need larger suits.

Kay Kamen's advertising and promotion office in Kansas City continuously developed new ideas and sales gimmicks for the Tim campaigns. Campaign tools supplied to retailers included clothing labels, celluloid and enameled buttons, Tim and Tim's Pup cutouts and signs, felt emblems featuring Tim as a sailor, cowboy, pirate, and aviator, and instruction kits for making a stuffed Tim's Pup, which was also sold ready-made. Shopping for knickers,

KAY KAMEN PROMOTED MERCHAN-DISE FOR THE OUR GANG COMEDY SERIES BEFORE HE TEAMED UP WITH WALT DISNEY AND MICKEY MOUSE. HERE HE IS PICTURED WITH THE FAMOUS GANG IN 1931.

caps, shoes, and socks in Tim's Official Stores was an exciting adventure for every boy in America between the ages of four and twenty. Little girls were provided for in their own department by Kamen with his Ruffles Doll Campaign that offered small, medium, and large Ruffles dolls, embroidered felt banners and plaques, Ruffles Scrapbooks, Fortune Books, luncheon sets, celluloid buttons, and other promotional merchandising material. It was the Tim's Stores format that later would be helpful in forming the Mickey Mouse Clubs and magazines with their codes of ethics, good health tips, patriotism, and nonsense games and riddles.

The Tim Campaign ceased when Kamen joined Disney in 1932 but was revived again in the 1940s, exhorting patriotic (and well dressed) young boys to sign up for the Pie-Eater's Club again to help Tim and his new pal Superman to bring about an end to the war and to work in salvage and scrap drives on the home front. Kamen's first real task was the creation of a Mickey Mouse press book. This advertising campaign book was centered around the Mickey Mouse cartoons and suggested advertising art, radio program and contest ideas, as well as tie-ins with manufacturers and their products. The promotional material that was available included paper Mickey and Minnie masks, flicker books, balloons, celluloid pin back buttons, posters, pennants, and lobby decorations with written instructions for theater managers, and lists of activities to be utilized by the Mickey Mouse Clubs. The 48-page pressbook, sent to 15,000 film exhibitors around the world, was entitled "The Exhibitors' Complete Campaign for Walt Disney's Mickey Mouse and the Silly Symphonies." Published by United Artists Pictures Corporation with the assistance of United Artists advertising director Hal Horne, the pressbook was an instant success for Walt Disney Enterprises. Hal Horne, as a licensee of Kay Kamen, later published the famous *Mickey Mouse Magazine.*

A suggestion made by a merchandise buyer from Montgomery Ward heralded the turning point in Mickey Mouse merchandising for Kay Kamen. It resulted in the legendary 1933 alliance of the Mickey Mouse image with the Ingersoll-Waterbury Clock Company of Waterbury, Connecticut, to manufacture watches and clocks bearing Mickey's likeness. This deal and many others like it, such as the one with the National Dairy Company, which sold ten million Mickey Mouse ice-cream cones, and Kay Kamen's successful Globetrotter Bread Campaigns for bakers, pushed Mickey Mouse over the top as one of the world's leading supersalesmen.

Kay Kamen became Disney's sole and exclusive representative for Walt Disney Enterprises in 1933, called by some the worst year of the Depression. Borgfeldt's exclusive licensing contract was canceled in 1933, though this company continued to manufacture and distribute Disney character merchandise until 1941. William Banks Levy's exclusive contract was also nullified in 1933, but as a licensee he persisted in England, beginning the Odhams Press *Mickey Mouse Weekly* in 1936. Levy joined the Disney Studios in Hollywood at a later date with the title "Worldwide Sales Supervisor of Disney films." Kay Kamen subsequently sent his nephew George Kamen to Great Britain to maintain and enforce worldwide licensing control, and he set about tightening and structuring the Kamen influence abroad. This included watching over the uniformity of Disney merchandise as to artwork and style.

Kay Kamen Ltd. created a new standard for the world of Mickey Mouse merchandise by establishing headquarters in

OFFICIAL MICKEY MOUSE STORE PINBACK CELLULOID BUTTON.

prestigious Art Deco–style offices at Rockefeller Center in New York. The West Coast offices were at the Disney Studios in Hollywood. The organization included a network sales office to handle licensed manufacturers and distributors, a department for retail store exploitation, and a production department for advertising, packaging, and promotion. Design and artwork was supplied free of charge to licensees to ensure that the images of Mickey Mouse and his friends were consistent with the cartoon film characters who might change, sometimes almost imperceptibly, from film to film.

Disney and Kamen both agreed that licenses were not to be granted for products deemed undesirable for children. Licensees were also to be canceled if they raised prices arbitrarily. Products like cigarettes, laxatives, or liquor were also turned down by Kay Kamen Ltd. Kamen insisted not only on top quality merchandise but that it be made available at Depression prices, the philosophy being that every kid who went to a dime store should be able to buy a Mickey Mouse product.

The financial arrangement Kamen had with Disney made him a millionaire, and enabled him to maintain luxuries such as a private railway car home-based in Omaha, which he used in his ceaseless cross-country business travels on behalf of Disney. Kamen also set up his sales offices not just in London but also in Toronto, Lisbon, Milan, and Paris. Offices were established on the continents of South America and in Australia. The fun-loving Kay Kamen always went first class, staying only at the best hotels. The agreement with Disney, first signed in 1933, structured the profits at 40 percent for Kamen and 60 percent for Disney, up to $100,000. Thereafter it was 50 percent for each. This split changed as time went on, though the licensing profits (based on a 2.5 to 10 percent royalty) soon exceeded the profits of the cartoon shorts, making Walt Disney and Kay Kamen happy partners in the merchandise marketplace. Some mutual friends jokingly described these two pals as the "Dime Store Kids."

Christmas 1933 saw America in the grip of the Great Depression, but thanks to Kamen it turned into a very bright season for Walt Disney. Mickey Mouse sales topped those of 1932. Every department

CARDBOARD POSTER FROM KAY KAMEN LTD., NEW YORK, SHOWING THE DISNEY CARTOON CHARACTERS AVAILABLE TO MERCHANDISERS FOR LICENSING IN THE POSTWAR YEARS.

ABOVE: MICKEY MOUSE AS A SALESMAN HELPED SELL $35 MILLION WORTH OF MERCHANDISE IN 1934, AS CLAIMED BY THIS 1935 KAY KAMEN PROMOTIONAL BROADSIDE. **RIGHT:** "TO BRING MORE BUYING CUSTOMERS INTO YOUR STORE," 1935 KAY KAMEN PROMOTIONAL BROADSIDE. **BELOW:** "THE SWEETEST MUSIC OF ALL IS THE JINGLE OF YOUR CASH REGISTER," 1935 KAY KAMEN PROMOTIONAL BROADSIDE.

store in America was demanding Mickey Mouse as the main merchandising theme for Christmas. Some merchandisers and retailers said that Mickey Mouse had taken over from Santa Claus in the minds of some children. *Advertising Age Magazine* applauded Kay Kamen for putting the toy industry back into the ballpark, calling him the "King of Character Merchandise." Kamen put out the first of his seven Walt Disney Merchandise Catalogs in 1934. These illustrated and identified literally thousands of licensed toys and products featuring the Disney characters. The catalogs were also issued in 1935, 1936–1937, 1938–1939, 1940–1941, 1947–1948, and 1949–1950. As source books for Disneyana these are often photocopied from originals today and are utilized by the more avid collector. In their own time, Kamen's organization sent them to manufacturers and retail merchants around the world, which numbered into the thousands.

Kamen printed a promotional broadside in 1935 stating that "in 1934 Mickey Mouse helped to sell $35 million worth of merchandise"—an astronomical feat in another bad year of the Depression. Mickey and his group of earliest friends, Minnie, Pluto, Horace, Clarabelle, and Goofy, now were obliged to help sell the Three Little Pigs, the Big Bad Wolf, and Donald Duck, a new cast of Disney characters that Kay Kamen was eager to launch in the marketplace. The August 1935 issue of *Toys and Novelties* magazine reported the following under the headline "Glad-handing Mouse Rescues Any and All":

Toy makers and merchants can point to many instances where, single-handed, Mickey Mouse drove off lurking receivers with the same vigor he exerts in defending Minnie in the movies. Back of the scenes, directing Mickey's snap-dash rescue of toy makers and merchants from the Depression, is Kay Kamen of the Walt Disney Enterprises. Unmindful of the bromidic warning against putting all the eggs in one basket, Kamen has built his worldwide organization on a single character, Mickey. True, the Disney inkpot and facile pen produce other members of Mickey's family but Mickey stays far enough ahead to keep it a one-man show. Glad is Mickey to help anyone with promotion of his wares. Outstanding perhaps as a single promotion feature is New York's annual Thanksgiving Parade wherein one of Manhattan's leading department stores displayed the genial mouse in proportions fifty feet high. Cooperating in this standout feature were a prominent rubber company and a famous designer of marionettes.

The magazine article went on to elaborate that Kay Kamen's merchandising offices contain artists, publicity-promotion men, and designers, all there to assist licensees and stores as well with sales posters, decorations, and full selling campaigns.

One of Kay Kamen's most successful merchandising ideas was the use of Disney characters to promote various brands of packaged bread. Mickey Mouse was featured in the very first bread campaign, followed by Snow White Bread in 1938. In 1939, Kamen developed a "campaign for bakers" for *Pinocchio*, the Disney animated feature film that was released in 1940. One feature of the campaign was a paper Pinocchio circus tent that bakers could use as a permanent advertising display centerpiece.

Advertisements were placed in local papers, coaxing children to send in a coupon in order to become a member of the Pinocchio Circus. Once signed up as official members they would receive a paper tent with a Ringmaster's guide to help set it up, a Ringmaster's Certificate, and a Ringmaster's hat. Local bakeries also would insert one of sixty different nature cards featuring *Pinocchio* characters performing a variety of circus stunts, slipping these into their loaves of Pinocchio Bread each day. The Ringmaster's Guide Book also showed how children could mount these pictures and cut them to form an easel. The Pinocchio Bread campaign also offered window displays, lithographed store signs, truckside panel posters, and pinback buttons.

Kamen carefully developed the characters from *Snow White and the Seven Dwarfs* to promote products.

A typical store sign would feature Snow White herself presenting Walt Disney's Pinocchio Bread. Signs, balloons, and banners featured Doc, Grumpy, Dopey, and the other dwarfs with Mickey Mouse or Donald Duck. With the advent of Disney's two greatest animated feature-length films, *Snow White* and *Pinocchio*, the parade of licensed characters multiplied, and graphics on toys and other children's products often featured characters from the two films in various surprising combinations along with many of the other cartoon and Silly Symphony characters: Donald Duck dancing with Dopey, or Snow White patting the head of Figaro the Cat, is a familiar sight to Disneyana enthusiasts today. The artwork on the signs and the waxed bread wrappers from the Kay Kamen campaigns make them desirable as collectibles. Bread picture cards and bread end-seals are also collected for Disneyana scrapbooks today. In terms of dating items, it should be noted that in 1939 Walt Disney Studios moved to its new Art Moderne quarters in Burbank and that in the process of reorganization eliminated its ancillary company, Walt Disney Enterprises. After 1939, copyright notices on most merchandise read "Walt Disney Productions" or just "W.D.P."

During World War II and into the postwar years, it became clear that Mickey Mouse had been superseded by Donald

MICKEY MOUSE MAGAZINE, VOL. 1, NO. 7, NEW HAVEN DAIRY COMPANY, NEW HAVEN, CONN., MAY 1934.

Duck, who became the new cartoon superstar at the studio. Donald also dominated the character merchandise market. The Donald Duck Bread campaign was a standout success, featuring waxed bread wrappers with Donald and his nephews Huey, Louie, and Dewey. The May 1947 issue of *Playthings* magazine reported that a food product, as with toys and other industries, was always a winner when it featured Walt Disney characters. Attesting to his popularity, Donald Duck poses proudly on the cover of this issue of the "National Magazine of the Toy Trade," in front of a display of litho on tin cans featuring Donald Duck offering up orange or grapefruit juice. Inside the magazine an advertisement for "Donald Duck in a Box" declared it "a sure-fire seller in his inimitable sailor outfit, smartly styled by the Arranbee Doll Company." A Spear Products Company ad touted Oak-Hytex balloons with Donald, Mickey, Pluto, and new friend Bambi. The Model-Craft Character Molding and Coloring Sets were "a year-round seller" and featured Donald, Mickey, Bambi, and the new South American character, the parrot José Carioca. Model-Craft, Inc., cited its exclusive Disney franchise of twelve characters, boasting "they're emblazoned on attractive boxes and colorfully displayed with plenty of SELL!"

Kay Kamen had made transitions from the Depression to World War II and then into peacetime. After the war years, he began making business trips by airplane to Stockholm, Copenhagen, London, and Dublin. The October 28, 1948, issue of *Time* noted that "Kay Kamen, who heads a private company that makes no financial reports, last week reported the 1948 gross at $1 million, of which he said, Disney would get $700,000 (approximately half the production cost of *So Dear To My Heart*)—Kamen, $300,000."

A Kamen Ltd. poster produced at this time and sent to manufacturers as a guide for character art design, featured Mickey, Minnie, Pluto, Morty and Ferdy (Mickey's nephews), Donald Duck and nephews Huey, Louie, and Dewey, Goofy, Snow White and the Seven Dwarfs, Panchito (the pistol packin' Mexican rooster), José Carioca, Donald (now in a south-of-the-border sombrero), Pablo Penguin, the Flying Donkey, Flower, Thumper, Bambi, Friend Owl, Pinocchio, Jiminy Cricket, Geppetto, Cleo, Figaro, Timothy Mouse, Dumbo, Fiddler, Fifer, and Practical Pig, Hiawatha, Elmer Elephant, Ugly Duckling, Pedro the Plane, Toby Tortoise, Max Hare, a Funny Runny, a Llama, and a Grasshopper. A notice on the poster warns

that the drawings were not for reproduction; instead manufacturers were advised to make rough sketches of their merchandise and/or advertising layouts based on the poster drawings, and return them to Kay

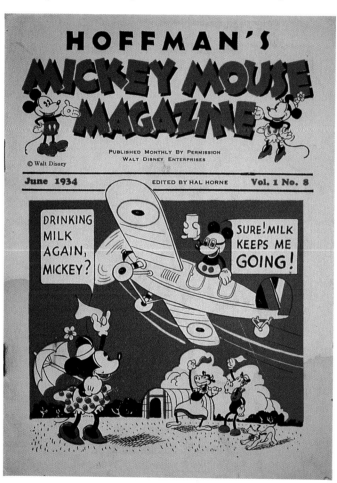

MICKEY MOUSE MAGAZINE, VOL. 1, NO. 8, EDITED BY HAL HORNE FOR HOFFMAN'S MILK PRODUCTS, JUNE 1934.

Kamen Ltd. for execution of the finished art. In red letters the Kay Kamen poster also states: "All Finished Art Must Be Done by Our Own Staff Artists and Approved by Us!"

Ruth Ivener, vice-president of K. K. Ltd., received Kamen's last letter in the New York office. Dated October 26, 1949, it was sent from Paris on Hotel George V stationery. This letter, with a flurry of business instructions, included a joking reference to Kamen's ongoing phobia about flying. On October 28, 1949, Kay Kamen (then fifty-six) and his wife Katie died in an Air France plane crash over the Azores. After his untimely passing, many of his better ideas were dropped by the restructured Disney merchandising organizations that followed. However, the decade of the fifties was influenced by Kay Kamen with the Cinderella merchandise featured in the 1949–1950 Disney Merchandise Catalog, Kamen's last. Ruth Ivener, who went to work as a merchandise representative for Ham Fischer, creator of Joe Palooka, after her boss died, kept his personalized notes, postcards, and telegrams sent to her from all over the world, one of which, on Beverly Wilshire Hotel stationery and dated April 17, 1944, contains only the cryptic lyric, "South of the Border, Down Mexico Way" penned in Kamen's distinctive script with illustrated musical notes and the cheery sign-off, "Hasta la vista, Mi Amigo!"

SIX

MICKEY MOUSE AT THE FIVE-AND-TEN: THE MERCHANDISE PHENOMENON

ABOVE: WALT DISNEY IS SURROUNDED BY THE FAMOUS CHARLOTTE CLARK PLUSH MICKEY MOUSE DOLLS IN THIS STUDIO PHOTOGRAPH, TAKEN IN EARLY 1930. THE DOLL WITH THE RATLIKE TEETH (SECOND ROW, RIGHT) IS THE ENGLISH MICKEY MOUSE, PRODUCED BY DEAN'S RAG BOOK COMPANY, LTD., LONDON. OPPOSITE: FLEXIBLE, WOOD-JOINTED MICKEY MOUSE DOLL WITH PAINTED COMPOSITION HEAD WAS AVAILABLE IN 7¼ AND 9¼ INCH SIZES, AND IN THREE DIFFERENT COLORS: RED, YELLOW, AND, AS SHOWN, DEPRESSION GREEN. THE TOY WAS DISTRIBUTED IN THE EARLY 1930S BY THE GEORGE BORGFELDT CORP., NEW YORK.

The first deal for the use of the Mickey Mouse image on a product was made in the autumn of 1929, when Walt Disney encountered a man in a hotel lobby in New York City who asked him if he could use Mickey on a child's school note tablet, and offered him $300 on the spot. This event piqued Disney's interest in making other merchandising deals. George Borgfeldt & Co. of New York became the first officially licensed company to manufacture large quantities of Mickey Mouse toys. These novelty items were distributed throughout America in 1930.

In 1930 Charlotte Clark produced her wondrous line of stuffed Mickey Mouse dolls, which captivated both children and adults. Initially these were giveaways to friends, Disney Studio employees, and guests who visited the studio. Eventually, Walt Disney, who loved the dolls, helped Clark establish a factory. Charlotte Clark, who was a recognized specialist in selling novelty dolls to toy manufacturers, was put in charge of six sewing machine operators. These original Mickey dolls were first sold at Bullock's and at May Co. department stores that Depression Christmas. The five-dollar price tag threw mothers into a state of apprehension when their child asked Santa to leave them one under the tree. If five dollars was a bit much during the Depression, parents could choose less expensive Mickey Mouse toys, including the first wood-jointed doll, which featured a painted wood composition head that moved up and down when the wire tail was pulled. This toy, designed by Disney artist Burton Gillett, was distributed by the Borgfeldt Company.

Mickey and Minnie Cloth Dolls

Mickey Mouse velvet and cloth dolls were first made in 1930 in California by Charlotte Clark. Minnie was first produced in 1931. The first doll was designed from a series of sketches made by Clark's nephew, Bob Clampett, a fourteen-year-old who watched Mickey Mouse cartoons at Saturday afternoon matinees. Aware of the copyright-trademark status of Mickey, Charlotte Clark gave a sample Mickey doll to Walt Disney himself, who gave his immediate go-ahead for her to continue to produce them. Department stores, toy shops, and other outlets began

to demand more and more of these hand-made dolls. Borgfeldt & Co. also manufactured and distributed a Mickey Mouse cloth doll to fill the vacuum, but the workmanship on their version of the Clark doll was not up to Disney's expectations.

Finally, after much thought on the subject, Walt Disney authorized the McCall's Company of New York to offer the Clark doll pattern to the public. Disney wanted every child to have a Mickey doll but he knew that many in the Depression could not spend five dollars to purchase a doll. Now parents had only to send in ten cents to receive the printed Mickey Mouse pattern #91 in the mail from *McCall's* magazine. It was suggested that the doll pattern, which was also available in yarn shops, dime stores, and sewing centers, be made of flannel for the pants and cotton for the body. Many of these early primitive pattern dolls were so well executed that it is hard to tell the difference

between them and the manufactured originals, which only on occasion have "Walt Disney Mickey Mouse" marked on the bottom of one of the cloth feet. Many seamstresses and housewives in need of cash during the Depression began to produce Mickey dolls to sell at Christmas time. Sometimes these were produced in volume and in disregard of any licensing authorization from Walt Disney Enterprises. The McCall dolls could be made in three sizes. The packaged patterns were sold from 1932 to 1939, when the appearance of Mickey Mouse began to change. Today sewing hobbyists will sometimes make new dolls for collectors. Again, these are home-sewn by hand, often using the original 1930s McCall pattern. Usually made with new and cheaper or synthetic materials, these are not always the most attractive pieces.

Margarete Steiff & Company, Inc., executed very fine stuffed Mickey dolls in the 1930s. They often have

long black whiskers added, a lengthy tail, and are made in velvet, broadcloth, and other better quality materials. A manufacturer's tag is usually to be found set in one ear; they also sometimes have the original orange cardboard tag strung around the collar. Steiff dolls are also often marked on the bottom heel of one foot. The Steiff Mickeys and Minnies, which were produced in Germany, were sold in England and the United States, and are eagerly sought after by doll collectors as well as Disneyana collectors. The Steiff Mickeys range in size from $4\frac{1}{2}$ to $16\frac{3}{4}$ inches.

The Knickerbocker Toy Company of New York City manufactured first-rate Mickey and Minnie dolls. Some of them were actually designed for the company by Charlotte Clark: and one of the good features was the brightly painted orange wood-composition clown-style shoes. There are some delightful Mickey carnival figurines that are about a foot high with movable arms. These may be made entirely of painted composition wood. Knickerbocker also began adding

outfits to their Mickey Mouse dolls, offering the doll-buying public Mickey in a Spanish toreador costume, in a polka-dot clown suit, and in a variety of Wild West cowboy gear, including sheepskin chaps, a kerchief, a cowboy hat, guns in holsters, and carrying a rope lariat. A die-cut tag attached to each doll by a string read: "Mickey Mouse—licensed by Walt Disney Enterprises for the Exclusive Manufacture by the Knickerbocker Toy Company."

Knickerbocker also added a Charlotte Clark–designed Pluto, Goofy, and a number of Donald Ducks, sometimes in his typical sailor's outfit and sometimes in a sombrero and a Mexican serape. Charlotte Clark also created wonderful Mickey, Minnie, Donald Duck, Pluto, and other Disney character dolls for the Gund Manufacturing Company beginning in 1947 and up to 1958. Charlotte Clark came to be regarded by Walt Disney almost as a member of his own family. When she died at the age of seventy-six on December 31, 1960, there were many who mourned the lady affectionately known as "the Mother of the Mickey Mouse doll."

Dean's Rag Book Company, Ltd., of Great Britain, which had made children's

rag-books since 1903, created some unusual Mickey and Minnie cloth dolls in the 1930s. These featured long spider arms and legs, rat teeth, white saucer eyes with black pupils, flat feet, and baggy shorts. Some complained that these Mickeys and Minnies resembled pit bull dogs rather than cute mice. The dolls infuriated Walt Disney when he first saw them, and he instructed William Levy, his London agent, to stop exporting the doll to America. However, collectors today consider them unique and are fascinated by their ratty look. The Dean Rag Mickey and Minnie Mouse dolls were made of velvet and velour and had small felt ears and five-finger felt gloves. They were available in a variety of sizes.

ABOVE: TWO-GUN MICKEY PLUSH VELVET DOLL DESIGNED BY CHARLOTTE CLARK FOR KNICKER-BOCKER TOY CO., NEW YORK, 1936. BELOW: CHARLOTTE CLARK DESIGNED THIS CLASSIC MICKEY MOUSE DOLL IN THE EARLY 1930S FOR KNICKER-BOCKER TOY CO.

Mickey Mouse in Toyland: Tin Litho and Trains

Lithographed-on-tin action windup comic character toys are considered among the most desirable collectibles in today's Disneyana marketplace. Like cartoons, these three-dimensional character figures jiggle and wiggle, walk or beat a drum, push a baby carriage, ride a motorcycle, or sometimes squeak or sound a bell. A German tin-litho toy like the Mickey-and-Minnie-Riding-a-Motorcycle depicts two toothy, smiling rodents on a motorbike, complete with Dunlop whitewall tires. This very handsome and rare toy was manufactured by the Tipp Company in 1928 for an English marketplace. The Mickey Mouse Hurdy-Gurdy tin-litho windup features a thin, five-fingered Mickey cranking the organ, while a tiny Minnie sings and dances on top to a plink-plank-plunk tune. Manufactured in 1931 by the Johann Distler Company of Nuremberg, Germany, this toy always causes a stir when it is being offered at a show or put forth at auction. Made-in-Spain lithographed tin-action toys manufactured by Isla are also considered rare. One charming toy has Mickey having a cigar lit by a Felix the Cat lookalike. Another has Minnie Mouse pushing a baby carriage with the same Felix-like cat under a blanket inside.

Litho-on-tin toys were manufactured in the millions during the 1930s, mostly in the United States and England. One of the more attractive pieces by today's standards is the Lionel Mickey Mouse Circus Train set. Finding one of these sets under the Christmas tree in 1935 must have seemed a wonder to boys and girls and their enthusiastic fathers. Ward Kimball considers this set to be among the best pieces of Disneyana. With a bright red windup or battery-operated Commander Vanderbilt streamliner engine, and with flashing headlights and ringing bells, the toy train was stoked by a swiveling, coal-shoveling Mickey Mouse. The 32-inch train set includes three attachable lithographed metal cars—a dining car, a circus car, and a band car. The train set came with a free-standing painted composition Mickey as Circus Barker, as well as a colorfully lithographed cardboard circus tent. The cost of two dollars for this set was quite a buy, even in the wake of a depression. The images on the cars included Mickey, Minnie, Horace, Clarabelle, Pluto,

A GRINNING, RODENT-LIKE MICKEY MOUSE OPERATES A HURDY GURDY WHICH MAKES A MINIATURE, DETACHABLE MINNIE MOUSE DANCE TO A RINKY-DINK TUNE. A RARE COLOR LITHOGRAPHED TIN WINDUP ACTION TOY MADE BY THE JOHANN DISTLER COMPANY, GERMANY, 1931.

LITHOGRAPHED TIN MICKEY AND MINNIE ON A MOTORCY-CLE WINDUP TOY, 10 INCHES LONG, 6 INCHES HIGH, AND 2 INCHES WIDE. MANUFACTURED BY TIP & CO. IN GERMANY, INITIALLY MADE TO SELL IN GREAT BRITAIN IN THE EARLY 1930S.

MICKEY THE MUSICAL MOUSE FEA-TURES MINNIE AND MICKEY WITH BABY CARRIAGE, COMPLETE WITH BABY MICKEY PLAYING HORN, AND A HURDY-GURDY MICKEY; THE HEADS MOVE TO A TUNE WHEN THE HANDLE AT THE BACK IS TURNED. MADE IN GERMANY FOR EXPORT IN 1930.

RIGHT: THE MICKEY MOUSE CIRCUS TRAIN FEATURED A RED WINDUP COMMODORE VANDERBILT O-GAUGE LIONEL STREAMLINER ENGINE, AND A TEN-DER STOKED BY MICKEY MOUSE HIMSELF. A TRIP MECHANISM ON THE CENTER TIE OF THE 84 INCHES OF TRACK KEPT HIM MOVING UP AND DOWN. THE BAND CAR, THE CIRCUS CAR, AND THE DINING CAR ARE VERY DETAILED AND BRIGHTLY COLORED LITHOGRAPHED TIN. THE SET CAME WITH A PAINTED COMPOSITION FIGURE OF MICKEY MOUSE AS A CIRCUS BARKER, A MINIATURE SUNOCO GAS STATION, CARDBOARD CUTOUTS OF MICKEY AND MINNIE, AND A GAILY DECO-RATED, 15-INCH HIGH AND 18-INCH WIDE CARDBOARD CIRCUS TENT. AVAILABLE IN STORES IN 1935, THE LIONEL CORP. OF IRVINGTON, N.J., SOLD THE SET FOR JUST $2 WITH ALL PIECES INCLUDED.

MICKEY MOUSE AND FELIX THE CAT LIGHT THEIR CIGARS ON SPARKS GENERATED BY FRICTION OF FLINT ON SANDPAPER; TIN-LITHOGRAPH LIGHTER MANUFACTURED BY ISLA OF SPAIN, C. 1930.

FRONT AND BACK OF AN ENGLISH-MADE MECHANICAL BANK. WHEN MICKEY'S EAR IS PRESSED A RED METAL "TONGUE" EMERGES TO ACCEPT A COIN WHICH MICKEY SWALLOWS. COLOR LITHOGRAPHED ON METAL, C. 1931. MARKED "BY EXCLUSIVE ARRANGEMENT WITH THE IDEAL FILMS LIMITED."

RAT-TOOTHED, FIVE-FINGERED MICKEY MOUSE WINDUP WALKER TOY MADE IN GERMANY IN 1930 AND 1931 BY THE JOHANN DISTLER CO. OF NUREMBERG. THE EARLIEST EUROPEAN IMAGES OF MICKEY DIFFER FROM HIS AMERICAN COUNTER-PARTS BECAUSE IN MANY CASES THERE WAS NO CONTACT WITH THE DISNEY STUDIOS, AND THE DESIGNS WERE CREATED HAPHAZARDLY, DRAWN FROM VIEWINGS OF CARTOONS.

MINNIE MOUSE PUSHES A SEATED FELIX THE CAT IN A CARRIAGE WINDUP TOY, MADE FROM LITHO-GRAPHED TIN, MANUFACTURED IN SPAIN IN 1930.

LITHOGRAPHED TIN MICKEY MOUSE SLATE DANCER HAS A WINDUP MECHANISM WITH A CRANK. MADE IN GERMANY IN 1930 AND 1931 BY JOHANN DISTLER CO.

Fifer and Fiddler Pig, along with monkeys, tigers, and a befuddled-looking Disney circus elephant. Wells O' London under the Brimtoy Brand made a version of this train set featuring a "Silver Link" engine and a beautifully executed litho-on-tin circus tent. Manufactured in 1935 and 1936, it easily stands alongside the American Lionel set as among the best of Disney collectibles.

The most famous Mickey Mouse toy of the thirties is the Mickey Mouse handcar, manufactured by Lionel. With painted wood composition figures of Mickey at one end and Minnie at the other, this bell-ringing car,

which had the two mouse characters pumping away in a see-saw motion, first rode the tracks around the Christmas tree in 1934. The Lionel Corporation, which had its factories in Irvington, New Jersey, began to produce the fanciful handcar in May of that year. The company was astonished by the success of this specialty item during the Christmas season. Initially there were 350,000 orders from stores, but they could manufacture only 253,000 in the first year. *Toys and Novelties* magazine acclaimed the handcar as the biggest event of the previous toy year in their February 1935 issue.

A headline in the *New York Times* on January 22, 1935, read: "Mickey Mouse Saves Jersey Toy Concern: Carries It Back to Solvency on His Railway."

The *New York Herald Tribune* stated: "Mickey Mouse Puts Bankrupt Firm Back on Its Feet."

If not for the Mickey Mouse handcar, the Lionel Train corporation, which was heading into bankruptcy, would have become just another sad story in the annals of the Great Depression. Lionel formally thanked Walt Disney for creating the wonderful Mickey and Minnie Mouse characters. The March 1935 issue of *Fortune* magazine also gave its salutations to the mouse who had kept "the proverbial wolf from the Lionel Factory gates." The inspired Mickey handcar novelty train, which sold for just one dollar, led Lionel to follow up with an Easter Bunny handcar and a Disney Santa handcar for the Christmas season of 1935 and seasonally thereafter. The Santa handcar featured a painted wood composition Santa Claus standing opposite a Christmas tree; and in

the toy sack on his back a tiny Mickey Mouse peeked out. The Lionel Donald Duck car produced in 1936 had a composition long-billed Donald and Pluto, who stuck his head in and out of a metal doghouse as the car traveled around the track.

Made in Japan: The Bisque Figurines

Made in Japan hand-painted bisque figurines were sometimes mounted on cellophane-wrapped candy containers sold at the dime stores. Single bisques were also used as prizes at games of chance at carnivals and amusement parks. Bisque is unglazed porcelain that has been fired once, after which it can be hand-painted. In the 1930s, millions of the cheap five-and-ten-cent store novelty knickknacks were available. Depression housewives put these figurines on display shelves, in potted plants, or used them as stuffing for Christmas stockings; they were never thought of as fine collectibles. Collector and toy specialist Bernard C. Shine has identified hundreds of different forms of Mickey and Minnie bisque figurines, as well as many delightful examples of Pluto, Goofy, Horace, Clarabelle, and other members of the Disney clan.

Often these bisque figurines came in band sets, with Mickey playing a drum, a banjo, a tuba, an accordion, holding a songbook, or waving a baton. Other sets depicted Mickey with a baseball bat, a mitt, or holding a ball. Some sets have musical variations, such as two Mickeys and two Minnies playing instruments. What is charming about these bisques is that they are often

the size of actual mice—and the larger ones look more like happy rats. There is a rare bisque Mickey military set with the separate little mice carrying a flag, a gun, and a sword; and there are other sets of the famous duo that feature Mickey carrying a walking stick and girlfriend Minnie with an umbrella. Another set shows the mouse couple sitting in tiny wicker chairs having tea at

ABOVE: BISQUE TOOTHBRUSH HOLDER FEATURING DONALD, MICKEY MOUSE, AND MINNIE MOUSE, HAND-PAINTED AND MADE IN JAPAN, C. 1934. LEFT: 9-INCH-TALL MICKEY MOUSE PAINTED BISQUE WITH MOVABLE ARMS IS THE LARGEST OF THE UBIQUITOUS 1930S NOVELTY ITEMS IMPORTED FROM JAPAN BY GEORGE BORGFELDT CORP. IT IS MARKED "MICKEY MOUSE" ON THE BASE AND "WALT E. DISNEY" ON THE BACK, C. 1934. RIGHT: MICKEY PLAYS A FRENCH HORN AND MINNIE A CONCERTINA. TINY HAND-PAINTED BISQUE FIGURINES MADE IN JAPAN, C. 1933.

Mickey Mouse Band Minnie poses with her violin, Mickey a Sax, a little mouse with accordian, another with a mandolin. Minnie and Mickey 5½ inches tall, little mice in proportion. Colored porcelain. Shpg. wt., 1 lb. 4 oz.
49 F 9110 4 for 29c

a wicker table, along with a full setting of miniature china! Collectors prize the sets when they are found in the often brightly colored cardboard boxes that often feature primitive images of Mickey and Minnie lithographed or silk-screened onto paper label stick-ons.

There are toothbrush holders of Mickey and Minnie sitting on a couch, or just a singular standing mouse figurine, or Mickey with Pluto showing Mickey wiping the dog's nose with a rag. Children loved this particular toothbrush holder. One bisque has a long-billed Donald Duck standing between Mickey Mouse and Minnie Mouse. These figural pieces always had plenty of space for a toothbrush or a tube of Mickey Mouse toothpaste. Very popular in the thirties, the bisque holders continue to fascinate collectors.

The tiniest and one of the rarest Mickey bisque figurines is just one

inch high. The largest Mickey Mouse bisque stands 8¾ inches on a fully formed bisque base. Some of the figurines have movable arms and heads, and stand 4, 5, 6, and 7½ inches high. Painted in a variety of color combinations—brown shoes with chartreuse pants, red shoes with sky blue pants, red pants with green or yellow shoes—these characters often will have a license number imprinted on them like "Des Pat 8302 by Walter E. Disney" or "W.D. Ent." They are often stamped "Made in Japan" on the bottom. The George Borgfeldt Company of New York imported these from 1932 to 1941, distributing them internationally. Production

ceased after war broke out with Japan.

Rare bisque or porcelain Mickey Mouse figurines with grinning, toothy rat faces were also produced in Germany. In 1934 Adolf Hitler branded Mickey Mouse "a pest" and proceeded to ban him, reasoning that Disney's cartoon character had a bad influence on Germany's youth. Mickey, along with the innovative Bauhaus design school in Germany, was seen as decadent. The

focus was on war machinery and a rigid, strident military complex. A funny mouse had no place in a fascist regime. Hitler ordered all toy companies producing Mickey Mouse items to stop manufacturing them and to destroy all molds as well.

The Celluloid Toys

Celluloid is a lightweight, thin but fragile, flammable plastic that was developed in the early years of the twentieth century as a substitute for shell, ivory, bone, and other natural materials. Many excellent figural and action windup Mickey Mouse or Donald Duck celluloid toys were manufactured in Japan during the 1930s. In this material we find Mickey together with Minnie doing high acrobatic turnabouts on wire stands, or Mickey walk-

ABOVE: MICKEY HELPS HIS LOYAL PAL PLUTO BLOW HIS NOSE ON THIS FIGURAL MICKEY MOUSE TOOTH-BRUSH HOLDER, C. 1933. TOP: HAND-PAINTED "BABY MICKEY" BISQUE FIGURINES IN BLUE AND RED NIGHTSHIRTS FLANK A TIN LITHO "LOLLIPOP" PAIL FEATURING RED AND ORANGE CLAD "BABY MICKEYS" ON THE SIDE. BISQUES WERE MADE IN JAPAN AND IMPORTED BY GEORGE BORGFELDT CORP. PAIL IS MARKED "HAPPYNAK SERIES—GREAT BRITAIN—PERMISSION WALT DISNEY MICKEY MOUSE LTD."

ing, nodding, shaking, or riding on a flat platform on wheels. There were celluloid baby rattles and bathtub floatables. It should be noted that celluloid was also used as a major ingredient in nitrate film stock. The use of the term "cel" to describe the thousands of drawings hand-inked and opaqued on thin, clear sheets made from cellulose nitrate was derived from the celluloid brand name. After 1940, cellulose acetate, which is nonflammable, was used by animation studio painters and inkers for cartoon cels. The earliest cels were often destroyed or washed off and used again and again; today the surviving cels and special limited edition cels are sought by collectors as art.

The George Borgfeldt Company of New York was the chief distributor of celluloid toys. These were often Mickey, Minnie, or Donald figures with movable arms or nodder heads. The "nodder" toys look somewhat flat as opposed to the more hollow and bulbous full-figurals. Examples include a windup carousel with a figure of Mickey beneath a spinning umbrella: When

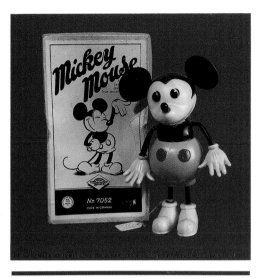

6-INCH CELLULOID MICKEY MOUSE TOY WAS MANUFAC-TURED BETWEEN 1929 AND 1932 BY THE RHEINISCHE GUMMI UND CELLULOID FABRIK COMPANY IN GERMANY. IT HAS A SIMPLE VIBRATING MECHANISM, WHICH IS NOTED ON THE ORIGINAL BOX IN GERMAN, ENGLISH, FRENCH, AND SPANISH. THIS RARE FIVE-FINGERED MICKEY, TYPI-CAL OF THE EARLY EUROPEAN MANUFACTURERS, HAS TIN EARS AND A WIRE TAIL.

the toy is wound up, tiny rotating celluloid Mickeys interspersed between gaily colored celluloid balloons spin out from the umbrella. Another version of this whirligig features Donald Duck. There is a Mickey celluloid as a walker on a rocking horse; Mickey in a cart being pulled by Tanglefoot; Horace or Pluto and Mickey and Donald rowing in a canoe. Boxes for the toys, like those of the bisque sets, have crudely primitive but attractive graphics on them, always illustrating the toy inside. Some staunch collectors think that it is most desirable to find such a toy in the original box. But more often than not the fragile celluloid is unprotected and discolored or damaged. These tiny toys, manufactured in minute sizes from less than an inch to 2 inches (small), 4 inches (medium), and 7 to 8 inches (large) were sold all over the country for pennies and nickels and quarters. A George Borgfeldt Company trade advertisement proclaimed:

You see them in the talkies! Now there is a demand to take them home. Feature Mickey Mouse and Minnie Mouse toys in celluloid and other materials in your toy department as they will be the big drawing cards for 1931.

The Borgfeldt Company also produced and distributed Japanese-made Mickey Mouse tape measures and Annie dress pins made of celluloid. Similar toddler novelty items were made in Great Britain by

Cascelloid, Ltd., of Leicester, including teething rings and baby rattles, soap dishes, egg-timers (Mickey holding a tiny hourglass filled with sand), and Mickey dolls. Other more durable plastics like Catalin, Bakelite, Insurok, or Plaskon, made of phenolic resin, were utilized in the manufacture of miniature Mickey, Minnie, Donald, or Pluto charms for bracelets or necklaces to be attached to dime store rings, or as giveaways in sold-over-the-counter boxes of caramelized popcorn. They were also amusement park prizes or thrown into bins in a penny-arcade machine. Piled up in heaps along with hard candies, a miniature mechanical derrick might scoop one up or, if you were having a particularly lucky day, you might

ABOVE: HAND-PAINTED MADE IN JAPAN MINNIE AND MICKEY CELLULOID FIGURES ARE 5 INCHES TALL WITH MOVABLE HEADS AND ARMS ATTACHED BY ELASTIC BANDS. MILLIONS OF THESE AND OTHER VARIATIONS OF DISNEY CHARACTER CELLULOID FIGURES AND TOYS WERE DISTRIBUTED TO RETAILERS IN AMERICA BY GEORGE BORGFELDT CORP. DURING THE DEPRESSION ERA.

win several for a penny.

Celluloids are among the most lifelike of all the pieces of Disneyana; and because of their fragility and rarity are among the most prized and expensive Disney collectibles in the marketplace. With fine detailing and imaginative designs, these often sell into the four figures today if they are perfect and still have their paper labels intact, which might read: "Walt E. Disney—Made in Japan."

NEAR RIGHT: A CELLULOID MICKEY MOUSE DOLL FIGURINE, RIDING A WOODEN HOBBY HORSE WITH A TINY BELL, MADE IN JAPAN, DISTRIBUTED BY GEORGE BORGFELDT CORP., EARLY 1930S. FAR RIGHT: MICKEY RELAXES WHILE DONALD ROWS A BOAT—RARE CELLULOID TOY IS 6 INCHES LONG, HAND PAINTED, AND MADE IN JAPAN, C. 1932. OPPOSITE: CELLULOID WINDUP ACTION TOY MADE IN JAPAN FOR IMPORT AND DISTRIBUTION BY BORGFELDT CORP., C. 1932. MICKEY'S HORSE TANGLEFOOT PULLS THE TIN WAGON.

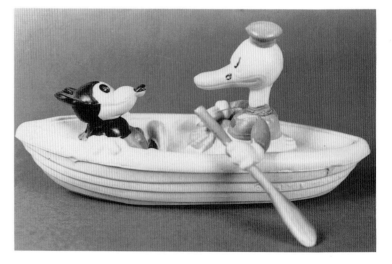

Mickey Mouse Timepieces

For boys in the Depression an aspect of the symbolic passage into manhood was to exchange their knickers for a pair of full-length trousers. Receiving a watch upon graduation from one's parents was also part of this ritual. Whether at a graduation ceremony, on a birthday, or for Christmas, a Mickey Mouse comic character wristwatch from the Ingersoll-Waterbury Clock Company of Waterbury, Connecticut, was *the* thing for a boy or girl to receive. With Mickey's yellow-gloved hands pointing to the time, 11,000 of these were sold at Macy's New York store on one day.

Mickey Mouse Ingersolls sold for $2.98 at Macy's and later for $2.69 at Sears, Roebuck. Featuring two chromium die-cut Mickey images on the links on either side of the watch face, it came in an orange cardboard box decorated with black and white Mickeys, Minnies, Horace Horsecollars, Clarabelle Cows, and Plutos racing about. It was a bright idea at the Ingersoll Clock Company, which in 1933 was filing for bankruptcy, to put the image of Mickey Mouse on the World War I Army surplus watches then in the company's inventory. From June of 1933 to June of 1935 two and a half million Mickey Mouse watches were sold by Ingersoll, which gladly paid Walt Disney a quarter of a million dollars in licensing fees.

Disneyana collectors insist that a "number one" Mickey Mouse Ingersoll watch is something they must own, and they will pay several hundred dollars to find one in the original box. Teenagers and young adults in the thirties seemed to prefer the

MICKEY MOUSE WRISTWATCH NUMBER ONE WAS MANUFACTURED BY THE INGERSOLL-WATERBURY CLOCK CO. OF WATERBURY, CONN., IN 1933. IT CAME WITH A CHROME-PLATED LINK WRISTBAND AND IS SHOWN HERE WITH ITS ORIGINAL BOX.

Mickey Mouse pocket watch with a Mickey chromium fob to the smaller wristwatch. On the back of the watch there was a die-embossed figure of Mickey Mouse enclosed in two circles with the legend "Ingersoll-Mickey Mouse." Mickey Mouse watches are regarded by collectors and the general population alike as the most popular use of the Mickey Mouse image on a product. This continues to be true even in today's market, whether it's an original Ingersoll or a new Seiko.

By the late 1930s, the Ingersoll watches became rectangular rather than round and utilized a less implike, mischievous Mickey than the original. Nevertheless these are still desirable among collectors, and the boxes, in royal blue with a large Mickey graphic, are very bright and cheery. The Mickey Mouse lapel watch, sold by Ingersoll in 1937, came in black enamel and featured a happy Mickey Mouse on the reverse side. Discerning collectors regard this watch as a first-rate example of a beautiful Mickey Art Deco timepiece.

In 1933, the Ingersoll-Waterbury Clock Company also produced two table-model Mickey Mouse clocks, one electrical and the other a windup. Painted Depression green (a grayish-green color) on metal, the face shows Mickey with hands pointing to the hour and minute and features a smaller secondhand mechanism with three miniature Mickeys chasing after each other. A lithographed paper band on three sides of the electric clock shows Mickey Mouse and his friends jumping about. By 1934, Ingersoll realized through customer complaints that it had left out one very important ingredient for a clock—an alarm! This oversight was corrected with a "wake-up alarm system" from 1934 on. Another new feature that year was the animated "wagging head" Mickey on an alarm clock. The Century of Progress World's Fair held in Chicago from 1933 to 1934 could not get enough Mickey

Mouse timepieces to sell to its customers; the progressive, futuristic Chicago Fair offered a special Mickey Mouse watch and clock display. A Mickey Mouse watch was also put into a time-capsule buried in the ground at the New York World's Fair of 1939, giving it the important status of a "necessity" in terms of living in modern times. By 1957 the Walt Disney Company estimated that 25 million Mickey watches had been sold.

The best Mickey Mouse collector timepieces include the first watch, the pocket watch, the electric and windup clocks, all from Ingersoll-Waterbury in America or from Ingersoll, Ltd., in London, and all manufactured in 1933. The 1934 Mickey Mouse wagging head rounded alarm clocks, which came in red or green, are also important pieces. A British merchandising catalog from the 1930s pictured an ad for a store display for retail merchandising of Ingersoll, Ltd., Mickey Mouse watches and clocks. Beneath the display was an image of a boy and girl on their knees,

their arms reaching out to the sun, which is just coming over the horizon. The sunrise, with its beams of light, is a Mickey Mouse clock. On the road leading to this Art Deco Mickey Mouse sun are the words, "Every boy and girl worships Mickey Mouse." The advertisement states that 9,500,000 English children all love Mickey Mouse and *want* a Mickey Mouse watch or clock of their very own.

A French Mickey Mouse alarm clock with a wagging head has a red-gloved Mickey almost racing at or against the concept of time. These rounded clocks came in painted red, blue, cream, or gray metal cases and were produced from 1936 through 1969 by the Bayard Company of France without changing a single aspect of the design or manufacture. In the 1960s nostalgia revival, which embraced the fashion of wearing Mickey Mouse watches, some very

attractive production pieces were originally made as prototypes for Ingersoll-Waterbury by artist–toy dealer Al Horen but were never produced in volume. Horen sold these collectible watches showing Mickey embracing Minnie amidst fluttering red hearts at Renninger's Antique Market in Adamstown, Pennsylvania, in the sixties and seventies. Called "love-in" watches, they are regarded as art pieces that have become rare treasures. Certainly, they are hard to find today.

TOP RIGHT: UNIQUE MICKEY AND MINNIE "LOVE-IN" POCKET WATCH CRAFTED BY AL HOREN, A PENNSYLVANIA ARTIST, AS A PRODUCTION MODEL FOR THE 1960S "NOSTALGIA" MARKETPLACE. THIS TIMEPIECE WAS NEVER MASS PRODUCED AND THE PROTOTYPES ARE NOW REGARDED AS RARE COLLECTORS' ITEMS, WHEN THEY CAN BE FOUND. RIGHT: THE 1937 MICKEY MOUSE LAPEL WATCH IS A RARITY TODAY, SINCE THE INGERSOLL-WATERBURY CLOCK CO. PRODUCED IT IN LIMITED NUMBERS. IT SOLD ORIGINALLY FOR $1.50. THE REVERSE SIDE OF THE WATCH FEATURES A COLOR ENAMEL MICKEY MOUSE. LEFT: CELLULOID-ENCASED, ART DECO STYLE WINDUP DESK CLOCK MEASURES ONLY 2 INCHES HIGH. THIS RARE MICKEY MOUSE TIMEPIECE WAS PRODUCED IN 1934 BY INGERSOLL-WATERBURY.

OPPOSITE: THE FIRST MICKEY MOUSE CLOCK, PRODUCED BY INGERSOLL-WATERBURY, SOLD FOR $1.50 IN 1933. THE METAL CASE WAS PAINTED DEPRESSION GREEN, AND A PAPER BAND PASTED ON THE SIDE FEATURED LITHOGRAPHS OF MICKEY MOUSE AND HIS FRIENDS.

SEVEN

"HOME SWEET HOME" MICKEY

Mickey Mouse for Tots

One of the first things a baby sees is Mickey Mouse on a rattle, as a doll, or in a picture on the nursery wall. The Mickey image is as omnipresent today as it was in the 1930s and the decades that followed. Youngsters now have the chance to see and talk with a lifesize Mickey Mouse with a gigantic head at any one of the Disney theme parks in California, Florida, France, or Tokyo. One bemused collector of Mickey Mouse toys stated, "That face, that image, has become so familiar to me that it wouldn't surprise me in the least to see Mickey Mouse, the size of a human-in-the-flesh walking down the street." Children exclaim that there is something magical about Mickey, more so than any other single cartoon image they have encountered. To the world at large Mickey Mouse has, like Pinocchio, *become* real.

Some wonderful tot merchandise from a variety of manufacturers was produced in the thirties, forties, and fifties. These items are the Disney collectibles of today. While some of these toys are scarce, others were mass produced and are somewhat more available in the Disneyana sellers' market. Hemco Moulding, a division of the Bryant Electric Company of Bridgeport, Connecticut, manufactured children's cocoa mugs, sectioned feeding plates, cereal bowls, and Mickey Mouse dish sets in a sturdy early plastic called Beetleware. Beetleware was produced in red, white, blue, yellow, cream, and green. Little Orphan Annie Ovaltine shake-up mugs, Captain Midnight cups and shakers, Skippy cereal bowls and spoons, and other send-away premiums of the thirties and forties were also made of this "new and unbreakable" plastic material.

ABOVE: MICKEY MOUSE IS ON BABY'S FIRST DRINKING MUG, MADE OF BEETLEWARE IN DEPRESSION GREEN BY THE HEMCO MOLDING DIVISION OF THE BRYANT ELECTRIC COMPANY OF BRIDGEPORT, CONN., IN 1935. HEMCO ALSO PRODUCED CEREAL BOWLS, FEEDING DISHES, AND MINIATURE PLAY TEA SETS IN GREEN, RED, AND YELLOW "SAFETY" PLASTICS. OPPOSITE: TOY WASHING MACHINE WAS MANUFACTURED IN LITHOGRAPHED METAL BY THE OHIO ART COMPANY, BRYAN, OHIO, C. 1934. MANY OF THESE MICKEY MOUSE "WASHER" TOYS INCLUDED A CRANKABLE WOODEN WRINGER.

GET MY SWELL SILVERPLATED
MICKEY MOUSE SPOON
WITH MY PICTURE EMBOSSED ON THE HANDLE!

POST-O
The NEW Wheat Cereal

LEFT: MICKEY'S IMAGE IS EM-
BOSSED ON THE HANDLE OF THIS
SILVERPLATED SPOON, MADE BY
WM. ROGERS & SON, A DIVISION OF
INTERNATIONAL SILVER COMPANY,
MERIDEN, CONN., AND OFFERED IN
1937 FOR ONLY 10¢, PLUS A BOX
TOP FROM POST-O WHEAT CEREAL.
BELOW: WM. ROGERS & SON ALSO
PRODUCED A CHILD'S DRINKING CUP
IN STERLING SILVER WITH A DIE-
EMBOSSED MICKEY, C. 1934.

In 1937 either children or their doting parents could send in a box top from Post-O-Wheat Cereal to General Foods and receive in the mail in a cardboard box a 5½-inch silver-plated Mickey Mouse cereal spoon. A small child's fork and knife set first produced in 1934 by Fairfield Silver Plate had embossed Mickeys and Minnies on them. The William Rogers & Son sterling silver Mickey Mouse drinking cup, on which a child's name and birth date were often engraved, is considered a fine collectible. The Salem China Company of Salem, Ohio, put out a quality line of Mickey Mouse dishware to attend to baby's eating needs. A three-piece set included a mug, a bowl, and a sectioned dinner plate.

Blankets, coverlets, bibs, towels, washrags, sheets, pillowcases, and other fabric "useables" with Disney characters imprinted on them were distributed by Smith, Hogg & Company, Inc., of New York, Boston, and Chicago. The Seiberling Latex Rubber Products Company produced Mickey Mouse rubber crib dolls with movable parts, as well as hot-water bottles in

A MINNIE MOUSE SAFETY WOOD
BLOCK, ENAMELED AND EMBOSSED
WITH ROUNDED CORNERS, HALSAM
PRODUCTS CO., CHICAGO, 1935.

the shape of Mickey Mouse in a sleeping outfit, Mickey Mouse playpen balls, and squeeze-whistle latex Mickey dolls. The American Latex Corporation of New York made a notable contribution to babydom with Mickey baby panties. Celluloid rattles for babies were produced by the Amloid Company of Lodi, New Jersey. The Mengel Corporation of St. Louis, Missouri, introduced Mickey Mouse playroom rockers, a backyard slide, and a seesaw youngsters and adults alike admired. The rockers, which employed big, painted wood jigsaw cutouts of Mickey, were initially distributed by the George Borgfeldt Company of New York.

Machine-carved, painted wood Mickey Mouse "safety" alphabet blocks were first produced in 1935 by the Halsom Products Company of Chicago, packaged in a beautiful litho-on-cardboard box with a happy Mickey running and an eager Minnie on the chase. These sets came with 9, 16, 20, 30 or 50 blocks featuring Mickey, Minnie, Pluto, Horace, Clarabelle, and other characters and were painted in primary colors like orange, green, red, and blue.

Eminently collectible in the Disneyana field and found everywhere in America in

the 1930s are the Made in Japan children's play chinaware tea sets featuring Mickey, Minnie, Donald, and the gang running, jumping, rowing, singing, or playing instruments. This cheap chinaware was imported and distributed by the Borgfeldt Corporation of New York in boxed sets in an amazing variety, with dinner and dessert plates, cake plates, grille (or sectioned) plates, covered specialty serving pieces, cups and saucers, teapots, creamers, and sugar bowls. Boxes were often brilliantly decorated with repeat images of the Disney characters; others were distributed in plain cardboard boxes with paper labels. Often the sets included an unusual Silly Symphony character like Elmer Elephant along with the images of Mickey, Minnie, Donald, or the Three Little Pigs and the Big Bad Wolf; other sets were figural, Mickey's head being the teapot top, his right arm the spout. Most of the pieces were marked on the bottom "Mickey Mouse—Copyright by Walt E. Disney—Made in Japan."

Limoges of France produced a brilliant line of Disney dishes for children, including complete tea sets, cake plates, cereal bowls, and drinking mugs. Faïencèrie D'Onnaing was another French company whose imported Disney dishware is delicately decorated in fast-action scenes in beautiful colors. The Paragon China Company of Great Britain produced sturdy baby dishware with images of Mickey and fanciful slogans alongside. Mickey Mouse china sets

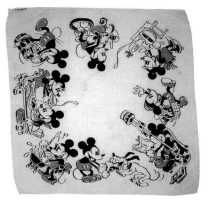

SUNDAY NEWS COLOR SUPPLEMENT AD FOR BLOOMINGDALE'S DEPARTMENT STORE SALE OF WALT DISNEY CHARACTER SWEATERS MADE BY KARINETTE, INC., NEW YORK. SEPTEMBER 7, 1947.

RIGHT: HOMEBODIES MICKEY AND MINNIE ON A HERMANN'S HANDKERCHIEF. BELOW: WHEN IT RAINS GET YOUR DONALD DUCK "DRY IN ANY WEATHER" ENDORSED JACKETS FROM NORWICH KNITTING COMPANY, NORWICH, N.Y. THIS PINBACK BUTTON, C. 1935, HAS AN ORIGINAL BACK PAPER LISTING THE MANUFACTURER AS ORANGE MFG. CORP/NEWARK, N.J. OPPOSITE: THIS HANDKERCHIEF BOX SHOWS MICKEY, MINNIE, DONALD, PLUTO, ELMER ELEPHANT, DOPEY, AND TWO DUCK NEPHEWS IN MARCH FORMATION. MADE BY HERMANN HANDKERCHIEF CO., NEW YORK, IN 1940.

were made in the early 1930s in Bavaria and imported by the Shumann China Company of New York. These fine "ready for use by children" cereal bowls, plates, cups, and saucers were stamped on the bottom "Authorized by Walter E. Disney—Made in Bavaria." Movie theater managers offered Bavarian Mickey Mouse pieces as prizes at Saturday movie matinees and special Dish Night at the Movies contests. The movie theaters also gave away adult ceramics, including bud vases, ashtrays, canister sets, jewelry trays, and other items, all with a Mickey Mouse image on them. Wade, Heath & Company Limited of Burslem, England, also produced tea sets, cups, saucers, creamers, and sugar bowls featuring Mickey Mouse, Minnie Mouse, Pluto, Donald, Horace Horsecollar, Clarabelle the Cow, and the other friends.

Wearables for Boys and Girls

A Mickey Mouse, Minnie Mouse, or other early Disney character image on clothing is a continuing fashion trend for today as Mickey & Co. and other newly licensed clothiers supply the constant demand. It is hard to walk down the street without seeing children and adults alike wearing a Mickey T-shirt or sweatshirt. Mickey wearables were initially considered as fare only for tots and children, though in the Depression decade Buddy Ebsen sported a Mickey Mouse sweatshirt when he tap danced on a New York tenement rooftop with

Donald Duck Jackets DRY IN ANY WEATHER NORWICH KNITTING CO. NORWICH, N.Y.

Eleanor Powell in the MGM musical *The Broadway Melody of 1936*. In *The Broadway Melody of 1938*, it was Donald Duck who was represented on an adult-size T-shirt on the silver screen.

Disneyana collectors as well as those who specialize in retro-clothing regard antique Mickey wearables as prize pieces today, when they can find them. Original sweatshirts, pullovers, pajamas, scarves, mittens, or sweaters with Mickey images on them are now scarce, as much of the clothing was worn out, while other items were discarded or given away to the ragman.

BELOW: "IN CONFERENCE," A 1932 PUZZLE WITHIN A PUZZLE, FROM THE EINSON-FREEMAN COMPANY, NEW YORK. THREE BOYS AT PLAY IN THE DINING ROOM, TWO IN SHIRT AND TIE, AND ONE IN HIS MICKEY MOUSE PULLOVER SWEATSHIRT, WHICH WAS PROBABLY MANUFACTURED BY THE NORWICH KNITTING CO. **RIGHT:** MICKEY MOUSE LANDS A BIG FISH ON THIS BOYS' RAYON TIE FROM D. H. NEUMANN CO., NEW YORK, FROM THE LATE 1930S.

boys' belts, suspenders, slippers or moccasins, rubber boots, jumpsuits, girls' pocket purses, boys' and girls' hats, pajamas with repeat patterns of Mickey Mouse and his friends, umbrellas with composition or Bakelite Mickey or Minnie figurine handles, raincoats, jewelry, and hair barrettes.

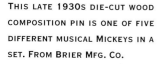

THIS LATE 1930S DIE-CUT WOOD COMPOSITION PIN IS ONE OF FIVE DIFFERENT MUSICAL MICKEYS IN A SET. FROM BRIER MFG. CO.

Accessories like ties, kiddy umbrellas, children's jewelry, handkerchiefs, and pocketbooks can be found more often, while shirts, galoshes, socks, or belts are less apt to show up in the markets. Colorful litho-on-cardboard boxes such as the ones for Mickey Mouse "undies" are thought of as very desirable by collectors because of their unusually strong graphics and colors.

Among the great variety of early children's wearables featuring Mickey Mouse, Minnie Mouse, Pluto, or other members of the original family are all-wool sweaters (with a character, usually Mickey, centered on the front), boys' ties, boxed sets of handkerchiefs,

Mickey Mouse All Over the House

A child growing up in the Depression could have his or her entire room decorated with Mickey and the gang. The centerpiece of such a room might be the tabletop desk from the Kroehler Manufacturing Company of San Francisco, which specialized in producing fine children's furniture in the 1930s. This Mickey Mouse desk and other pieces from Kroehler, like the Mickey bookshelves or end tables, featured a Mickey Mouse painted wood cutout on one side and a Minnie Mouse jigsaw on the other. The desk also included a Mickey, Minnie, or Pluto stool.

A child's room might also utilize sun-tested and waterproof Mickey Mouse

ENGLISH-MADE PAINTED LEAD FIGURINE WITH MATCH HOLDER AND ASHTRAY, C. 1930.

UNITED WALLPAPER FACTORIES, JERSEY CITY, N.J., PRODUCED MICKEY MOUSE WALLPAPER IN 1935 AND 1936.

BELOW: MINNIE MOUSE AND MICKEY MOUSE GLASS TUMBLERS, FROM LIBBEY-OWENS GLASS CO., TOLEDO, OHIO, 1936.

ABOVE LEFT: MICKEY MOUSE RELAXING AT HOME ON A HAND-EMBROIDERED COTTON PILLOWCASE. DISNEY SEWING PATTERNS WERE OFFERED FOR A VARIETY OF SOFTWARE GOODS IN THE EARLY 1930S THROUGH VOGUE NEEDLECRAFT COMPANY, NEW YORK. ABOVE RIGHT: THIS MICKEY MOUSE SERIES #98 PILLOWCASE, FROM VOGUE NEEDLECRAFT, WAS AVAILABLE IN RETAIL SEWING STORES AND YARN SHOPS IN 1931. HAND-EMBROIDERED BY OLGA HEITKE OF IRVINGTON, N.J., IT FEATURES MICKEY AND MINNIE SHARING A PATCHED UMBRELLA IN A RAINSTORM.

LEFT: The cigarettes stand upright in these Mickey and Minnie porcelain ashtrays, hand painted in Japan in the early 1930s.

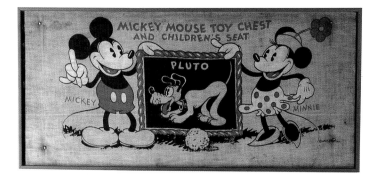

BELOW: This Mickey Mouse toy chest, made of lithographed wood and corrugated cardboard, and measuring 26 x 13 x 16 inches, has a top covered in printed cotton (left) that doubles as a children's seat. From the Odora Company, New York, c. 1935.

ABOVE: Art Deco style Mickey Mouse radio. The cabinetry is constructed of painted wood trimmed in metal. Made by Emerson Radio and Phonograph Corp., New York, 1934.
BELOW: Giveaway pinback button for the Mickey Mouse Emerson radio, c. 1934.

wallpaper and trim from the United Wallpaper Factory, Inc., of Jersey City, New Jersey. A toy chest manufactured by the Odora Company, made of cardboard and wood with a fabric cover, could also serve as a child's windowseat.

Lucky lads and lasses in the Depression could tune into their favorite radio programs on a square, boxlike, four-tube "Baby" Emerson radio made of a pressed wood called Syroco. Model 411 came in two versions, unpainted and lightly varnished and "painted all-in-color," both versions featuring Mickey in relief on all four sides playing different musical instruments. Emerson Radio and Phonograph Company also manufactured two Art Deco radios (model 410), one in black enamel with an aluminum cutout of Mickey as a speaker grille, with Minnie, Pluto, Horace, and Clarabelle on separate aluminum strips at the corners; the other was in cream and green enamel.

Alongside a child's bed on a night table might be a painted plaster lamp of Mickey sitting in an overstuffed chair from the Soreng Manegold Company of Chicago. This tabletop lamp came with a paper lamp shade with, of course, a Mickey Mouse litho on it. A figural bisque Mickey Mouse toothbrush holder with a Mickey Mouse toothbrush held in one arm would sit on the dresser. A child would remove the brush just before bedtime, brush his teeth, and carefully return the brush to the Mickey holder. Rarely did these cartoon-character bisque toothbrush holders sit on a bathroom sink, since they could so easily fall over and break.

For the bathroom, boxed Mickey Mouse figural soap was available at drugstores from the Lightfoot Schultz Company of New York, and Mickey Mouse toothpaste came from the Kent Dental Laboratories of Philadelphia. Boys and girls could brush their hair with fine Mickey Mouse hairbrushes, which came in sturdy decorated cardboard boxes from the Hughes-Autograf Brush Company of New York. On the floor of the room you could find one of the colorful Mickey-in-action-adventure

rugs, which might show Mickey throwing a snowball at Donald, or Mickey in a cowboy outfit riding his horse Tanglefoot, pursued by Peg Leg Pete. These rugs were made by the Alexander Smith Company of Yonkers, New York. Mickey Mouse linoleum with all the characters was produced by several American firms.

In the kitchen Mickey Mouse turned up on tablecloths, napkins, tea towels, colorful Catalin napkin rings, cookie jars, hot-dish holders, dishware, ceramic planters, glass tumblers, and as salt and pepper shakers. The square, factory painted cream and Depression-green enamel "baby" Emerson Mickey Mouse radios found their way into many middle-class kitchens, which were often painted in those same easy to clean soft 1930s colors.

The living room or parlor seldom went Mickey Mouse, but an occasional Mickey chalk or composition amusement park figure might be found standing atop a mantle or the family console radio. Glazed ceramic figurines of Disney characters and painted-on-metal, porcelain, or glass figurine ash-receivers were popular novelty store-bought souvenirs that were proudly displayed on blue-mirrored end tables or on small glass or Lucite knickknack shelves. These novelties would also serve as decoratives for a post-Prohibition barroom, game room, or den.

Nonlicensed, Japanese-made Mickey Mouse look-alike ceramic planters, match holders, ashtrays, and pincushions were a rage in the dime stores, selling in the millions in a period when such a famous mouse could take on a number of image variations and look-alike identities. An embroidered *Vogue* or *McCall's Needlecraft* pillow from a Mickey Mouse sendaway or a sewing-center appliqué transfer added a note of fun and color to a sofa or chair, the graphics featuring Mickey and Minnie caught in a rain shower or Mickey reading under a shaded lamp, snuggled into an overstuffed armchair while eating from a box of chocolates.

EIGHT

FUNTIME MICKEY

Merchandise in the toy industry is not meant to be just seasonal but is usually geared to specific time points and references. Certainly back-to-school in autumn leads into Halloween and then to Thanksgiving and the Christmas season, when many stores in the United States claim to do more than one-third of their total yearly business. Easter awakens the spring buying season, while summer, as vacation time, presents other opportunities in the sales marketplace.

22-in. Mickey Mouse Shooting Gallery
17½-in. sturdy colorful, tripod type, target. 6 rubber tipped vacuum cup darts! 7⅝-in. enameled steel gun with powerful spring.
49 F 5669—Shpg. wt., 3 lbs. 8 oz... **89c**

Pin-the-Tail on Mickey: Games and Targets

The very best in Disneyana graphics are found on the boxes and boards of games. The Mickey Mouse Target manufactured by Marks Brothers is a first-rate example of the type of design and excellent color lithography that attracts collectors to these original Pop Art works. A child given a gift of this dart board in 1934 at Christmas or on his or her birthday would be overjoyed. It came with a black metal gun, six wood and rubber suction darts, and a rubber-tipped three-legged stand.

The Quoits Gameboard made by Chad Valley of Birmingham, England, has exactly the same straightforward Mickey Mouse image as the American dart set. A red circle in the center with the number 1000 substitutes for Mickey's shorts, but he is wearing

ABOVE: MICKEY MOUSE BAGATELLE GAME, COLOR-LITHOGRAPHED PAPER ON CARDBOARD, WOOD, AND METAL, MANUFACTURED BY MARKS BROTHERS COMPANY OF BOSTON, MASS., 1934. **LEFT AND OPPOSITE:** MICKEY MOUSE TARGET GAME, OFFERED BY SEARS, ROEBUCK FOR 89¢ IN 1934, CAME WITH TARGET, SPRING GUN, SUCTION DARTS, AND THREE-LEGGED WOOD STAND. FROM MARKS BROTHERS.

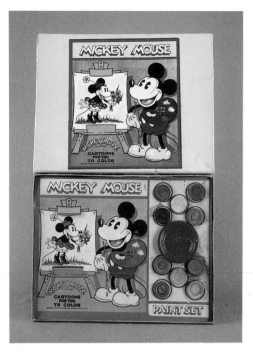

MICKEY MOUSE PAINT SET (WITH OPEN BOX TOP) WAS MANUFAC-TURED IN THE EARLY 1930S BY MARKS BROTHERS, BOSTON, MASS.

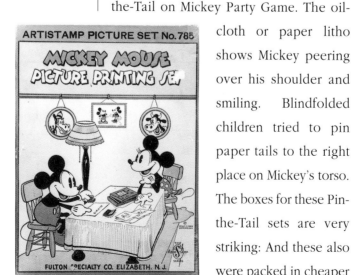

MICKEY MOUSE PICTURE PRINTING SET FROM FULTON SPECIALTY CO., 1935.

his big yellow clownlike shoes and his yellow gloved hands rest on his hips. Mickey stands smiling, and behind him are bright red, yellow, and blue circles. The American board (which came in two sizes) was thick cardboard cut in a circle, while the diamond-shaped English board had metal hooks attached for the quoits.

The bright blue background and the red, yellow, and black Mickey graphic on the Mickey Mouse Bagatelle Game, made of wood, metal, lithographed paper, and cardboard, shows Mickey with one gloved hand lowered and one held up as if he were playing catch. This happy Mickey graphic image was repeated on the Mickey Mouse Hoop-La Game and the Pin-the-Tail on Mickey Party Game. The oil-cloth or paper litho shows Mickey peering over his shoulder and smiling. Blindfolded children tried to pin paper tails to the right place on Mickey's torso. The boxes for these Pin-the-Tail sets are very striking: And these also were packed in cheaper

LITHOGRAPHED METAL STAMP PAD, FROM FULTON SPECIALTY CO., 1935.

picture envelopes with the same graphic.

Prized items in the world of Disneyana collecting are a number of the games produced in the 1930s by Marks Brothers of Boston, which in addition to the bagatelle, hoop-la, and the pin-the-tail games sold a circus game with colorful images of Mickey and Minnie with horses, lions and seals, a topple Mickey in which children could shoot down Mickey and Minnie, a Mickey Mouse kite, a squeeze toy, a bean-bag, miniature pinball games, soldier sets, and a Mickey Mouse Rollem' Game. The splendid Scatter Ball Game, also from Marks Brothers, shows eight repetitions of Mickey with images of Minnie, Pluto, Clarabelle, and Horace on the box and board in the colors most associated with Mickey—yellow, red, blue, and black.

Other producers of Disney games for the children's market of the 1930s include the Einson-Freeman Publishing Corporation of New York, which made Mickey Mouse puzzles, and the Fulton Specialty Company of Elizabeth, New Jersey, which made Be Your Own Printer sets that came with litho-on-metal ink pads and Mickey Mouse rubber stampers. American Toy Works of New York, Parker Brothers Inc., of Salem,

LEFT: MARKS BROTHERS MADE THIS OIL-CLOTH 22 X 28 INCH PIN-THE-TAIL-ON-MICKEY AS PART OF THE MICKEY MOUSE PARTY GAME SET (ABOVE) IN 1935.

Massachusetts, and the Milton Bradley Company of Springfield, Massachusetts, also produced games featuring Mickey and the original gang. American-made products were happily augmented in the market-place by foreign licensees like the Vera Company of Paris, which manufactured and exported to America beautiful puzzles and other games.

If these or some other games, toys, or a wristwatch were wrapped in Mickey Mouse Christmas or birthday paper, more often than not they would be accompanied by a Mickey Mouse greeting card from Hall Brothers (Hallmark Cards), which had offices in the Empire State Building in New York and was headquartered in Kansas City, Missouri. These fine Disney graphics of Mickey or one of his pals are collected with zest. The Mickey Mouse portrayed on Hall Brothers cards of the 1930s is wonder-ful in his impishness.

Seaside Play

Summer sand pails, sand-sifters, toy water pumps, and sand shovels in Technicolor litho-on-tin from the Ohio Art Company of Bryan, Ohio, were extremely familiar items at the beaches during the thirties and for-ties. Collectors enjoy them today for their Mickey cartoon-art style, showing Mickey and Minnie, Horace, Clarabelle, and Pluto at play on the beach or in the water, on a picnic outing, in a parade or selling lemon-ade. A particularly novel big-sized sand pail shows Mickey pushing Minnie in a wicker boardwalk rolling chair with "Atlantic City" written in big letters. Ohio Art also pro-duced wonderfully crafted children's play-time tea sets, snow shovels, drums, carpet sweepers, and other play items in tin-litho. The Paton Calvert Company, Ltd., of London produced similar and equally beau-tiful litho-on-metal seaside pails, children's tea sets, money boxes, and tin drums with the marking "By Permission of Walt Disney (Mickey Mouse) Ltd."

ABOVE: LITHOGRAPHED TIN AND WIRE-SCREEN SAND SIFTERS, WHICH CAME WITH A COLORFUL METAL FISH SAND MOLD AND SAND SHOVEL, WERE MANUFACTURED FOR SEASIDE FUN BY THE OHIO ART COMPANY, 1934. **BELOW**: LARGE-SIZED MICKEY-MINNIE-PLUTO LITHOGRAPHED TIN SAND PAIL, OHIO ART COMPANY, 1938.

ABOVE LEFT: LITHO-ON-TIN SAND PAIL SHOWING MICKEY MOUSE WITH A DONALD DUCK SANDPAIL. THE PAIL, WHICH ORIGINALLY CONTAINED CANDY LOLLIPOPS, AND SHOVEL WERE MANUFACTURED IN GREAT BRITAIN AS PART OF THE "HAPPYNAK SERIES." **LEFT**: DONALD TESTS THE WATER ON THIS LARGE LITHOGRAPHED METAL SAND SHOVEL WHILE TWO OF HIS NEPHEWS LOOK ON. FROM OHIO ART COMPANY, 1939.

R. H. Macy & Company's Santa Claus handed out copies of "Mickey Mouse and Minnie at Macy's" to children during Christmas 1934. Kay Kamen instigated this promotional giveaway, which was so popular that another book, entitled "Mickey Mouse and Minnie March to Macy's" (below), was given out at Macy's during the 1935 Christmas season.

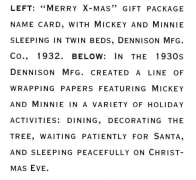

ABOVE: "We're in the money!" A Depression-era Christmas greeting card with book-style folds, from Hall Brothers, Kansas City, Mo., 1935. **RIGHT:** "Wheeeeee" greeting card, Hall Brothers, 1934.

LEFT: "Merry X-mas" gift package name card, with Mickey and Minnie sleeping in twin beds, Dennison Mfg. Co., 1932. **BELOW:** In the 1930s Dennison Mfg. created a line of wrapping papers featuring Mickey and Minnie in a variety of holiday activities: dining, decorating the tree, waiting patiently for Santa, and sleeping peacefully on Christmas Eve.

Merry Christmas with Mickey and Minnie

The Christmas season is the biggest one for toy manufacturers; and the many toys featuring Mickey engaged in Christmas activities originally found under the tree on Christmas mornings by children in the thirties, forties, and fifties are eagerly sought by collectors today who have developed a new appreciation for these artful, themed objects. The Mickey Christmas specialty items on many Disneyana collectors' "most wanted" lists would include in addition to a good selection of Disney greeting cards from Hall Brothers, the spectacular Mickey Mouse light sets from Noma Electric Corporation. These Mazda tree lights have varicolored Beetleware shades featuring decal appliqués of the early Disney characters engaged in Christmas pursuits. Some, where Mickey, Minnie, Pluto, and Donald are playing at wintertime snow sports, are particularly engaging. Mickey Mouse was a perennial giant balloon in the Macy's Thanksgiving Day Parade during the Depression, bringing cheer to children and their families and the legions of unemployed who watched the parade go by as they drank a cup of coffee and ate a cruller offered by the Salvation Army. R. H. Macy also had Santa Claus present children who visited him during the Christmas season of 1934 with a giveaway Big Little–type book entitled *Mickey Mouse and Minnie at Macy's*. Another tiny book, *Mickey Mouse and Minnie March to Macy's*, was given out in 1935. Both of these books tell the story—in words and ink drawings—of Macy's huge Thanksgiving Day Parade.

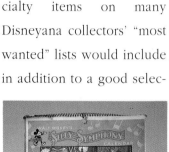

LEFT: *THE NIGHT BEFORE CHRISTMAS*, A 1933 SILLY SYMPHONY CARTOON, IS THE ILLUSTRATION FOR THE DECEMBER 1938 SUNSHINE BEER CALENDAR, E. C. STASHINSKI, DISTRIBUTOR, MT. CARMEL, PA. RIGHT: MICKEY MOUSE CHRISTMAS TREE LIGHTING SET FROM NOMA ELECTRIC CORP., NEW YORK. MAZDA LIGHTS INSIDE ARE COVERED WITH COLORFUL BEETLEWARE SHADES WITH DECAL APPLIQUÉS OF THE DISNEY CHARACTERS IN HOLIDAY SCENES. SHOWN WITH THE ORIGINAL BOX, THIS SET WAS SOLD IN 1936 TO ADD MICKEY MOUSE CHRISTMAS CHEER IN THE GREAT DEPRESSION.

Fun in the Snow

In January, after the merrymaking at Christmas, when heavy snow begins to fall, reluctant children must be sent back to the schoolroom. But as the icy chill of Old Man Winter settles in, there is always some time to be found for fun in the snow.

If a child's Christmas gifts included a Mickey Mouse snowsuit from Mayfair Togs, Inc., of New York, Mickey Mouse mittens, Mickey Mouse rubber boots, or a Mickey Mouse scarf, then he or she could romp about in style and warmth in a fully guaranteed Mickey product. For indoor fun children could play with their Christmas gift toys and games, or venture out on the frozen iceponds wearing Mickey Mouse ice skates. And, for gliding down a snow bank, there was a Mickey Mouse or Donald Duck sled from S. L. Allen and Company, Inc., of Philadelphia. This company boasted in its merchandise advertisements: "The makers of the famous Flexible Flyer now include a complete line of sleds incorporating the designs and names of the outstanding Walt Disney characters." The Mickey Mouse sled came in 30" and 32" sizes, and the Donald Duck model, showing Donald with Huey, Dewey and Louie, was 36" long. Later, a 40-inch-long Snow White and the Seven Dwarfs model was added for bigger children. These snowsleds were sturdily constructed of wood and steel, and were sold in great volume in the 1930s.

Mickey or Donald often appeared on film cavorting in winter activities and sports just like any other kid, and one of the best of these Mickey wintertime cartoons is called *On Ice* (1935). In stories, coloring books, games, and as illustration on

ABOVE: DIE-CUT *MICKEY MOUSE BOOK FOR COLORING* (10 ½ x 14 INCHES) WAS PUBLISHED IN 1936 BY THE SAALFIELD PUBLISHING COMPANY, AKRON, OHIO. RIGHT: "COME ON EVERYBODY, LET'S GO SLEDDING," SAYS MICKEY, ON THIS PAMPHLET FOR A MICKEY MOUSE SLED MANUFACTURED BY THE MAKERS OF THE FAMOUS FLEXIBLE FLYER, S. L. ALLEN & CO., PHILADELPHIA, 1935.

children's winter outdoor toggery—scarves, mittens, hats, sweaters, or snowsuits—Disney characters were engaged in winter play, whether it be an image of Mickey hurling a snowball at a flustered Donald Duck or, perhaps, another of Mickey and Minnie skating over the ice or skiing down a snowy slope. Mickey Mouse and his friends were enthusiastic about their wintertime activities—and the world happily joined in the snow fun.

ABOVE: MICKEY MOUSE SKI JUMPING, GLASS-COVERED MINIATURE BAGATELLE GAME FROM MARKS BROTHERS, C. 1934.

RIGHT: DETAIL FROM THE PAMPHLET ACCOMPANYING S. L. ALLEN & CO.'S MICKEY MOUSE WOOD AND METAL SLED (BELOW), 30 INCHES LONG AND MADE IN 1935.

A Spooky Mouse

Halloween is always a scary, mysterious, and wondrous time for children; and during mischiefmaking or trick or treating in the thirties, boys and girls came dressed up as their beloved mouse characters Mickey and Minnie. The painted black-and-white lifesize Mickey-Minnie face masks made of stiff molded cheesecloth by the Wornova Manufacturing Company of New York were indeed fright-ening to many. Mickey had a big rat-face, while the Minnie Mouse mask bore a full set of rat-like choppers. Collectors prize these wonderful masks; and if they can find a vintage thirties outfit in the original box with the full costume intact, that is a real plus. Sometimes these masks are squashed, mangled, or torn in places; but they can be artfully reshaped and restored with a bit of paste, water, and extra cheesecloth or burlap.

TOP: A STIFF, MOLDED CHEESE-CLOTH MICKEY MOUSE HALLOWEEN MASK, STAMPED INSIDE "WOR-NOVA—LICENSE FROM WALT DISNEY" AND MADE BY WORNOVA MFG. CO., NEW YORK, 1934. ABOVE: DONALD DUCK MASK FROM 1936. TOP RIGHT: GUM-BACKED HALLOWEEN PAPER SEAL, FEATUR-ING A TRADITIONAL MICKEY AGAINST A SMILING PUMPKIN. DENNISON'S MANUFACTURING CO., FRAMINGHAM, MASS., 1935. RIGHT: KIDS OF THE DEPRESSION-ERA DRESSED UP FOR HALLOWEEN IN THEIR MICKEY MOUSE, MINNIE MOUSE, DONALD DUCK, POPEYE, OLIVE OYL, AND OTHER FAVORITE COMIC STRIP CARTOON CHARACTER OUTFITS.

MICKEY AND MINNIE PULLING AT A WISHBONE FOR VALENTINE'S DAY. HALL BROTHERS GREETING CARD, 1932.

Valentine's Day and Eastertime

On Valentine's Day there were many Mickey Mouse or Minnie Mouse greeting cards produced by the indomitable Hall Brothers of Kansas City and New York that could be sent to a boy or girl from their "secret" sweetheart, or to teachers, parents, and other relatives. A Charlotte Clark Mickey or Minnie doll was a popular favorite at Easter, in case a Depression kid had missed out on one at Christmas. The Paas Dye Company of Newark, New Jersey, sold attractive packages of Mickey Mouse transfers for Easter eggs, with a bright graphic of Mickey, the Funny Little Bunnies, and Donald Duck, who as a duck could easily enter the Easter markets at the dime store.

RIGHT: "MAN-EGG-KINS" CUTOUT DONALD DUCK KIT FOR DRESSING UP EASTER EGGS, PASS DYE CO., NEWARK, N.J., LATE 1930S. BELOW: MICKEY MOUSE "TRANSFER-O-S FOR EASTER EGGS." PASS DYE CO., C. 1935.

1936 HALLMARK EASTER GREETING CARD. INSIDE IT READS: MICKEY HAS HIS HANDS FULL BUT STILL HE COMES TO SAY SOMEONE YOU KNOW IS WISHING YOU A HAPPY EASTER DAY!

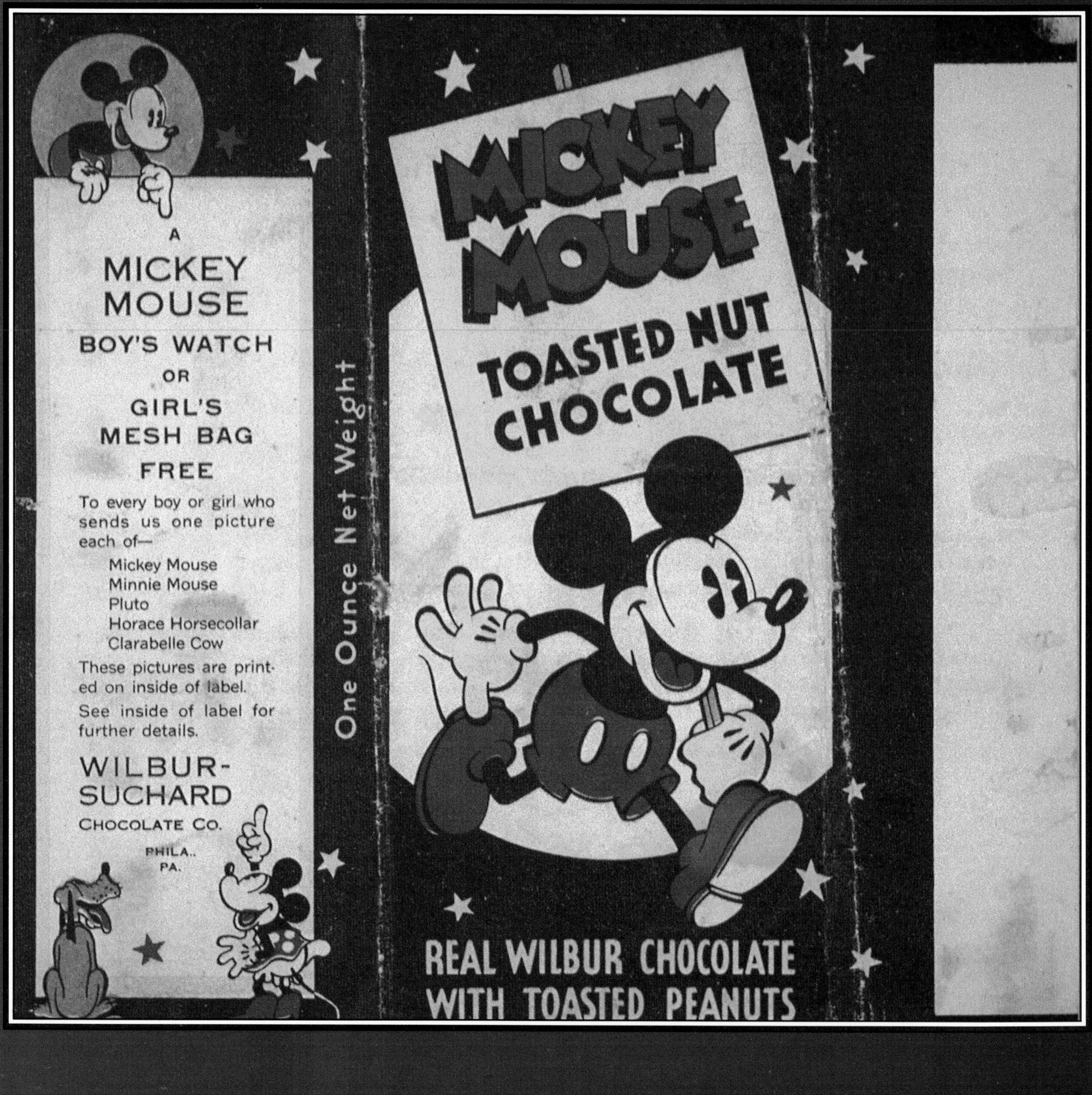
A
MICKEY
MOUSE
BOY'S WATCH
OR
GIRL'S
MESH BAG
FREE
To every boy or girl who sends us one picture each of—
Mickey Mouse
Minnie Mouse
Pluto
Horace Horsecollar
Clarabelle Cow
These pictures are printed on inside of label.
See inside of label for further details.
WILBUR-SUCHARD
CHOCOLATE CO.
PHILA., PA.
One Ounce Net Weight
MICKEY MOUSE
TOASTED NUT CHOCOLATE
REAL WILBUR CHOCOLATE
WITH TOASTED PEANUTS

NINE

BUY THIS BREAD

The merchandising campaigns created by Kay Kamen for retail-store exploitation of Mickey Mouse products included large cut-out displays and promotional giveaway booklets, posters, and store window signs, campaign newspaper advertising, and other ephemera that are seen as important aspects of collecting Disneyana. Pinback buttons, rulers, Mickey play money, paper masks, balloons, T-shirts, and other giveaways, including the 145-page illustrated storybook *Mickey Mouse and the Magic Carpet*, were available to movie exhibitors and retailers to encourage box-office receipts and product sales.

Particularly collectible are some of the food products and their packaging. The Glaser Crandell Company of Chicago manufactured what is now a rare and desirable piece—the Mickey Mouse Jam jar. After the jam was eaten and the jar washed, it could be reused as a bank. The screw-on metal top with the face of Mickey against a red background had a punch-out die-cut slot in Mickey's mouth for coins. The words "Feed Mickey for Wealth— Eat Jam for Health" are imprinted on the cap. The glass jar itself has Mickey and Minnie in relief. Usually such items would have been saved and used; but more often than not the colorful jam label disappeared as soon as the jar was washed. The label features an ecstatic Mickey Mouse eating a jam sandwich, while Minnie is handing him a jar of Mickey Mouse jam. When such a jar is found with the label intact, it can sell well into the hundreds of dollars, providing the colors on the label and the tin cap are still bright and clean and

ABOVE: MICKEY MOUSE "BUY THIS BREAD" STORE WINDOW POSTER, C. 1934. OPPOSITE: WRAPPER OF A MICKEY MOUSE TOASTED NUT CHOCOLATE BAR, MADE BY WILBUR-SUCHARD CHOCOLATE CO., PHILADELPHIA, 1934.

not faded by sunlight. These jars are found without the label, but many were just thrown away like any other product container once the jam was eaten.

Action Mickey Mouse store displays to sell this jam product (which cost 25¢) were produced by the Old King Cole Company of Canton, Ohio, and sold to retail stores through Kay Kamen Ltd. They were available as window and showroom displays for jam or jelly and for dozens of other products. These large figures of Mickey, Minnie, Clarabelle, Horace, Pluto, Goofy, Donald, and other Disney characters gave added charm and always a boost to any retail store in the 1930s that featured a Mickey Mouse product. The Mickey Mouse Bubble Gum

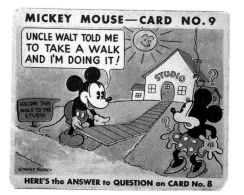

MICKEY MOUSE—CARD NO. 9

UNCLE WALT TOLD ME TO TAKE A WALK AND I'M DOING IT!

HERE'S the ANSWER to QUESTION on CARD No. 8

MICKEY MOUSE—CARD NO. 93

IS THAT WHAT YOU DO WHEN YOU GET ANGRY?

SURE, I STAMP MY FOOT!

HERE'S the ANSWER to QUESTION on CARD No. 92

MICKEY MOUSE—CARD NO. 79

WHO'S AFRAID OF THE BIG BAD WOOF!

HERE'S the ANSWER to QUESTION on CARD No. 78

MICKEY MOUSE—CARD NO. 77

YOU CAN'T MAKE IT, MICKEY! THAT ICE IS CRACKED!

THAT'S AN ICE CRACK TO MAKE, MINNIE!

HERE'S the ANSWER to QUESTION on CARD No. 76

Company picture insert cards, collected and traded eagerly during the 1930s, are again collected today. There are two series, one from 1933 to 1935, numbered 1 to 96 (with two albums) and the other, "Mickey Mouse with the Movie Stars," numbered 97 to 120. These have fine graphics, funny gags, and the colorful lithography (on cardboard) make them appealing.

The first of the successful promotional campaigns produced by Kay Kamen Ltd., in 1934–1935, featured Mickey Mouse "Buy This Bread" posters, themselves artfully executed lithographs. There were other litho store pieces, including cardboard display signs, window stick-ons, and free Globetrotter Bread Campaign Scrapbooks in which to paste your Mickey Mouse bread insert-picture cards. Post Toasties (General Foods) lithographed cardboard store display signs, as well as other bread signs and advertising, are sought after today and occasionally featured in rare-poster auction sales. The original Post Toasties Disney character cutouts, usually in yellow, red, brown, or black, taken from the back of the cereal box, are

Post Toasties

Corn Flakes

MADE OF CORN GRITS SUGAR AND SALT

POSTUM COMPANY, INC.
BATTLE CREEK, MICHIGAN
DIVISION OF
GENERAL FOODS CORPORATION
NET WEIGHT 13 OZS.
MADE IN U.S.A.

CUT-OUTS
ON BACK
AND SIDES

ABOVE: 1930s POST TOASTIES CORN FLAKES, WITH MICKEY ON THE BOX COVER. POSTUM COMPANY DIVISION OF GENERAL FOODS, BATTLE CREEK, MICHIGAN. LEFT, FROM TOP: MICKEY MOUSE GUM CARDS NO. 9, 93, 79, AND 77.

plentiful in the marketplace and still reasonably priced items for collectors. Mickey or Minnie and other comic or cartoon character cutouts were the only toys a poor child of the Depression had to play with. Mickey on roller skates, leading a band, as a circus barker, at bat, or playing instruments could bring a smile to the face of a hungry child. Cutouts of Disney characters were often saved and stored in boxes or scrapbooks; but an entire, uncut Post Toasties box is a rare find. An empty Mickey Mouse product box in good condition is a desirable item in today's popular-culture marketplace. Mickey Mouse litho candy tins are prized items; but so is a paper wrapper from a Mickey Mouse "Toasted-Nut-Chocolate" bar made and distributed in 1934 by the Wilbur-Suchard Chocolate Company of Philadelphia.

Beginning in 1937, the National Biscuit Company packaged Mickey Mouse Cookies in colorful boxes that show Mickey being chased by Donald, Pluto, and Silly Symphony characters Max Hare and Clara Cluck. The retail store cookie posters, which show Mickey holding up a sign

ABOVE: Post Toasties were on sale at the grocery store for 10¢ a box, as advertised in this 1933 litho-on-cardboard store display sign. **RIGHT:** A full, uncut back and two side panels from a 1934 Post Toasties box features cutouts of Mickey playing the accordion, the xylophone, the bass fiddle, the drum, and the tuba while Minnie "tra-la-las." These box cutouts of Disney characters were sometimes the only toys children of the Depression had to play with. **BELOW, LEFT TO RIGHT:** Post Toasties cut-out toys of Mickey and his loyal pal Pluto, Minnie with her ukulele, listening to Mickey play the harmonica, and a roller-skating Mickey.

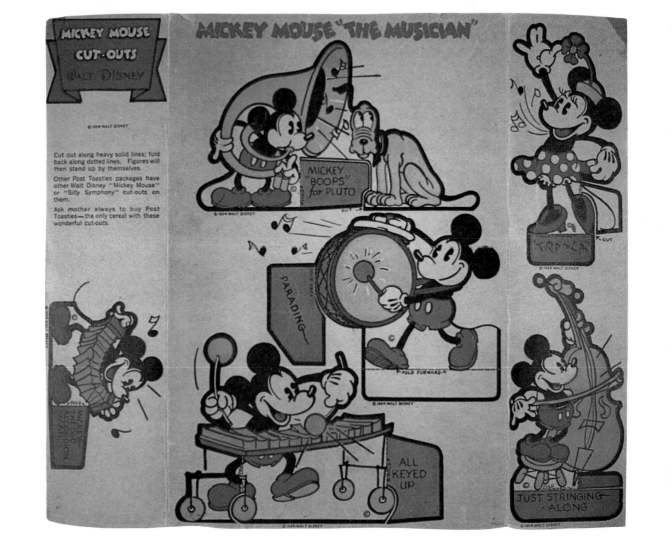

stating "We're At The Grocery Now!" are excellent lithographs. The paper Mickey Mouse Comic Cookie Hat from an early 1930s cookie campaign is a choice item. A jar of Crosse & Blackwell's Mickey Mouse Marmalade depicts Mickey and Minnie Mouse on its label squeezing a giant orange into a miniature replica of—what else?—an identical Mickey Mouse Marmalade jar!

Presumably this repetitive theme party went on into infinity until it disappeared, just like the graphic decal on the Little Orphan Annie Ovaltine cups and shakers.

Mickey Mouse has been a sponsor for gasoline companies, appearing on Nu-Blue Sunoco ink blotters and big-sized canvas gas-station banners and posters, in Standard Oil travel brochures and maps and the "more wholesome" milk of the National Dairy Products Company. The "dairy campaigns" launched by Kay Kamen for Disney created one of the most successful licensing

deals. Milk and cheese sales skyrocketed when National Dairy and an affiliate called Southern Dairies used Mickey Mouse to sell their product. Yoo-Hoo ice-cream cones and Yoo-Hoo ice-cream-in-a-cup were sold in the millions due to national advertising promotion programs put together by Kay Kamen. Other interesting products include Mickey Mouse soda-pop from California, which had a short-lived, though active, promotional campaign in the thirties. The dark green bottle with Mickey on the label is indeed a striking product image.

ABOVE: MICKEY, DONALD, PLUTO, MAX HARE, AND CLARA CLUCK RACING AROUND A NABISCO COOKIE BOX, NATIONAL BISCUIT COMPANY, 1936. BELOW: THE THREE LITTLE PIGS, THE BIG BAD WOLF, AND PLUTO JOIN MICKEY AND MINNIE ON A MICKEY MOUSE COMIC COOKIES PREMIUM HAT FROM UNITED BISCUIT CO., 1934.

LITHOGRAPHED STORE WINDOW SIGN FEATURES MICKEY MOUSE COOKIES, A PRODUCT OF THE NATIONAL BISCUIT COMPANY, 1937.

TEN

BACK TO SCHOOL MICKEY

OPPOSITE: CARDBOARD DIE-CUT DISPLAY SIGN OF MICKEY MOUSE ASKS "HAVE YOU SEEN THE MICKEY MOUSE PENCIL BOXES AT THE BIG SCHOOL SALE?" USED AS PART OF "BACK TO SCHOOL" ADVERTISING CAMPAIGN, FROM THE DIXON CRUCIBLE CO. **RIGHT:** MICKEY MOUSE, GOOFY, AND PLUTO TAKE OFF FOR OUTER SPACE À LA BUCK ROGERS IN THIS BLUE, GOLD, AND BLACK LITHOGRAPH ON SIMULATED-COWHIDE CARDBOARD SCHOOL PENCIL BOX, LARGE SIZE, 9 X 5½ INCHES. **BELOW:** THE OPENED PENCIL BOX SHOWS THE EARLY DISNEY CHARACTER DECORATION. INCLUDED IN THE SCHOOL SET IS A MICKEY MOUSE RULER, MICKEY MOUSE PENCILS, CRAYONS, AN ERASER, A PEN, AND A PENNY BANK. PRODUCED IN 1936 BY THE DIXON CRUCIBLE CO.

A schoolchild returning to class in September could bring along any number of back-to-school Mickey items available from the dime store or the department store in the Depression, the forties, or the fifties. This merchandise helped to brighten up things for students at school or at their desks at home. At the stores you could choose from a selection of silk-screened and lithographed Disney cartoon character cardboard pencil boxes manufactured by the Joseph Dixon Crucible Company of Jersey City, New Jersey. These rectangular or sometimes figural Mickey Mouse snap-shut boxes were marked "A Dixon Product" or "Dixon U.S.A.," and "Walt Disney Enterprises," and include Mickey Mouse pencils, a pen, a Mickey Mouse ruler, a Mickey Mouse eraser, crayons, a tin penny bank, a compass and sometimes a Dixon Mickey Mouse Map of the United States, which showed all the characters in different activities and outfits related to the particular

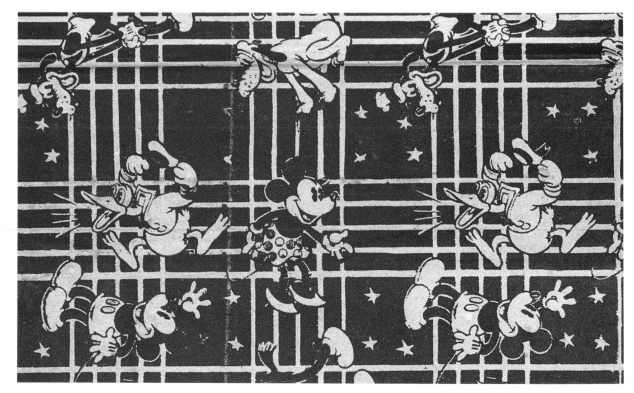

RIGHT: Red interior paper lining of pencil box with Disney characters made by Dixon Crucible Co., Jersey City, N.J. **BELOW:** Color lithography on cardboard die-cut novelty Mickey Mouse pencil box from Dixon Crucible Co., 1934.

geographical interests. These sturdy pencil boxes came in single, two (medium-size), and three-drawer (jumbo) sizes. Bright lollipop colored Catalin pencil sharpeners from Plastic Novelties, Inc., of New York with a decal appliqué of Mickey, Minnie, Pluto, Horace, or Clarabelle were sold separately out of merchandise bins at the dime store.

Mickey Mouse easel blackboards in several styles and sizes were produced by the Barricks Manufacturing Company of Chicago and by the Richmond School Furniture Company of Muncie, Indiana. The InkoGraph Company Ink-D-Cator fountain pen, which sold for one dollar in the Depression featured a Mickey head at the top of the pen. Retractable pencils with a Mickey head were produced by InkoGraph as well. The Geuder Paeschke and Frey Company of Milwaukee, Wisconsin, manufactured litho-on-tin or sheet metal wastepaper baskets, flower pots, bread boxes and cake covers, all with

"Your favorite Disney characters on them." A Geuder Paeschke and Frey Mickey Mouse lunch kit from the thirties had a removable eating tray insert. This metal, oval-shaped box had Mickey, Minnie, Horace, Clara Cluck, and Morty and Ferdy lithographed in bright colors. Hinged tin-litho boxes for crayon sets made by the Transogram Company of New York and stamp pads made by the Fulton Specialty Company of Elizabeth, New Jersey, also had a Mickey Mouse image on them.

School note tablets, such as those produced by the Powers Paper Company of Springfield, Massachusetts, had bright covers with fine Disney graphics, which showed Mickey and his friends in school activities or at playtime games. And so it was that the good little mouse showed children at school how to develop penmanship, to write letters, address envelopes, spell or multiply on a blackboard—and, in general, to practice good scholarship and manners and learn to be a good sport.

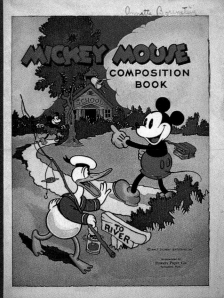

ABOVE: ALPHABET BLOCKS WERE MADE BY THE HALSAM PRODUCTS CO., CHICAGO, C. 1935. **RIGHT:** MICKEY MOUSE COMPOSITION BOOK FROM THE POWERS PAPER CO., SPRINGFIELD, MASS., 1935.

BELOW AND DIRECTLY OPPOSITE: BOTH ENDS OF THE MICKEY MOUSE/MINNIE MOUSE PAINTED PLYWOOD TABLE-DESK FOR HOME STUDYING FROM KROEHLER MFG. CO., 1935.

LEFT: CHILDREN'S BENCH FEATURES A PAINTED PLYWOOD MINNIE MOUSE ON ONE SIDE AND A MICKEY MOUSE ON THE OTHER, COMPANION PIECE TO THE KROEHLER MFG. CO.'S MICKEY MOUSE/MINNIE MOUSE TABLE-DESK. THERE WAS ALSO A PLUTO THE PUP STOOL, A BOOKCASE, A HANGING RACK FOR COATS, AND OTHER KIDDIE FURNITURE, SAN FRANCISCO, 1936.

DIRECTLY OPPOSITE AND ABOVE: FRONT AND BACK OF KAY KAMEN GIVEAWAY: A WOODEN SCHOOL RULER ADVERTISING YOO HOO ICE CREAM, KAY KAMEN LTD., 1934.

RIGHT: DONALD DUCK AND MICKEY MOUSE LITHOGRAPHED TIN CRAYON BOX, MANUFACTURED BY THE TRANSOGRAM CO., NEW YORK, IN 1946.

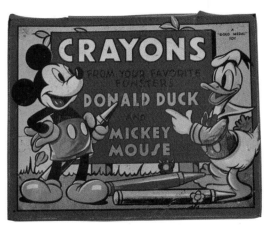

RIGHT: MICKEY MOUSE "STAND-UP" BLACKBOARD, MANUFACTURED BY THE RICHMOND SCHOOL FURNITURE CO., MUNCIE, INDIANA, C. 1936.

ELEVEN

MICKEY MOUSE BOOKS

Mickey Mouse storybooks from the 1930s, 1940s, and 1950s, with their brightly colored covers, were usually profusely illustrated, and are collected by Disney-ophiles as well as antiquarian book specialists. Collectors find enjoyment in owning these pieces of historic Disney, and some read them over and over again, taking utmost caution in their handling and keeping them far removed from a child's sticky fingers.

The "Mickey Mouse Book," considered by con-noisseurs to be the first Mickey Mouse book, is actu-ally in a magazine format. It was written by Bobette Bibo, the book publisher's eleven-year-old daughter, who enti-tled her fictionalized account of Mickey Mouse, "The Story of Mickey Mouse." "Mickey Mouse Book," published in 1930 by Bibo and Lang, is only fifteen pages long and includes a Mickey Mouse game, a march, and a song. Marked "Copyrighted by Walter E. Disney," the cover shows a typical early black-and-white drawing of Mickey Mouse, one hand on hip, the other thrust upward, with Mickey standing in a white circle against a plain Depression-green background. This "book" had a print run of 100,000 and was first sold at dime stores. Many were giveaways when parents bought a Charlotte Clark Mickey Mouse doll for their children. Of special interest to Disneyana collectors is the fact that the cover of this book was drawn by Ub Iwerks.

In the very early years of the creation of Mickey Mouse, Walt Disney had problems finding a publisher who could distribute Mickey books nationally. The David McKay Company of Philadelphia and New York was the one to finally agree to Walt Disney's demands and eccentricities. McKay published the first commercial book, which arrived on the market in 1931. The cover of *The Adventures of Mickey Mouse* shows Mickey strumming a banjo to a dancing Minnie, while on the back cover Horace plays an elongated accordion and Clarabelle, with a tambourine and cowbell ringing, dances to the tune. This original storybook tells the tale of Mickey, who lived in a hole-in-the-wall, running scared from an aggressive Claws the Cat. Other barnyard characters in this story are Henry Horse, Carolyn Cow, Patricia Pig, Clara Cluck, and Donald Duck. It should be noted that only two references to a Donald Duck character were made in this book,

OPPOSITE: "MICKEY MOUSE BOOK" (ACTUALLY IN MAGAZINE FORMAT) WAS THE FIRST BOOK PUBLISHED ABOUT MICKEY MOUSE, FEATURING A STORY WRITTEN BY BOBETTE BIBO, THE ELEVEN-YEAR-OLD DAUGHTER OF THE PUBLISHER. THIS RARE 15-PAGE BOOK IN-CLUDES A MICKEY MOUSE GAME, A MICKEY MOUSE SONG, AND A MICKEY MOUSE MARCH, AS WELL AS SEVERAL BEAUTIFUL ILLUSTRA-TIONS, PRINTED IN BLACK AND GREEN. PUBLISHED BY BIBO AND LANG, NEW YORK, 1930.

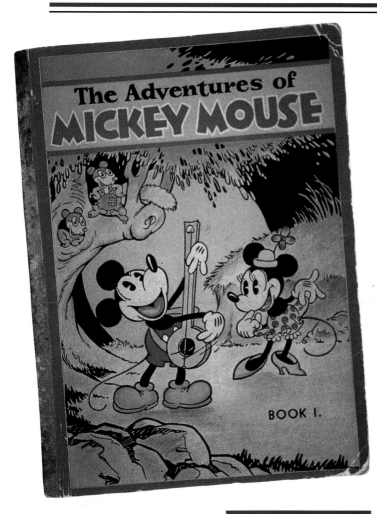

MICKEY MOUSE STORY BOOK BY WALT DISNEY, DAVID MCKAY, NEW YORK, 1931.

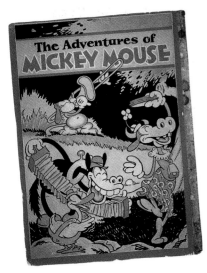

ABOVE: *THE ADVENTURES OF MICKEY MOUSE*, BOOK 1, PUBLISHED IN 1931 BY DAVID MCKAY, NEW YORK. THIS ILLUSTRATED BOOK TELLS THE STORY OF THE ORIGINAL BARNYARD CHARACTERS, INCLUDING HENRY HORSE, CAROLYN COW, PATRICIA PIG, ROBERT ROOSTER, CLARA CLUCK, AND A VERY EARLY MENTION OF A DONALD DUCK. IN 1978 THIS BOOK WAS REPRINTED WITH A DIFFERENT COVER IN HARDBACK BY DAVID MCKAY ON THE OCCASION OF MICKEY MOUSE'S FIFTIETH BIRTHDAY. **LEFT:** THE BACKCOVER SHOWS HORACE HORSECOLLAR, CLARABELLE COW, AND DONALD DUCK.

OPENING PAGES TO *THE ADVENTURES OF MICKEY MOUSE*, BOOK 2, DAVID MCKAY, 1932.

and although an odd variety of ducks are seen in the illustrations, there is no actual Donald as we know him.

In 1931, McKay also published *Mickey Mouse Series #1*, an album of newspaper comic strip reprints, and *The Mickey Mouse Storybook*, illustrated with stills from the cartoon shorts. *Mickey Mouse Series #2* was issued in 1932; *Series #3*, in color from the Sunday strips, in 1933; and *Series #4* in 1934, all published by McKay. Sold originally in bookstores for 50¢ were McKay's *Mickey Mouse Illustrated Movie-Stories*; *The Adventures of Mickey Mouse—Book #2*, both published in 1932; and *Mickey Mouse Stories—Book #2*, published in 1934.

In 1978, McKay published *Walt Disney's Mickey Mouse Story Book Album*, with color and black-and-white illustrations featuring stories from the 1931–1934 cartoons, and the "all-in-color" 50th Anniversary Edition of *Walt Disney's Adventures of Mickey Mouse*, a reprint of the original *Adventures of Mickey Mouse Book #1*, *Adventures of Mickey Mouse Book #2*, and *Mickey Mouse and His Horse Tanglefoot*.

Dean and Sons Ltd., in London, published the first *Mickey Mouse Annual for Boys and Girls* in 1931, and this series continued through the fifties. The colorful, thick, cardboard-covered books, chockfull of color pictures, stories, comics, poems, games, and crosswords, delighted the chil-

dren of Great Britain. William Collins published storybooks in England as well, including *Mickey Mouse and Mother Goose*, *Mickey Mouse in Giant Land*, *Mickey Mouse Nursery Stories*, and *Mickey Mouse Bedtime Stories*.

Blue Ribbon Books, Inc., of New York published *The Pop-Up Mickey Mouse* and *The Pop-Up Minnie Mouse* in 1933, each with three beautiful Pop-Ups. Blue Ribbon Books coined the term "pop-up" in the 1920s, registering the phrase in 1933 as their official trademark. A large-sized Pop-Up storybook format included *Mickey Mouse in King Arthur's Court*, *Mickey Mouse in Ye Olden Days*, and *The Pop-Up*

Silly Symphonies. In 1934, Blue Ribbon published *The Mickey Mouse Waddle Book*, which featured cutouts of Mickey, Minnie, Pluto, and Tanglefoot "walking" right out of the book on a slanted ramp. It is rare to find the Disney character "waddlers" intact or unpunched. Usually when these books are found they are missing. However, even without the waddlers walking the book is still a desirable collector's item.

Disney educational books were welcomed by parents and teachers because

they helped children to learn to read. "Readers" like *Mickey Mouse and His Friends* by Walt Disney and Jean Ayer, published in New York in 1937 by Thomas Nelson and Sons, and the schoolbook series from D. C. Heath and Company of Boston, which included titles like *School Days in Disneyville, Mickey Never Fails,* and *Mickey Sees the U.S.A.,* were favorites of schoolchildren of the 1930s and 1940s. Kay Kamen licensed the Whitman Publishing Company of Racine, Wisconsin, to publish hundreds

of books, usually printed on pulp paper and sold at J. J. Newberry's, Woolworth's, S. S. Kresge's, McCrory's, and other dime stores. With their bright graphic covers, these books sold into the hundreds of thousands of copies. Whitman's large-size picture books, coloring and paint books, and cut-out paper doll books were a boon for just one dime in the Depression–World War II era.

Big Little Books published by Whitman included many Mickey Mouse titles, along with their other series of cartoon or comic-strip characters like Little Orphan Annie, Popeye, Dick Tracy, Flash Gordon, Buck Rogers, Skeezix, Skippy, Chester Gump,

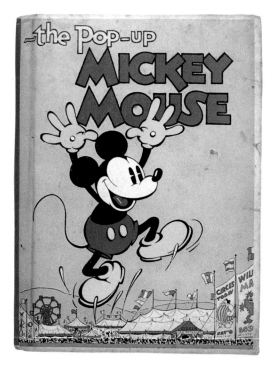

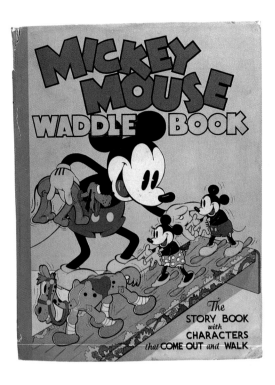

Moon Mullins, and the Katzenjammer Kids. Measuring approximately 3³/₄ x 4¹/₂ inches, these "novelized" picture books were usually about 300 to 500 pages in length. Big Little Books were produced with the idea in mind that a boy or girl would put them into a Mackinaw pocket or perhaps a lunch box or school bag.

For ten cents, the Big Little Books featured Mickey Mouse acting the role of a mail pilot, a detective, a newspaper editor, a cowboy, or a hunter searching for hidden treasures. The first Mickey Mouse Big Little Book, published in 1933, was simply entitled *Mickey Mouse*. The cover illustration has Mickey Mouse in his typical posture:

ABOVE: WALT DISNEY'S *MICKEY MOUSE HAS A PARTY*, A SCHOOL READER FROM WHITMAN, 1938.

ABOVE: *A MICKEY MOUSE ALPHABET BOOK*: "26 SMILES FROM A TO Z," WHITMAN, 1936.

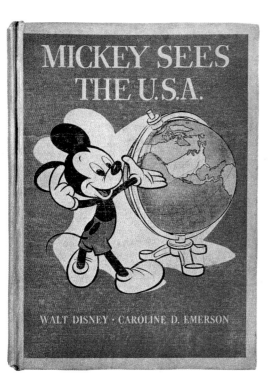

LEFT: *MICKEY MOUSE SEES THE U.S.A.*, BY WALT DISNEY AND CAROLINE D. EMERSON, D. C. HEATH, 1939. **RIGHT:** *MICKEY MOUSE AND HIS FRIENDS*, A HARD-COVER STORYBOOK BY WALT DISNEY AND JEAN AYER, THOMAS NELSON & SONS, NEW YORK, 1937.

OVERLEAF: CIRCUS SCENE POP-UP, ONE OF THREE POP-UPS IN THE *POP-UP MICKEY MOUSE* ILLUSTRATED STORYBOOK PUBLISHED BY BLUE RIBBON BOOKS, NEW YORK, IN 1933.

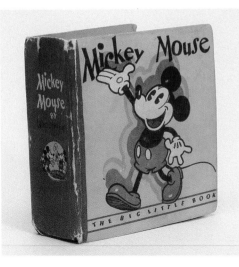

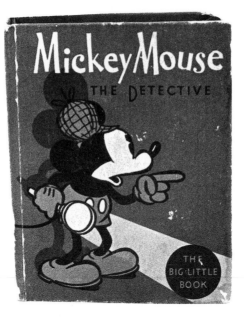

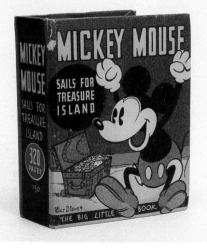

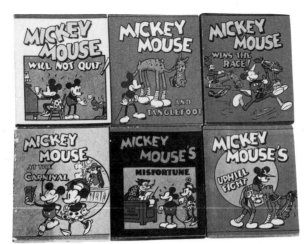

arm up, hand on hip. The second edition of this Big Little Book shows Mickey in a more relaxed pose, with one hand extended outward rather than upward, while the other is pointing at his belly.

Over the years Kay Kamen engineered tie-ins with a number of companies that issued limited editions of Mickey Mouse Big Little Books as premiums for their products, which included Kolynos Toothpaste and Cocomalt, a chocolate powder to be mixed with milk.

In 1934, Whitman published a set of six Wee Little Books (3 x 3¹⁄₂ inches), which were only 40 pages long and were attractively packaged in a sturdy cardboard Mickey Mouse Library container. The titles, each of which tells a single story reprinted from the newspapers are: *Mickey Mouse and Tanglefoot, Mickey Mouse's Uphill Fight, Mickey Mouse Wins His Race, Mickey Mouse Will Not Quit, Mickey Mouse at the Carnival, Mickey Mouse's Misfortune*

A Big Big Book (9¹⁄₂ x 7³⁄₄ inches), 316 pages, and entitled *The Story of Mickey Mouse*, was published by Whitman in 1935 and reprinted the following year with a different cover featuring Mickey and Minnie on a boat wearing nautical garb. In 1938, Whitman also published a series of 5¹⁄₂ x 5¹⁄₂-inch Better Little Books featuring Mickey Mouse. They include *The Story of*

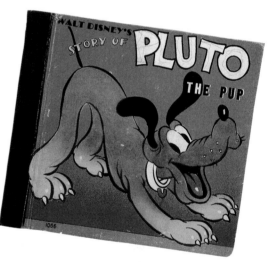

Dippy the Goof, The Story of Pluto, The Story of Minnie Mouse, The Story of Clarabelle, and others. Other series of Big Little Book–type novelty books were Fast Action Books from Dell Publishing Company and Little Big Books from Saalfield Publishing Company. Since these and the millions of other Disney books

were produced for quantity distribution in many countries throughout the world, they are still attainable through book dealers as well as at specialty antique shows and at paper ephemera shows. Comic book stores and comic book shows will also feature this type of Disney book.

ABOVE AND TOP: WALT DISNEY'S STORY OF CLARABELLE COW AND STORY OF PLUTO THE PUP, BOTH PUBLISHED IN 1938 BY WHITMAN.

TWELVE

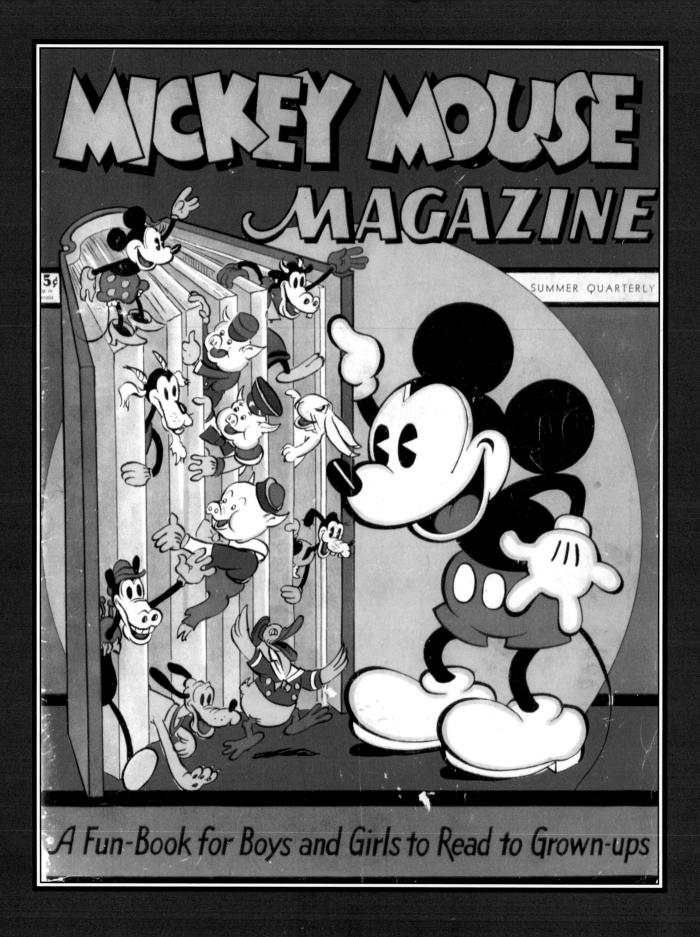

MICKEY MOUSE MAGAZINES

It was Kay Kamen who produced the first *Mickey Mouse Magazine* for Walt Disney enterprises in January 1933. Volume 1, No. 1 features stories along with Disney illustrations, games, jokes and puzzles. Kamen originally created this magazine to be just a promotional giveaway at department stores and movie theaters. The ninth issue, dated September 1933, is also the last of this first series. Measuring $5\frac{1}{4}$ x $5\frac{1}{4}$ inches, they are among today's hard-to-find magazines.

An advertising director at United Artists named Hal Horne, who had published Kamen's 1932 movie campaign book, was selected to produce the second *Mickey Mouse Magazine*. Not unlike the first series in size and format, it was part of Kamen's national campaign for dairies that used Mickey and Minnie and their pals

to get the kids to drink milk. The 24 issues, Volume 1, No. 1 (November 1933) through Volume 2, No. 2 (October 1935), are highly desirable as collectibles.

Hal Horne created the *Mickey Mouse*

Magazine again in May 1935, an event that had been orchestrated with a full national newsstand distribution deal. This new magazine was larger in format, and had a 300,000-copy print run. Unfortunately, only 150,000 of this first run were sold. At 25¢ per copy, parents considered them too expensive, especially in the hard times of the thirties. Subsequent editions were reduced in price to 10¢ as well as in size. After Horne's first nine issues (Summer 1935; October, November, December 1935; February, March, April, May, and June 1936), Kay Kamen pushed the circulation of the tenth issue and subsequent issues to an amazing 500,000 copies. The final issue, Volume 5, No. 12, was printed in September 1940.

In October 1940, the first *Walt Disney's Comics and Stories* was published. Much cheaper to produce and easy to distribute, comic books by that year were becoming a rage, taking the place of many thirties publications like the *Mickey Mouse Magazine* and eventually superseding the sales of the popular Big Little Books. *Walt Disney's Comics and Stories* was selling one million copies per issue within months, and became the best-selling comic book over the world. Issues of *Mickey Mouse Magazine* are considered highly collectible today, not just because they represent the most exciting and original period for Disneyana—the 1930s—but for their first-rate cover art, their illustrations, and the full-color advertisements featuring early Mickey Mouse merchandise such as the Ingersoll watch, Noma Christmas lamps,

Big Little Book titles, Mickey Mouse toothpaste, boys' scarves, ties, and sweaters, the famous Mickey Mouse Lionel handcar, and Post Toasties cereal.

The *Mickey Mouse Weekly* put out by William B. Levy in London had a large format (11 x 15 inches) and seems more like a color newssheet than a magazine, although the quality of paper was better than the pulp used in comic books. This weekly had an initial print run of 400,000 in 1936, going to 600,000 in the issues that followed. Offering games, crosswords, comics, advertisements, and such, the *Mickey Mouse Weekly* is collected today, particularly in the early editions. *Le Journal de Mickey*, a Mickey magazine from Hachette Publishers in Paris, published its first volume on October 21, 1934. *Topolino*, the Italian magazine, first appeared on newsstands and in stores in Italy in December of 1932. These latter two are still being published, which is a testimony to the timeless power of Mickey Mouse.

Disneyana paper material would certainly include the Disney comic books, which are fully catalogued and valued in the annual editions of *Overstreet's Comic Book Price Guide*, and the song folios and Mickey Mouse song sheets from the Disney shorts or animated features for songs such as "Mickey Mouse's Birthday Party" or

"Mickey Mouse and Minnie's in Town."

More difficult to obtain and more expensive to buy are the movie posters and lobby cards and the advertising signs and campaign promotional materials for products and toys. Some of these utilized high quality lithography on poster stock and are considered as "art" posters in today's marketplace. The official bulletins and newsletters from the Mickey Mouse Clubs from 1930 on are also sought-after paper ephemera.

Mickey Mouse Bread and Gum card sets, 1930s movie and radio magazines and national magazines like *Collier's* or *Liberty*, which featured Mickey on their covers, are all seen as desirable pieces of Disney memorabilia. Articles about Mickey Mouse and his creator Walt Disney in 1930s issues of

LEFT: "CARTOON CHARACTERS WILL MAKE YOU A FORTUNE," PROMISES THE NOVEMBER, 1933 ISSUE OF *MODERN MECHANIX*, VOL. 11, NO. 1. BELOW LEFT: THE NOVEMBER 6, 1937, ISSUE OF *COLLIER'S*, THE NATIONAL WEEKLY MAGAZINE, SHOWS MICKEY ON THE COVER HAVING HIS RICKETY SOAP-BOX AUTO CHECKED OUT FOR SAFETY BY GOOFY AND DONALD DUCK.

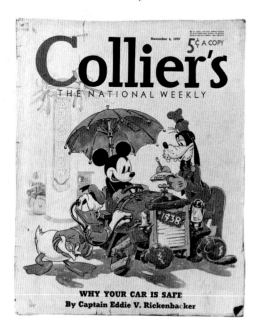

McCall's, Woman's Home Companion, the *Atlantic Monthly, Cosmopolitan*, the *New Yorker, American Magazine, Woman's Day, Ladies' Home Journal*, and *Fortune* are valuable sources of information for collectors and for the growing number of Disney scholars, as well as for museum curators and libraries.

Special Christmas promotion pamphlets published by Kay Kamen Ltd. for retailers and wholesalers and the original character merchandise catalogs, as well as

George Kamen's Mickey Mouse–Walt Disney Merchandise Catalogs published in England in the thirties and forties are among the most highly sought after printed materials in the field of Disneyana. These wonderful catalogs illustrate and document just what merchandise was available and which companies produced it. It could be said that these original compilations are the very first Disneyana books—but they came well before the word *Disneyana*.

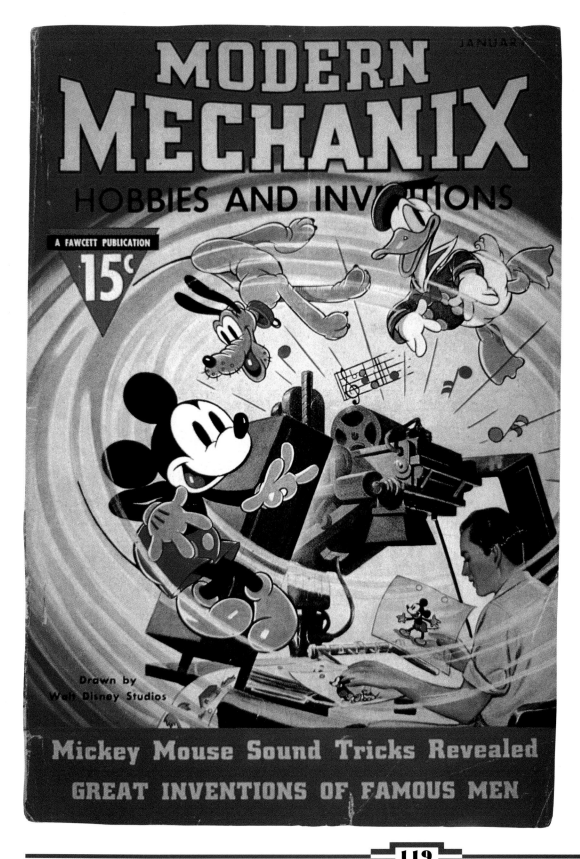

LEFT: COVER OF *MODERN MECHANIX*, VOL. 17, NO. 3, JANUARY 1937 IS "DRAWN BY WALT DISNEY STUDIOS." INSIDE, "MICKEY MOUSE SOUND TRICKS ARE REVEALED!" BELOW: THE DONALD DUCK SPECIAL ON THE COVER OF *LIBERTY* MAGAZINE, OCTOBER 1940. NOTE THE UNCLE SAM EAGLE ON THE HOOD AND THE LICENSE PLATE NUMBER, "U.S. 1776."

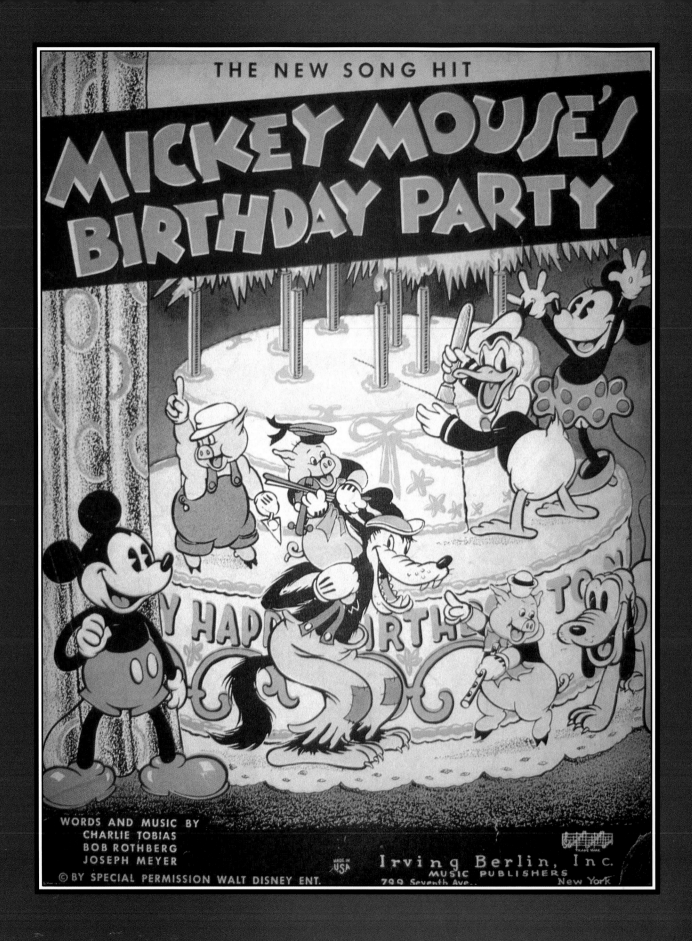

THIRTEEN

MICKEY MOUSE
MUSIC IN THE AIR

In the 1930s, many homes had upright pianos in the parlor or living room on which perched sheet music and Disney song folios purchased either from the music store or from the sheet-music counter at the five-and-dime store. At these establishments, an attractive piano-playing vocalist with flame-red lips, mascaraed eyes, and permanent-waved hair might be found crooning "Minnie's Yoo Hoo" in her best high soprano. Copies of this sheet music—Mickey Mouse's theme song, first introduced in the 1929 cartoon *Mickey's Follies*—were given to lucky members of the first Mickey Mouse Clubs. Other Mickey Mouse songs the dime store crooner might sing and play for you would include: "Mickey Mouse's Birthday Party," "Mickey Mouse and Minnie's in Town," "The Wedding of Mister Mickey Mouse," and "What! No Mickey Mouse? What Kind of a Party Is This?"

The last song, by Irving Caesar, was rerecorded in 1970 by band leader Phil Harris with some lyric variation:

Vote for Mickey Mouse,
And make him our next President:
To Congress he is sure to say,
"Meow, meow okay, okay,
Ja, ja, yes, yes, si, si, oui, oui,
How dry I am, have one on me,"
And then he'll cry,
"Give me the facts,
Give me my ax,
I'll cut your tax."
He'll show us all what can be done
When he's in Washington,
So, let's give Nixon's house,
To that slicky wacki, wicki,
Tacki, tricky Mickey Mouse.
Mickey Mouse!
Mickey Mouse!

The Disney music publishers included Villa Moret, Inc., Music Publishers from San

ABOVE: RCA VICTOR 78 RPM "ORTHOPHONIC" RECORDING OF "MICKEY MOUSE AND MINNIE'S IN TOWN," SUBTITLED "EL RATONCITO MICKEY Y MINNIE;" SONG BY ANN RONELL, PERFORMED BY DON BESTOR AND HIS ORCHESTRA, VOCAL REFRAIN BY THE DE MARCO GIRLS AND FRANK SHERRY. RCA VICTOR CO., CAMDEN, N.J., 1934. **OPPOSITE:** "MICKEY MOUSE'S BIRTHDAY PARTY" SHEET MUSIC, IRVING BERLIN, MUSIC PUBLISHERS, NEW YORK, 1936.

Francisco, Irving Caesar, Inc., and the major publisher of the 1930s decade, Irving Berlin, Inc., later known as Bourne Music Publishers. A variety of publishers have been used by Disney since 1940 up to the present. Some early Silly Symphony song folio hits were "Lullaby of Nowhere,"

WHAT! NO MICKEY MOUSE?
What kind of a party is this?

by IRVING CAESAR

"Funny Little Bunnies," "The Penguin Is a Very Funny Creature," "The Wise Little Hen," "Ferdinand the Bull," "Rats" from the cartoon *The Pied Piper*, "You're Nothin' But a Nothin'" from *The Flying Mouse*, and the most famous Silly Symphony song of all time, "Who's Afraid of the Big Bad Wolf?" from *Three Little Pigs*, which caught on to such an extent that it became the anthem theme song of the Great Depression. The most popular all-time favorite songs from Walt Disney films include: "Some Day My Prince Will Come," "Whistle While You Work," and "Heigh Ho" from *Snow White and the Seven Dwarfs*; "When You Wish Upon a Star," "Give a Little Whistle," and "Hi Diddle Dee

Dee" from *Pinocchio*; "Der Fuehrer's Face" from the short *Der Fuehrer's Face*; "You Belong to My Heart" from *The Three Caballeros*; "Zip-a-Dee-Doo-Dah" from *Song of the South*; and "Bibbidi-Bobbidi-Boo" and "A Dream Is a Wish Your Heart Makes" from *Cinderella*.

Three songs that won Academy Awards were "When You Wish Upon a Star" (1940), "Zip-a-Dee-Doo-Dah" (1946), and "Chim Chim Cher-ee" (*Mary Poppins*, 1964). Disney sheet music is highly collectible for the splendid graphics which are decoratively framed and hung on the wall in a den, collectibles room, or music room. Sheet music is not as hard to come by as an original poster, lobby card or original stills, drawings or cels, as it was produced and sold in the millions when everyone in the family seemed to play the piano, accordion, or some other instrument. Sheet music falls into the category of ephemera and is to be found today at paper collectibles shows, antique shows, flea markets, nostalgia conventions, and antiquarian book sales.

Record collectors search

ABOVE LEFT: "WHAT! NO MICKEY MOUSE? WHAT KIND OF PARTY IS THIS?" SHEET MUSIC BY IRVING CAESAR, IRVING CAESAR, INC., MUSIC PUBLISHERS, NEW YORK, 1932. BELOW RIGHT: MARKS BROTHERS OF BOSTON MADE THIS MUSICAL MICKEY MOUSE PARTY-TIME HORN IN BRIGHT LITHO-GRAPHED CARDBOARD IN 1934.

with great intensity for the early Disney 78 rpm records. In 1934, the RCA Victor Company, Inc., of Camden, New Jersey, produced one of the first Disney records, using Frank Luther and his Orchestra to perform the Mickey hits. Many dance bands performed songs recorded from Disney movies. Original 78 rpm record albums of film music are very desirable, particularly those from *Snow White and the Seven Dwarfs*, *Pinocchio*, *The Three Caballeros*, *Dumbo*, *Saludos Amigos* and *Song of the South*.

The term "Mickey Mouse music" was derived from the ricky-tick sound of the early Disney cartoon soundtrack music, much of it written by Carl Stalling, a former organist and theater orchestra conductor. This type of orchestration came directly out of the 1920s orchestras that played in nightclubs or in Broadway shows. This fun-time sound, which was very popular on the radio and on phonograph records, included these 1920s hits that influenced the music used in early Disney cartoons: "I'm Just Wild About Animal Crackers" as recorded by Irving Aaronson and his Commanders, "The Japanese Sandman" as recorded by

RIGHT: LINEMAR, A DIVISION OF LOUIS MARX BROTHERS AND CO., NEW YORK, PRODUCED THESE WINDUP TOYS (FROM LEFT TO RIGHT): DONALD DUCK TIN LITHO WINDUP DRUMMER; MICKEY MOUSE WINDUP XYLOPHONE PLAYER (ATOP A TIN-LITHOGRAPH MICKEY MOUSE DRUM FROM OHIO ART COMPANY, 1934); AND PLUTO WINDUP HORN BLOWER AND BELL RINGER, C. 1950. BELOW: "A MARCH FOR MICKEY MOUSE" SHEET MUSIC, BY C. FRANZ KOEHLER, PUBLISHED BY BOSTON MUSIC COMPANY, 1932.

Paul Whiteman, "Sax-o-Phun" (a study in laugh and slap tongue) as recorded by George Olson, and "Horses" as recorded by George Olson.

College jazz babies of the 1920s loved this type of "flaming youth" rhythmic sound, but in the 1930s, the new hotel orchestras were featuring strings and a more sophisticated music to go along with

the repeal of Prohibition. The snobs of the 1930s frowned on some of the best music of the 1920s, calling it Mickey Mouse music—meant in a derogatory way. The term eventually worked its way into some dictionaries and was notated trite, slick, and commercial. In fact, the *Random House Dictionary of the English Language* had this definition for Mickey Mouse: "(often caps) slang. Trite and commercially slick in character: Mickey Mouse music. (After a cartoon character created by Walt Disney.)" However, some of the better composers of the 1930s did not forget to include Mickey Mouse himself in the lyrics of their songs. In 1934, when Ethel Merman first sang the renowned "You're the Top" from Cole Porter's Broadway show *Anything Goes*, the audience broke into wild applause when they heard:

You're a melody from a
      symphony by Strauss,
You're a Bendel bonnet—
A Shakespeare sonnet—
You're—Mickey Mouse!

Miss Merman continued her song tribute to Mickey Mouse in the movies when she sang the Mack Gordon–Harry Revel song "It's the Animal in Me" in Paramount's film *The Big Broadcast of 1936*. This lyric contained the musical observation:

Look at Mickey Mouse,
Look at Minnie Mouse,
They just live on love and cheese!

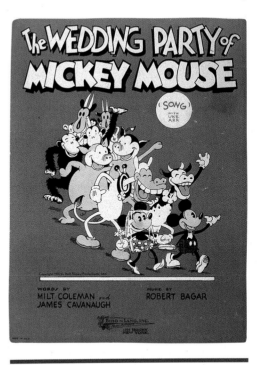

"THE WEDDING PARTY OF MICKEY MOUSE" SHEET MUSIC, WITH UKULELE ARRANGEMENTS, PUBLISHED BY BIBO LANG MUSIC PUBLISHERS, NEW YORK, 1931.

FOURTEEN

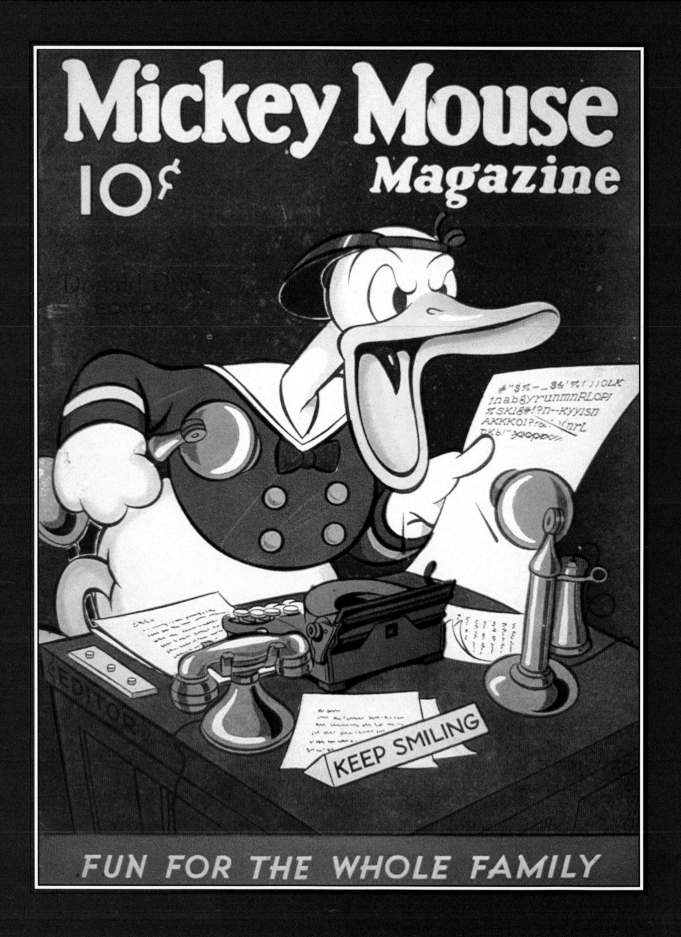

DONALD DUCK RAGE

Donald Duck is mentioned by name in *The Adventures of Mickey Mouse Book #1*, published by David McKay Company in 1931; but he did not actually take on his cartoon persona until June 9, 1934, the date the Silly Symphony cartoon *The Wise Little Hen* was released to movie theaters. So endearing to the public was this agitated, quacking duck, who some said resembled a long-billed gander in his little sailor-boy suit, that he stole the picture from the cooing Wise Little Hen with her bevy of chicks and from a lazy barnyard character called Peter Pig. Weary of a country in the grip of the Great Depression, angry moviegoers identified with Donald Duck, particularly when he twisted his bulbous feathery form into a rotating white, orange, and

blue ball while emitting a series of vitriolic quacks. These honking, quivering vocalizations were made by the muffled trickster voice of Clarence Nash, who continuously spoke as Donald Duck. After his introduction as a character in *The Wise Little Hen*, Donald Duck appeared as Mickey Mouse's sidekick in cartoons like *Orphan's Benefit*, and *The Dognapper*, in 1934, *The Band Concert*, and *On Ice*, in 1935, *Mickey's Circus*, 1936, and *The Clock Cleaners*, 1937.

As Mickey Mouse became less the mad, impish rodent and more the virtuous, happy-go-lucky good little boy-scout model of a mouse—mostly to satisfy the millions of mothers in the 1930s who were writing letters to Walt Disney claiming that their children seemed bent on imitating all of Mickey's actions, whether

good or bad—it seemed appropriate to create a new cartoon character star, one who could encompass and express the emotion of venomous anger. And so Donald Duck came into being in 1934. Even as early as 1931, Walt Disney himself had said that he felt "caught in a trap with a good mouse," who as a top Hollywood movie-star idol and icon could no longer perform the more off-color stunts that might in any way be construed by the public as either mean-spirited or openly hostile. Good Mickey could no longer mischievously bang on a cow's teeth or pull at a sow's teats as he had in *Steamboat Willie.*

The obvious answer to this profound moral dilemma, as Disney saw it, was to create new barnyard characters who could express some of the rage at the world the masses were feeling in those hard times. Disney heartily explained: "The Duck could blow his top and it was Donald—and Pluto the Pup with his gnashing teeth and sullen expressions—who gave us an outlet for our crazy shenanigans and gags!"

In his scholarly book *The Art of Walt Disney*, published by Macmillan in 1942 and now a rare collectible, Robert D. Feild said of Donald Duck, "He was probably the most garrulous incoherence of all time and we, the public, have been obliged to overlook his precocity and accept him as one of us because we recognize, particularly in his moments of despair, a gentle heroism that we would wish to emulate."

An interview by Howard

ABOVE: DONALD DUCK IN A BELLIGERENT MOOD, FROM *THE ADVENTURES OF DONALD DUCK,* GROSSET & DUNLAP, 1936. BELOW LEFT: DONALD DUCK BISQUE FIGURINE, 3 INCHES, HAND-PAINTED AND MADE IN JAPAN, 1930S.

Sharpek with a noted psychiatrist in the May 9, 1942, issue of *Liberty* magazine entitled "Donald Duck's Biggest Moments" helped to explain Donald's popularity in the mid-Depression years. The psychiatrist called him "opaquely symbolical of every small frustrated man in an era of continuous frustration." In the same article, Walt Disney offered up another philosophical treatise about his obstreperous cartoon duck creation, "Life to Donald is just a hat with a brick underneath it just waiting for him to come along for the thud!"

Dime Store Donald: Merchandising the Duck

After Donald's triumph in *The Wise Little Hen*, Kay Kamen licensed Donald Duck to eager manufacturers and merchandisers in the same aggressive manner he had with Mickey Mouse. By 1935, Donald Duck soap, Donald Duck ties and handkerchiefs, and other merchandise began to appear at dry goods stores and dime stores. Disneyana collectors seek out Donald Duck

memorabilia from the 1930s, 1940s, and 1950s with the same interest they hold for Mickey Mouse merchandise, and there are those collectors who prefer Donald over Mickey, and choose to collect Donald above all the other Disney characters.

In the world of cartoons, the duck character is seen as the predecessor to other troublesome birds like Daffy Duck and Woody Woodpecker; but for these latter two there is little contest compared to the longevity and enormous popularity of Donald Duck. In addition, in the area of merchandising, neither Daffy nor Woody was exploited in the way that Donald Duck was. Collectors of Donald Duck often have a penchant for the longer-billed, longer-necked Donald of the mid-thirties, and still

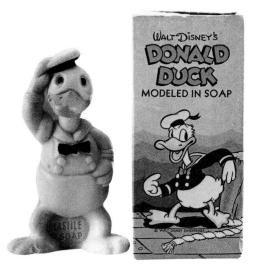

DONALD DUCK MODELED IN CASTILE SOAP, SHOWN WITH THE ORIGINAL BOX, LIGHTFOOT SCHULTZ CO., NEW YORK, 1938.

others prefer the wide-eyed, short-billed, and better proportioned Duck of the late thirties, forties, and fifties.

Donald Duck as a comic-strip character began on Sunday, September 16, 1935, with the Silly Symphony version of *The Little Red Hen*, written by Ted Osborne and drawn by Al Taliaferro. The Silly Symphony Sunday pages featured Donald beginning August 30, 1936; but it wasn't until February 7, 1939, that Donald took the lead in his own strip, with Bob Karp thinking up the humorous situations and Al Taliaferro doing the Donald Duck penciling and inking. This arrangement continued until others took over the inking and Al Taliaferro died in 1969. Donald Duck took hold as a comic-book character in a profound way from 1942 through the 1960s, with Carl Barks operating as the top Donald Duck artist and writer for Dell Comic Book Publications. Barks's comic characters included Daisy Duck, Huey, Dewey, and Louie, Uncle Scrooge, Gus Gander, Gyro Gearloose, and, of course, Mickey Mouse. The first Mickey Mouse comic book was *Mickey Mouse versus the Phantom Blot* in 1941. Donald Duck's first original full comic book, other than the 1936 and 1937 Sunday reprints in black and white (Whitman/Kay Kamen Publications, 1938), is generally thought to be *Pirate's Gold* (1942), written

ABOVE: LONG-BILLED "SIAMESE TWIN" DONALD DUCK BISQUE TOOTHBRUSH HOLDER, HAND-PAINTED AND MADE IN JAPAN FOR DISTRIBUTION BY THE GEORGE BORGFELDT CORP., 1935. BOTTOM LEFT: DONALD DUCK BISQUE FIGURINE WITH MOVABLE ARMS, HAND-PAINTED AND MADE IN JAPAN FOR BORGFELDT CORP., 1935. BOTTOM RIGHT: LONG-BILLED DONALD DUCK BISQUE TOOTHBRUSH HOLDER, HAND-PAINTED AND MADE IN JAPAN, IMPORTED AND DISTRIBUTED BY BORGFELDT CORP. IN THE 1930S.

and drawn by Carl Barks and Jack Hannah. Barks-drawn Donald Duck comics and comic art are considered the most desirable by comic-book collectors.

The George Borgfeldt Company distributed a great number of Made in Japan Donald Duck painted bisque figurines and toothbrush holders from tiny to medium to large ($5^{3}/_{4}$ inches). As a three-dimensional figurine, Donald with his long orange bill, one eye shut, and sailor suit (not unlike Fleischer's Popeye the Sailor who also sported a "pop-eye" and seafaring togs) plays violins, trum-

pets, and accordions, rides a scooter, and rocks on a hobby horse. Larger painted Donald Duck bisque figurines with movable arms are the most exquisitely sculptured and detailed of these bisque pieces. The Donald Duck toothbrush holder, which features two likenesses of Donald, is sometimes referred to as the "Siamese-twin Donald" by collectors, many of whom regard it as tops in the design category. Another attractive bisque toothbrush holder has Donald in the center with a smaller Mickey and Minnie on either side.

Like the Mickey Mouse bisques, the Donald Duck bisques were produced in Japan in the millions for a mass market. And, like Mickey, Donald Duck also was marketed in celluloid as a windup action toy, in a wagon being pulled by Pluto, riding Pluto as if the dog were a hobby horse, jumping over a high wire, riding a scooter or crawling on his belly, nodding, or simply waddling. A whirligig toy features a large celluloid Donald under a spinning canopy of miniature celluloid Mickeys and Donalds, while the Donald Duck Carousel, a smaller

piece, has simple celluloid balls in various colors rotating over his head when wound up. Like the bisque figurines, these celluloids were distributed by the Borgfeldt Company and came in boxes with interesting graphics. Small Catalin pencil sharpeners, Catalin napkin rings with Donald Duck decals, and small celluloid tape measures were also in the marketplace in the 1930s. With the growing interest in early plastic materials today, these items are sought after by the Duck enthusiasts as

well as those who are collecting Celluloid, Bakelite, Catalin, Tenite, and other period plastics with company brand names.

In the Donald Duck line are children's porcelain tea sets—"a treat for the girlies"—as one advertisement put it, Roly-Poly banks, action and pull toys featuring Donald banging drums or playing the xylophone from the Fisher-Price Company, a Donald Duck toy phone by N. N. Hill Brass, a Seiberling latex Donald Duck with a movable head, Donald Duck lithographed tin sand pails and shovels from the Ohio Art Company, a Donald Duck sled, lamps, bookends and a host of other items.

Knickerbocker Toy Company created some excellent cloth Donald Duck dolls and painted wood-composition dolls featuring Donald as a band leader, a cowboy, a vaquero with serape and sombrero, or simply in his familiar sailor-boy attire. Charlotte Clark designed Donald Duck dolls for several manufactur-

ers, and some of these are quite splendid in their detail. Richard G. Krueger Company of New York made a variety of Donald dolls, some in velvet, as did the Character Novelty Company.

The tin-litho windup parade of moving Donald Ducks is led by the Schuco toy, manufactured in Germany in 1935. This toy, highly prized, is a rather mean-looking Donald wearing a felt outfit, and when he is wound up, he waddles and opens and closes his long orange bill. Windups by Marx and LineMar, which came packed in colorfully lithographed cardboard boxes, have Donald in some kind of action like playing a drum or riding a Disney "Dipsy" car.

One toy that brought a great deal of excitement to the Christmas season of 1936 was the Lionel Corporation's Donald Duck railcar. This follow-up to the Mickey-

Minnie handcar features Pluto with a moving head popping in and out of a metal doghouse, which is painted white with a Depression-green roof, while the long-billed painted composition Donald Duck stands quacking away on the other side. The railcar came in a handsome box with a 27-inch circle of standard gauge Lionel track. Not surprisingly, the flow of words coming out of Donald on the box are simply, "Quack! Quack! Quack!"

Donald Duck timepieces may not have the same interest as the original Mickey Mouse watches, but they are rare and attractively packaged. Originals, like most comic character timepieces of the thirties, forties, and fifties are avidly sought by watch collectors as well as by Disneyana enthusiasts. The first Donald Duck watch was produced in 1936 by Ingersoll-Waterbury Clock Company, and a fine pocket watch of Donald, also from Ingersoll, was made in 1939. Some of these Donald pocket watches have colorful decals of Mickey Mouse on the reverse side, while others are plain. No miniature ducks are to be found running around in

the second hand as in the mini-Mickeys that are found on the original Mickey Mouse watches. A later Donald Duck wristwatch appeared in 1947, a Daisy Duck in 1948, and a Huey Duck in 1949. A handsome blue alarm clock featuring Donald Duck

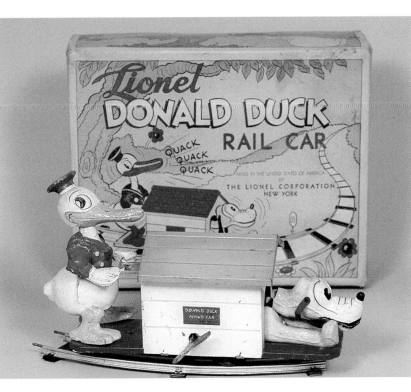

was produced in France by Bayard in 1969 for the new-wave nostalgia market that was then taking hold.

The first storybook to portray Donald Duck in pictures and text was *The Wise Little Hen*, published by David McKay in 1934. The first all–Donald Duck book was similar in size to the paint and coloring books sold in the dime stores.

THE DONALD DUCK RAIL CAR, SHOWN WITH ITS ORIGINAL BOX, FEATURED A COMPOSITION DUCK WITH PLUTO THE PUP IN A METAL DOGHOUSE, LIONEL CORP., IRVINGTON, N.J., 1936.

Entitled simply *Donald Duck*, it has sixteen linen-like pages with color illustrations of Donald. Marketed in 1935 by the Whitman Publishing Company, it is seen as an essential item for Donald Duck–Disneyana collectors, since it was the very first one in which he was featured as a star in his own right in the bookstores. An English adaptation of this book, published by William Collins & Sons, is primarily the same story but entitled *Mickey's Nephews*. A larger-than-life Mickey and his nephews and a much smaller Donald are depicted on the cover. Donald Duck had not yet become a cartoon star in England as he had in the United States. It was not until the advent of World War II that Donald became a worldwide celebrity.

Donald first appeared in a Whitman Big Little Book in 1933, in a collection entitled "Mickey Mouse Presents Walt Disney's Silly Symphony Stories" that also included Peter Pig, Benny Bird, and Bucky Bug. A 1937 Silly Symphony Big Little Book features Donald, but the 1939 Big Little Book

ABOVE: DONALD DUCK BIG LITTLE BOOKS, WHITMAN, 1937. RIGHT: DONALD ON THE COVER OF *MICKEY MOUSE MAGAZINE*, VOL. 3, NO. 6, MARCH 1938. BOTTOM: "SILENCE! ARTIST AT WORK!" DONALD DUCK PAINTS AN IMAGE OF MICKEY MOUSE ON THE LID OF THIS ENGLISH-MADE COOKIE TIN, MARKED "BY PERMISSION OF WALT DISNEY (MICKEY MOUSE) LTD.," C. 1948.

Donald was on the cover of many *Mickey Mouse Magazine*s, either by himself or sharing honors with his pal Mickey.

There was no holding down Donald Duck once he entered the world of merchandising and promotion with Kay Kamen at the helm. Donald Duck's march into the stores included Ohio Art paint sets, Parker Brothers' games; and salt and pepper shakers, planters, cookie jars, and baby dishes produced by the American Pottery Company of Los Angeles and the Leeds China Company of Chicago. The Kay Kamen campaigns found receptive consumers for Donald Duck, who had major success with food products that included Donald Duck Bread, Donald Duck Chocolate Syrup, Donald Duck Coffee, Donald Duck Mayonnaise, Donald Duck Sandwich Spread, Donald Duck Peanut Butter, Donald Duck Apple Sauce, Donald Duck Mustard, Donald Duck Chili Sauce, Donald Duck Catsup, Donald Duck Rice, Donald Duck Popcorn, and, his most popular, Donald Duck Grapefruit or Orange Juice. Canned vegetables like corn, peas, lima beans, succotash, and others also utilized Donald Duck on their food labels. Boxes, wrappers, tins, packages, and other ephemera like

Donald Duck and His Misadventures stars Donald all by himself. Donald went on as a stellar attraction in over a dozen Whitman Big Little Books from 1939 to 1949 and, as some of the titles indicate, provided young readers with his own inimitable brand of comic fun and excitement: *Donald Duck in Such a Life!*, *Donald Duck Forgets to Duck*, *Donald Duck Hunting for Trouble*, *Donald Duck Sees Stars*, *Donald Duck Gets Fed Up*, *Donald Duck Off the Beam*, *Donald Duck Up In the Air*, and *Donald Duck Says Such Luck!*

Whitman published *Donald Duck's Cousin Gus*, *Donald Duck's Better Self*, and *Donald Duck's Lucky Day* as part of their Walt Disney Picture-Story book series, given away as premiums or sold for a penny. Dell Publishing's Fast Action Books, just a bit wider but not as thick as Big Little Books, had Donald Duck appearing in at least four titles, and D. C. Heath Company of Boston published three Donald titles in their 1940s schoolbook-reader series. They were *Donald Duck and His Friends*, *Donald Duck and His Nephews,* and *Donald Duck Sees South America,* (featuring José Carioca)

DONALD DUCK EDIBLES (LEFT TO RIGHT): DONALD DUCK FLORIDA GRAPEFRUIT JUICE, DONALD DUCK POP CORN, DONALD DUCK COLA, DONALD DUCK CHOCOLATE SYRUP, AND DONALD DUCK FLORIDA ORANGE JUICE.

THE MAY 1947 ISSUE OF *PLAYTHINGS* FEATURES DONALD DUCK PREENING ON THE COVER, CONFIDENT THAT HIS IMAGE WILL SELL TRUCKLOADS OF CANNED FRUIT JUICE. THIS ISSUE OF THE TOY TRADE'S NATIONAL MAGAZINE INCLUDES ADS FOR DONALD DUCK TOYS AS WELL AS FOR LATTER-DAY OSWALD THE RABBIT AND ANDY PANDA RUBBER SOFTIES (WALTER LANTZ CHARACTERS, FROM THE IDEAL NOVELTY AND TOY COMPANY), DIE-CUT PICTURE PUZZLES OF ELSIE THE COW (SELCHOW & RIGHTER CO.), A WOOFY WAGGER WOODEN PULL-TOY (FISHER-PRICE), BAMBI MODEL-CRAFT MOLDS (MODEL CRAFT, INC.), OAK-HYTEX BALLOONS FEATURING DONALD, MICKEY, PLUTO, BAMBI, THUMPER, AND FLOWER (OAK RUBBER CO.), AND BEN COOPER MASKS AND MASQUERADE COSTUMES OF DUMBO AND TIMOTHY MOUSE.

ABOVE: 1940S DIE-CUT CARDBOARD "OFFICIAL DEALER" STORE SIGN ADVERTISING DONALD DUCK ICY-FROST TWIN POPSICLES. LEFT: DONALD DUCK BUTTER CREAMS. COLOR LITHOGRAPHED CARDBOARD ADVERTISING SIGN, 10½ X 10½ INCHES, 1937.

store signs, cardboard displays, and window stickers from product campaigns featuring Donald are collected today by serious Disneyana collectors. In many areas of the country, Donald Duck products are still available; although the graphics have been updated for a new ongoing market.

ADVERTISING STORE SIGN FOR DONALD DUCK BREAD, CHROME-LITHO ON METAL, C. 1946.

THREE LITTLE PIGS, THE BIG BAD WOLF, AND THE GREAT DEPRESSION

1933 has been called the worst year of the Great Depression, and those who kept their jobs worked hard to keep the proverbial wolf from the door. In the 1930s, the Big Bad Wolf served as a euphemism for the landlord, the mortgage company, or the bill collector. Walt Disney, who saw the dire situations that most Americans were in, started work on his all-in-color cartoon version of the famous tale by the Brothers Grimm that centered around three pigs and a menacing wolf. The *Three Little Pigs* Silly Symphony cartoon opened in New York in 1933 at the Radio City Music Hall; and during three separate runs at the Roxy later that year, it grossed $64,000—an impressive sum for a cartoon in those days.

The story of the three little pigs and their frantic attempts to outwit the wolf, as well as their desperate search for security, captivated adults and children alike, who identified with them in those difficult times. Fifer, the first pig who played the flute, built a house of straw, while the second pig, Fiddler, went for a house made of twigs. Practical Pig built his home-sweet-home of red bricks and cement. Merrily and defiantly they sang "Who's Afraid of the Big Bad Wolf?" the cartoon theme song. Ultimately it was Practical Pig who saved the day when the Big Bad Wolf landed in a stew pot of bubbling, boiling water. Many who saw this cartoon thought of the wolf as "Old Man Depression" himself.

The jolly theme song, written by Frank Churchill, in effect became the theme song of the Depression, supplanting the more optimistic "Happy Days Are Here Again" and the dispirited "Brother Can You Spare a Dime?" Don Bestor's and Ben Bernie's dance orchestras in America and Henry Hall's orchestra in England recorded popular 78 rpm records of "Who's Afraid of the Big Bad Wolf?" *Three Little Pigs* is less than ten minutes long, but is often cited for its artful animation and the very advanced background settings of Albert Hurter. It was

BELOW RIGHT: "WHO'S AFRAID OF THE BIG BAD WOLF" SHEET MUSIC, PUBLISHED BY THE BOURNE MUSIC COMPANY, NEW YORK, 1933. MUSIC COMPOSED BY FRANK E. CHURCHILL WITH ADDITIONAL LYRICS BY ANN RONELL. **OPPOSITE:** WALT DISNEY'S THREE LITTLE PIGS GAME, "BASED ON THE MOVIE SENSATION," MANUFACTURED BY THE EINSON-FREEMAN COMPANY, NEW YORK, 1933.

seen by critics of the day as a real development in cartoon shorts in terms of plot and characterization, and for employing a more sophisticated sound synchronization. *Three Little Pigs* won an Academy Award for Disney as Best Cartoon Short Subject of 1932–1933. America took *Three Little Pigs* to heart in the 1930s; and in a 1934 Silly Symphony, the popular wolf character was put opposite Little Red Riding Hood in *The Big Bad Wolf.* This new gang appeared together with Mickey Mouse in animation with live-action in the movie *Hollywood Party* (M.G.M, 1934) starring Laurel and Hardy, Lupe Velez, and Jimmy Durante. The Disney menagerie in a Technicolor Silly Symphony sequence stole the show in this film. The Pigs were also featured with the Wolf in the 1936 Silly Symphony *Little Wolves,* and again in 1939 in *The Practical Pig.*

Three Little Pigs opened on May 27, 1933, just a month before Kay Kamen signed his first official merchandising contract with Walt Disney. Once installed as the sole

BIG TOOTHED, BLACK AND FURRY BIG BAD WOLF STUFFED DOLL FROM THE KNICKERBOCKER TOY CO., 1934.

licensing representative for Walt Disney Enterprises, Kamen lost no time marketing Three Little Pigs, the Big Bad Wolf, Little Red Riding Hood, and, eventually the three Wolf nephews to product manufacturers and merchandisers. Pig and wolf merchandise flooded the markets following Kamen's in-store promotional campaigns; and mother, father, and the children were only too happy to bring home one, two, or all three pigs in one form or another.

The Pigs themselves were cute, pink, cherubic innocents who had instant appeal to children, while the Big Bad Wolf scared them half to death. Some adventurous souls went out and bought a black, furry, spike-toothed Big Bad Wolf Knickerbocker doll that could leer at a child in his crib. The frightening aspect of the Big Bad Wolf determined

"The three little pigs"

FRAMED WALL PICTURE OF THE THREE LITTLE PIGS, PAINTED ON REVERSE GLASS, 8 x 12 INCHES. PRACTICAL PIG IS SHOWN BUILDING A SECURE HOUSE OF BRICK WHILE FIFER PIG AND FIDDLER PIG DANCE A JIG IN FRONT OF THEIR HOUSES OF STRAW AND TWIGS. THE BIG BAD WOLF LURKS BEHIND A TREE IN THE BACKGROUND. BATES ART INDUSTRIES, CHICAGO, 1934.

that most merchandise was centered around the Three Pigs, either as single entities or as a group.

A good many middle-class houses built in the 1920s and in the Depression era were small cottages with brick-faced chimneys that were placed architecturally right into the front of the house. A real cozy house like the brick one the Pigs lived in might also have a peaked Humpty-Dumpty-style roof that was made of slate or clay piping, and the windows would have wooden shutters on them. The building plans for these small homes could be purchased out of a send-away catalog during the Depression. Parents took delight in hanging up "reverse-painted" on glass pictures of the famous Disney Pigs, with the menacing Wolf looking at them in a drooling, hungry manner while hiding behind a tree. With these hung on the wall or with a porcelain Three Little Pigs ashtray set on a blue-mirrored endtable, the Disney characters had once again entered the home as a decorative theme. In the bar-room, Pop might serve beer in mugs to his pals on a Three Little Pigs litho-on-metal "Repeal" beer tray or play cards with a Three Little Pigs deck (and tally pads) from Whitman Publishing Company.

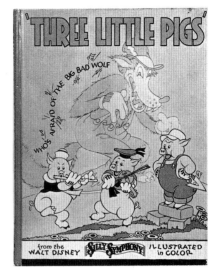

The security the three Little Pigs yearned for went hoof in hand with every-man's dream—that of being in possession of his home, be it a mansion, a cottage, or just a tiny dream bungalow. Having a roof over his head was all Practical Pig really needed in his life, but of course he had to work hard and sweat profusely to get it. Children in the Great Depression were lucky indeed when they were given a hard-back edition of *Three Little Pigs* from Blue Ribbon Books, Inc., of New York. Printed by the Jersey City Printing Company with beautiful color illustrations from the Disney

Studio staff of artists, this book helped instill in kids a fear of the Big Bad Wolf and helped them to realize the need for security in an uncertain world. This book was also printed in 1934 in England by John Lane, The Bodley Head Ltd., London. Blue Ribbon Books also published *The Big Bad Wolf and Little Red Riding Hood* with Disney Studio illustrations in 1934. David McKay Publishers put out their own version of Walt Disney's *Three Little Pigs* and *Little Red Riding Hood and the Big Bad Wolf* in both hard and soft covers in 1934.

General Foods' Post Toasties Cornflakes featured colorful graphic cut-out figures of the Three Little Pigs and the Big Bad Wolf on the backs of their red, yellow, and black cardboard cereal packages. Boys and girls enjoyed cutting these out and standing them up in action poses. These cut-out collectibles are sought after by today's collectors, and it is good fortune that so many were saved.

The Ingersoll-Waterbury Clock Company of Waterbury, Connecticut, issued a

ABOVE: PROHIBITION "REPEAL" BEER-TRAY FEATURING THREE DRINKING PIGS, A FREE-FLOWING BEER BARREL, AND A FRUSTRAT-ED AND LASCIVIOUS WOLF. COLOR LITHOGRAPHED METAL, 1933. **RIGHT, TOP TO BOTTOM:** *THREE LITTLE PIGS* BOOK, BLUE RIBBON BOOKS, NEW YORK, 1933; *THE BIG BAD WOLF AND LITTLE RED RIDING HOOD*, COLOR ILLUSTRATED STORYBOOK PUBLISHED BY BLUE RIBBON, 1934; AND *WHO'S AFRAID OF THE BIG BAD WOLF* SOFTCOVER BOOK PUBLISHED BY DAVID MCKAY OF PHILADELPHIA AND NEW YORK IN 1933.

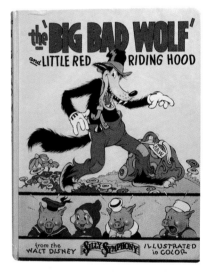

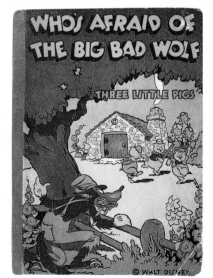

Three Little Pigs and Big Bad Wolf bright red alarm clock in 1934. The Big Bad Wolf's jaws snap open and close, his eyes blink, and his hairy arms and paws point to the time as he chases the Three Little Pigs around the dial. Boys in particular wanted the Three Little Pigs pocket watch

produced that same year; and it is a striking timepiece that collectors covet. A watch fob featuring Three Little Pigs was usually purchased separately from the pocket watch. A Big Bad Wolf wristwatch with the Wolf and the Pigs on the links was also available from Ingersoll in 1934. The graphic images on the alarm clock employ a full figure of the Big Bad Wolf, while the wristwatches feature only the Wolf's head, all against a red background with

twelve white numbers. In a 1935 Sears, Roebuck catalog advertisement, the wristwatch was offered for $2.98 and the pocket watch and alarm clock for a mere $1.39. Today, these timepieces are considered rare, and command high prices in the Disneyana collectors' arena.

George Borgfeldt & Co. bisque novelties produced in Japan featured the Three Little Pigs, each single figurine playing a horn, a drum, and a fiddle. These came in sets in boxes with primitive graphics of the pigs on them. The most common handpainted Japanese bisque toothbrush holder has the three standing Pigs all connected in one form, while another toothbrush figurine features Practical Pig sitting on a barrel building a red brick piano while Fiddler and Fifer play on either side of him.

A single, menacing Big Wolf was produced in bisque in medium and small sizes, and these were popular as carnival prizes in games of chance, where they were sometimes given as jokes to men who thought of themselves as "wolves" with the ladies. There were as well three tiny separate Pigs and a Big Bad Wolf that were pro-

duced as novelty decorations for children's birthday cakes. Three Little Pigs celluloid novelties and action toys were part of the George Borgfeldt & Co. offerings.

Seiberling Latex Rubber Products Company made a handsome hard-rubber Big Bad Wolf and three separate Pig dolls that came singly and in boxed sets. Both the Knickerbocker Toy Company and Richard G. Krueger, Inc., both of New York, produced stuffed Pigs, a Big Bad Wolf, and Little Red Riding Hood dolls. Knickerbocker often inserted a music box into the insides of one of these stuffed dolls. The tune that tinkled out was "Who's Afraid of the Big Bad Wolf?" Borgfeldt also manufactured a big-size plush Red Riding Hood doll; and Madame Alexander produced outfitted Pig dolls. Borgfeldt also distributed the German Schuco Toy Company's three felt on metal windups, which had one Pig drumming, another playing the fiddle, and another blowing into his fife.

A stunning Silly Symphony Christmas tree light set from the Noma Electric Company of New York features the Big Bad Wolf on the box along with the Three Little Pigs, the

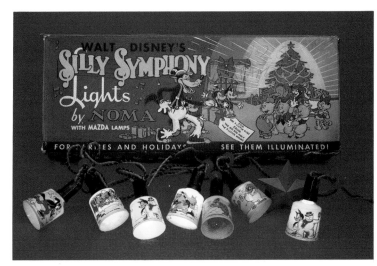

Three Little Wolves, Elmer Elephant, the Robber Kitten, Tillie Tiger, and Clara Cluck emblazoned on the box. Colorful Beetleware shades with decal appliqués of all the Silly Symphony characters in action scenes could be put over each tiny Mazda Christmas tree light bulb.

Disneyana collector pieces featuring the Three Pigs and the Wolf that are desirable would include: Pencil boxes featuring the Three Little Pigs and the Big Bad Wolf from the Joseph Dixon Crucible Company of Jersey City, New Jersey; Three Little Pigs litho-on-metal children's play sets, which include toy-sized tea sets, seashore sand pails, a laundry washbasin and scrubboard, watering cans, and drums from the Ohio Art Com-

pany; Three Little Pigs notepads from the Powers Paper Company of Springfield, Massachusetts; and a very rare Three Little Pigs Emerson Company table radio made of Syroco (pressed sawdust).

During the Depression a Three Little Pigs stationery set, with twenty-four sheets of paper and envelopes, could be purchased for a quarter. Kay Kamen Ltd. issued three individual litho on paper face masks of the Pigs, and one particularly menacing mask of the Wolf was manufactured by the Einson-Freeman Company. Given away free nationwide at toy and department stores and at cartoon showings to members of the Mickey Mouse Club, these masks are excellent graphics for framing today, and are sought-

after pieces of Disneyana ephemera. Pinback button giveaways featuring the Wolf alone with "Who's Afraid of the Big Bad Wolf?" printed above were offered free at screenings of *Three Little Pigs.*

Appearing in many household kitchens in the Depression and avidly collected today are the Three Little Pigs and Big Bad Wolf drinking tumblers put out by Sheffield Farms in an All-Star Parade series from a campaign to promote cottage cheese and other dairy products. Salem China Company of Salem, Ohio, provided beautiful chinaware sets for the children, including mugs for cocoa or hot milk, cereal bowls, and compartmented dinner plates, all featuring the Pigs and/or the Wolf. William Rogers International Silver Company made sets of forks and knives, spoons, and drinking cups for toddlers. In the nursery you might also find a Three Little Pigs windup lamp complete with a matching paper shade. When wound up the lamp—helping the baby into lullaby-land—played "Who's Afraid of the Big Bad Wolf?"

Girls might put Three Little Pigs handkerchiefs from the Hermann Handkerchief Company, Inc., of New York in their lithographed leatherette Three Little Pigs handbags from King Innovations, Inc., New York. Boys wore D. H. Neumann Company Three Little Pigs ties to school and could play either the Who's Afraid of the Big Bad Wolf? game from Marks Brothers or Walt Disney's Who's Afraid of the Big Bad Wolf? or The Red Riding Hood—Big Bad Wolf games, both produced by Parker Brothers. Full costume sets with masks for Halloween were sold at the five-and-dime, featuring sets for the Big Bad Wolf, all Three Little Pigs, and Little Red Riding Hood from A. S. Fischback, Inc., and Sarkman Brothers Company, both of New York, and from the Wornova Company.

Under the Christmas tree for boys in the Depression might be a Three Little Pigs flash-

light from the U.S. Electric Manufacturing Company of New York and a Who's Afraid of the Big Bad Wolf? toy printing set from the Fulton Specialty Company. The Ensign Ltd. of London produced a slide projector that came with hand-painted glass lantern slides that told the story of *Three Little Pigs* in visuals.

The Bates Art Industries of Chicago framed full-color pictures of the Three Little Pigs dancing a jig, singing at home, or riding atop a Big Bad Wolf hobby horse. Produced in the millions were the non-Disney china or bisque Made in Japan ver-

sions of the Three Little Pigs as knickknack figurines, ashtrays, and the like, available in the dime stores during the 1930s and adding to the mystique that surrounded the Disney short. These are not to be confused with the Borgfeldt Company licensed items, though some bear a striking resemblance to the Disney Pig or Wolf characters. Still, these are fun items to enjoy or collect as dime store whatnots.

Merchandise featuring the Three Little Pigs persisted through the forties and well into the fifties; the LineMar litho-on-tin windups, packaged in colorful boxes, are fine examples of later Disneyana. These and other items from *Three Little Pigs* fascinate Disneyana enthusiasts, some of them still able to remember the bad days of the Depression.

TOP: WHO'S AFRAID OF THE BIG BAD WOLF CELLULOID PINBACK BUTTON GIVEN AWAY AT SCREENINGS OF *THREE LITTLE PIGS*, 1933. LEFT: FIDDLER PIG AND BIG BAD WOLF. COLOR LITHOGRAPHED METAL WINDUP JUMPERS, MADE IN JAPAN FOR LINEMAR CO., C. 1949.

The Three Orphan Kittens, *The Robber Kitten*, and *The Tortoise and the Hare* were all published by Whitman Publishing Company, Racine, Wis., in 1935, and were written and illustrated by the staff of the Walt Disney Studios.

SIXTEEN

SILLY SYMPHONY PARADE

The Silly Symphonies introduced a number of interesting Disney cartoon characters into the world of sales and merchandising. Although these never had the impact of Mickey Mouse, Minnie Mouse, or Donald Duck; or the original gang of Horace, Clarabelle, Goofy, and Pluto; the Three Little Pigs and the Big Bad Wolf, they nevertheless turned up as toys, games, and books, and on dozens of food products licensed by Kay Kamen Ltd.

Kamen kept a close watch on the Silly Symphonies after the success of *Three Little Pigs*, looking for ways to utilize the characters to add to the merchandising list. These seventy-five short films, starting with *The Skeleton Dance* (1929) and ending with a remake of *The Ugly Duckling* (1939), won seven Academy Awards. There were enough characters in the series (twenty-eight in black and white, forty-

seven in color) to provide an army of characters for the merchandise markets.

The unique, charming Disney Silly Symphony characters of the 1930s include Clara Cluck, Bucky Bug, the Wise Little Hen, the Grasshopper, a Disney Santa Claus, Mother Goose, King Neptune, Old King Cole, the Peculiar Penguins, Polly and Peter, the Funny Little Bunnies, the Water Babies, Peter Pig, the Country Cousin mice, the Robber Kitten, the Three Orphan Kittens, King Midas, Max Hare, Toby Tortoise, The Ugly Duckling, the Flying Mouse, Wynken, Blynken, and Nod, and Little Red Riding Hood.

Of special interest to merchandisers were Elmer Elephant, the cartoon star of *Elmer Elephant*, a 1936 Silly Symphony, and his girlfriend, Tillie Tiger. Elmer and Tillie appear on N. N. Hill Brass Company

LEFT: Libbey-Owens Glass Co. made the drinking glasses offered as send-aways from dairy companies. The glasses featured Mickey Mouse and Silly Symphony characters, c. 1939. **BELOW:** Mickey Mouse presents cutouts of Walt Disney's Three Little Kittens on the back of a Post Toasties cereal box.

and Fisher-Price action-pull toys, on drinking tumblers, handkerchiefs, paint boxes, as bisque figurines and toothbrush holders, as dolls, and in books in which Elmer is the main character. Richard G. Krueger of New York produced what would now be regarded as rare character dolls of the Robber Kitten, the Three Orphan Kittens, Elmer Elephant, Miss Cottontail, and Toby Tortoise.

David McKay published beautiful books of the Silly Symphonies, including the first *Elmer Elephant* book in 1936, *The Wise Little Hen* (1934), *Peculiar Penguins* (1936), and *The Country Cousin* (1938). The Walt Disney Studios wrote the text and illustrated hardcover books published by Whitman in 1935 of *The Three Orphan Kittens, The Robber Kitten*, and *The Tortoise and the Hare*. In 1938, Whitman published *Timid Elmer*, a 5 x 5½-inch cardboard-covered book with black and white illustra-

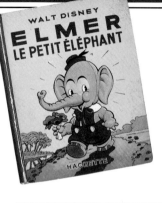

tions featuring Elmer Elephant, Tillie Tiger, and Tuffy Tiger, as well as similar editions featuring Practical Pig, the Ugly Duckling, and "Mother Pluto." Whitman Publishing Company of Racine, Wisconsin, put out four Silly Symphony Big Little Books: *Mickey Mouse Presents a Silly Symphony* (1934); *Walt Disney's Silly Symphony Stories* (1936), featuring Donald Duck, Peter Pig, Benny Bird, and Bucky Bug, and two others published in 1937 and 1939, both featuring Donald Duck. In 1933, Blue Ribbon Books published a handsome hardback storybook with Pop-Up illustrations of the Silly Symphonies *King Neptune* and *Babes in the Woods.*

In 1938, a special short, *Ferdinand the Bull,* based on Munro Leaf's famous story about a Spanish fighting bull who preferred relaxing and sniffing flowers, was released

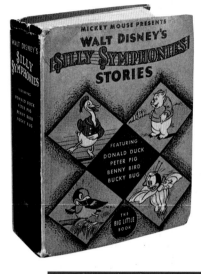

and won Walt Disney another Academy Award. Ferdinand was a very popular character with the public, and was produced as a "glazed leatherette fabric" stuffed doll manufactured by Richard G. Krueger; as a Knickerbocker Toy Company painted composition doll; as an attractive painted bisque "sitting-bull-with-flower" novelty figurine; and as a Louis Marx Company tin-litho windup toy with a spinning tail. Ferdinand also was a sculptured soap in the Lightfoot Schultz Company's attractively packaged character soap series, which included Donald, Pluto, Mickey, Peter Pig, and the Funny Bunnies.

Clara Cluck appeared as part of a set of nursery pull-toys in 1936 from Fisher-Price Toys, but the extent of the operatic hen on merchandise is unfortunately as scarce as a hen's tooth. Collectors may never enjoy, alas, a Clara Cluck watch or clock that made operatic hen noises on the hour or half hour.

It is not at all unusual to find Donald and Mickey or Pluto on various products and toys parading, running, or chasing after a variety of Silly Symphony characters in different combinations. Some of the Silly Symphony characters are rare, and collectors seek them out for that reason and because they add breadth and style to their Disneyana collections. One collector regards his Disney Little Red Riding Hood bisque figurine as the rarest in his collection, with Toby Tortoise in bisque a close second.

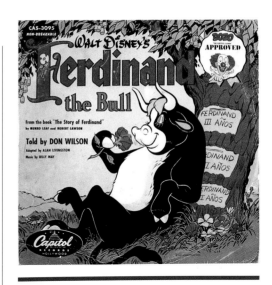

FERDINAND THE BULL, A SILLY SYMPHONY "SPECIAL SHORT," RELEASED IN 1938. THE CAPITOL RECORDS 78 RPM RECORDING FEATURES MUSIC BY BILLY MAY, NARRATION BY DON WILSON (JACK BENNY'S TELEVISION SIDEKICK), AND ADAPTATION BY ALAN LIVINGSTON FROM THE BOOK *THE STORY OF FERDINAND* BY MUNRO LEAF AND ROBERT LAWSON.

CLARA CLUCK, THE OPERATIC HEN AND STAR OF THE 1934 DISNEY SHORT *ORPHAN'S BENEFIT*. PAPER LITHOGRAPHED ON WOOD NURSERY PULL-TOY PRODUCED IN 1936 BY FISHER-PRICE TOYS, EAST AURORA, NEW YORK.

A SMALL HAND-PAINTED BISQUE FIGURINE OF FERDINAND THE BULL, MADE IN JAPAN FOR DISTRIBUTION IN THE U.S., 1938.

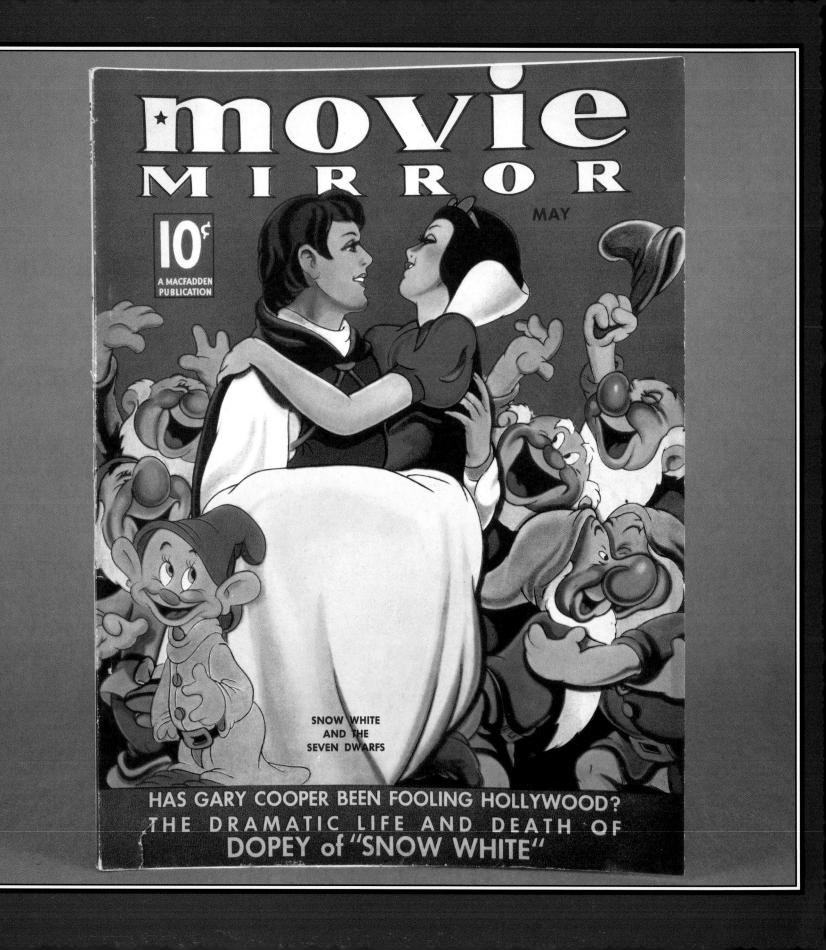

SEVENTEEN

DISNEY'S MASTERPIECE:
SNOW WHITE AND THE SEVEN DWARFS

The preparation for *Snow White and the Seven Dwarfs*, which is generally acknowledged to be Walt Disney's masterpiece, was begun in 1934 when Disney explained his dream of a feature-length animated film to a group of studio artists. The Disney story department began to develop the Grimms' fairy tale into a full concept, but actual work in animation did not start until 1936. Initially, Roy Disney dissented, thinking that such a project was foolhardy. He felt that such an endeavor could drive the studio into bankruptcy, emphasizing to his brother that they should all stay with a good thing, namely Mickey Mouse. He also predicted that it could never receive critical acclaim, and that audiences would shy away from an animated full-length fairy tale. He urged Walt to stay with the financially secure shorts, even though at that time the introduction of the double-feature in movie theaters was pushing cartoons off the screen.

The production cost, which was estimated to be $150,000, eventually accelerated to $1.5 million. Word around Hollywood in the mid-1930s had it that *Snow White* would be "Disney's Folly." Walt told his staff of artists that he remembered being strongly moved by a 1915 silent film version of *Snow White* starring Marguerite Clark. Walt remained steadfast and ignored the Hollywood doubters as well as his businessman brother. Many years later, Walt recalled:

As the budget climbed higher and higher, I began to have some doubts, too, wondering if we could ever get our investment back.

OPPOSITE: SNOW WHITE, THE PRINCE, AND ALL SEVEN DWARFS ARE FEATURED ON THE COVER OF *MOVIE MIRROR* MAGAZINE, VOL. 9, NO. 6, MAY 1938. THE FEATURE ARTICLE BY SARA HAMILTON IS ENTITLED "THE DRAMATIC LIFE AND DEATH OF DOPEY OF *SNOW WHITE*."

Then came a shocker. My brother, Roy, told me that we would have to borrow another quarter of a million dollars to finish the movie. I had to take the bits and pieces we had already done of the film to show the bankers as collateral, and I was sure, being bankers, they wouldn't view the footage with any understanding. I was plenty worried. On the appointed day, I sat along with Joe Rosenberg of the Bank of America, watching those bits and pieces on a screen, trying to sell him a quarter of a million dollars' worth of faith. After the lights came on, he didn't show the slightest reaction to what he'd just seen. He walked out of the projection room, remarked that it was a nice day—and yawned! Then he turned to me and said, "Walt, that picture will make a pot full of money." Well, as everyone knows, we got the loan, the picture did make money, and if it hadn't, there wouldn't be any Disney Studio today.

With the profits from *Snow White* Walt built the new Disney Studios in Burbank.

Walt Disney had been pondering the creation of a feature-length cartoon for some time. He and Mary Pickford had discussed a production of *Alice in Wonderland* in the early thirties, with herself in the title role and the rest of the cast animated characters drawn by studio artists. Another idea was to cast Will Rogers as Rip Van Winkle, but this project never came to fruition. "It took guts to do what Walt did," veteran animator Ollie Johnston said. "The story is based on the idea that the Queen is going to murder this girl. That's one drawing killing another drawing. Walt convinced us that this could be done so that it would be believable and we all believed him." The superior artistry that was being developed in animation at the studio through the Silly Symphonies convinced Disney that he must make a fully animated feature film. Nothing could stop him.

Snow White and the Seven Dwarfs premiered December 21, 1937, at the Carthay Circle Theater in Los Angeles to an audience filled with Hollywood luminaries. Judy Garland, Charles Laughton, and Marlene Dietrich, among others clapped spontaneously throughout, breaking into wild applause after seeing the wonder of multiplane Technicolor and an all-

F59-5-894

JANE WITHERS AT HOME IN 1938 HOLDING A DOPEY DOLL IN FRONT OF HER COLLECTION OF SNOW WHITE AND THE SEVEN DWARFS CHARACTER DOLLS. CHILD STAR WITHERS, ALONG WITH SHIRLEY TEMPLE, WAS AN AVID COLLECTOR OF MICKEY MOUSE DOLLS AND OTHER DISNEY TOYS IN THE 1930S AND CONTINUED TO COLLECT INTO HER ADULT LIFE.

animated feature film.

The general release for *Snow White* was on February 4, 1938, when it officially opened at the Radio City Music Hall in New York. It played for five weeks, doing good business at the box-office at a time when a movie theater ticket was ten cents for children and twenty-five cents for adults: In Paris it played for an astounding thirty-one weeks. During its first three months of release it has been estimated that more than twenty million people flocked to see it, and it grossed $8.5 million. The movie remained the all-time box-office champion until *Gone With the Wind* came along to surpass it.

The great success of *Snow White* was capped off on February 23, 1939, when Shirley Temple presented Walt Disney with an Academy Award consisting of one large Oscar for Snow White and seven miniature ones for each of the dwarfs. An all-time top grosser (to date, worldwide totals surpass more than $330 million in its many re-releases), *Snow White* was a hit again when it was released at over two thousand theaters on July 17, 1987, to celebrate the fiftieth anniversary of the movie. It was the first movie exhibited simultaneously in more than sixty countries including the USSR and China—and in more than ten languages.

Throughout the world the public of the 1930s and 1940s adored the seven dwarf cartoon characters, who all had individual identities: the original suggested names Wheezy, Shorty, Lazy, Sniffy, Gabby, Puffy, Jumpy, Shorty, Stubby, and Nifty were all discarded during the process of the film's creation in favor of Sleepy, Grumpy, Bashful, Dopey, Happy, Sneezy, and Doc. Snow White herself was thought of by the public as a star almost as if she were a real-life flesh-and-blood girl like Jane Withers, Deanna Durbin, Judy Garland, or Gloria Jean.

The voice of Snow White was supplied by Adriana Caselotti; and Marjorie Belcher, the wife of animator Art Babbitt and later famous as Marge Champion, was the model who posed for the drawings. Louis Hightower posed for the Prince; and it has been said that the face and manner of Joan Crawford were the inspiration for the beautiful Wicked Queen who demanded that her magic mirror refer to her alone as "the fairest of them all" over and above Snow White.

When the queen sought revenge on Snow White, whom the mirror called "the fairest," she drank a magic potion that temporarily transformed her into the gnarled Old Witch. Children in theaters were so frightened by this that some hid under their seats or ran out of the theater in tears. Not since the Big Bad Wolf had a character seemed so mean, malevolent, and monstrous. Indeed, it was the same studio artist, Norman Ferguson, who helped to create both of these cruel characters. Even to this day irate mothers and social groups complain about the cackling Old Witch and the dark forest scene in which the Huntsman threatens Snow White's life while taunting, grasping trees pull at her as if trying to tear off her tattered dress.

A *New York Times* editorial published August 5, 1987, on the fiftieth anniversary, called the film "irresistible . . . in the world of Snow White justice will out, goodness will triumph, true love will prevail. To see the movie after a lifetime that would seem to indicate otherwise is to see the scales tip toward optimism once again." Letters in response to the editorial and to an essay by Glenn Collins regarding parental fears of violence in the film ranged from amazed: "There is, indeed, hope for us all if the *New York Times* can devote an editorial to the return of *Snow White . . .*" to outraged: "My memories of *Snow White* are tarnished by the distaste I felt for a (cartoon) character who was cheerful about housekeeping for seven little men, including a sarcastic grump, and who lived only for the day when her fantasy Prince would come. Heigh-ho, it's off to work I go. When I get home, I expect my Prince to do half the housework!" John B. Archibald, an artist from Brooklyn, summed it up when he wrote, "Though there has been considerable debate over the suitability of this film for children, it is perhaps its ability to affect all my emotional responses that makes it just as effective today as when it was first released."

Snow White, Grumpy, Doc, Bashful, Sleepy, Sneezy, Dopey, and Happy Character Merchandise

Kay Kamen made preparations early in 1936 to begin the aggressive campaign to saturate the marketplace with mass-produced Snow White, Grumpy, Sleepy, Bashful, Sneezy, Doc, Dopey, and Happy character merchandise. This is one reason why certain Snow White items may be dated 1937, though the bulk of original Snow White merchandise is dated 1938.

Comic books, paint and coloring books, picture books, and a Big Little Book were printed and distributed well in advance of the film's release. Kamen's prerelease publication plan, used for many of the cartoons and for all of the later feature films, familiarized children with the characters, images, and plot (and, not the least important for Disney, helped establish the copyright for the characters before the film was released). Snow White and Dopey were the most popular characters in the film and consequently they are seen more either singly or together on products and toys. Many companies utilized the images of Snow White and all Seven Dwarfs or, in some instances, just the Seven Dwarfs.

By the time *Snow White* merchandise was in the marketplace at toy stores, five-and-dimes, department stores, and in food chains across the nation, it was clear Kay Kamen's genius for masterminding the sales campaigns for distributors and licensees with hundreds of ideas exploiting the new Disney characters was solidified. Kamen's

ABOVE LEFT: PREMIUM GIVEAWAY PINBACK BUTTON FOR MEMBERS OF THE SNOW WHITE JINGLE CLUB. AN INSERT IN THE BACK READS "WALT DISNEY ENTERPRISES, KAY KAMEN LTD., SOLE REPRESENTATIVE, 1270 SIXTH AVE., NEW YORK." BELOW: WEARING THIS LITHOGRAPHED PAPER MASK ON HALLOWEEN WOULD GIVE YOU AN INSTANTLY "GRUMPY" APPEARANCE. MASKS OF ALL THE CHARACTERS FROM *SNOW WHITE AND THE SEVEN DWARFS* WERE MADE BY THE EINSON-FREEMAN CO., 1937.

Rockefeller Center headquarters sold retailers specially ordered display pieces from the Old King Cole Company featuring Snow White and the Seven Dwarfs and including the forest animals, the cottage in the woods, and various scenic setups from the film. Kamen headquarters also issued a pinback button giveaway for the Snow White Jingle Clubs and litho-on-paper premium masks of Snow White, all Seven Dwarfs, and the Wicked Witch, made by the Einson-Freeman Company.

Hand-painted bisque sets of Snow White and all Seven

Dwarfs, often with their names on the front, were produced in Japan for George Borgfeldt & Co. in small, medium, and large sizes, boxed and unboxed. Some unique sets had the Seven Dwarfs playing instruments. Bisque figurines from *Snow White* were sold into the millions at the five-and-dime and were popular prizes at amusement parks. A Snow White bisque was sometimes pasted on circular pieces of cardboard that stood atop candy packets wrapped in cellophane and tied with ribbon. Larger size painted-chalk or plaster dolls of Snow White and Dopey were also produced by carnival supply companies.

The Seiberling Latex Products Company made painted hard-rubber figures of the Seven Dwarfs that have excellent detail, and each is identified with a name on its hat. Manufacturers realized the public would have difficulty naming all Seven Dwarfs, and even today the Dwarfs' names are used in popular crossword puzzles or trivia games. The Seiberling Snow White is quite rare: being hollow, it often crumbled or deflated, but the Dwarfs have a wonderful artistic quality. A painted white-metal set of Snow White and the Seven Dwarfs from J. L. Wright, Inc., of Chicago sold for twenty-five cents each at Gimbels, Marshall Field, Bullock's, B. Altman's, and other stores in 1938. Glass pottery companies like

ABOVE, LEFT AND RIGHT: Einson-Freeman Paper Par-T-Masks of Snow White and the Wicked Witch, offered by Procter & Gamble as a promotional tie-in for Camay soap, 1937.

Bisque figurines of Snow White and the Seven Dwarfs. Snow White is 6 ½ inches tall and the Dwarfs are 5 inches. These hand-painted, Made in Japan figurines were distributed in 1938 and 1939 by George Borgfeldt Corp., New York.

Evan K. Shaw, the American Pottery Company, Brayton's Laguna Pottery, and the Hagen-Renaker Company made very good eight-piece sets that are regarded as fine collectibles.

Twenty-inch-high Snow White stuffed dolls with molded, painted cloth faces and yarn hair were produced by the Richard G. Krueger Company, Inc., which also made one-foot-high dwarfs. Fawn, the little deer, was included in this desirable product line, and also available were a number of dolls of Disney forest rabbits, chipmunks, and birds. The Knickerbocker Toy Company and the Chad Valley Company produced Snow White and the Seven Dwarfs doll sets; and Knickerbocker included the Wicked Queen and forest creatures as well. Madame Alexander created Snow White and the Seven Dwarfs dolls and marionettes. Her Snow White doll was produced from the same mold as the company's Princess Elizabeth doll. The Wicked Queen, the Huntsman, and the Prince were also available as marionettes from Madame Alexander. The Ideal Novelty and Toy Company of New York made a complete stuffed set of Snow White and the Seven Dwarfs and a composition Snow White doll, which used a Shirley Temple face mold, minus the Shirley dimples.

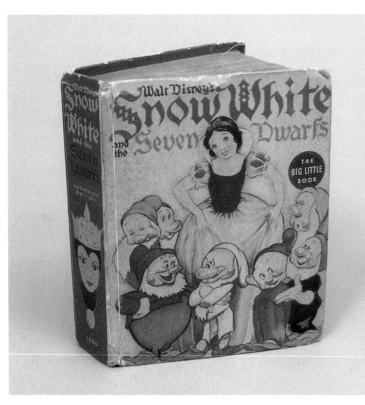

TOP LEFT: RUBBER DOPEY DOLL, 6 ½ INCHES TALL, WITH A PAINTED YELLOW SUIT AND PURPLE HAT AND SHOES. MANUFACTURED BY THE SEIBERLING LATEX PRODUCTS CO., OF AKRON, OHIO. ALL SEVEN DWARFS WERE AVAILABLE WITH SNOW WHITE SOLD SEPARATELY OR IN BOXED SETS, 1938. LEFT: *SNOW WHITE AND THE SEVEN DWARFS* BIG LITTLE BOOK FEATURES THE WICKED QUEEN ON THE SPINE AND THE WICKED WITCH ON THE BACK COVER, WHITMAN PUBLISHING COMPANY, 1938.

Storybooks from Grosset & Dunlap, the David McKay Company, and other publishers were produced in large numbers in several editions. Whitman Publishing Company produced at least five linen-like books, cut-out doll books, coloring books, boxed book sets, a Big Little Book, and stories and titles featuring each character in the film including: *The Story of Snow White, The Story of Dopey, The Story of Doc, The Story of Bashful, The Story of Sneezy, The Story of Sleepy, The Story of Happy*, and *The Story of Grumpy*.

William Collins of Great Britain published a number of books for the British trade, and the Tower Press of London put out novelty cut-out books and transfer-story books. RCA Victor produced the soundtrack recording, Decca records produced a 78 rpm record-album set of the songs recorded by Lyn Murray and His Orchestra and Chorus, and the sheet music from *Snow White* published by the Irving Berlin Company of New York includes: "Whistle While You Work," "Some Day My Prince Will Come," "One Song," "With a Smile and a Song," "I'm Wishing," "A Silly Song," "Heigh Ho, Heigh Ho (It's Off to Work We Go)," "Dig Dig Dig," and "Bluddle-uddle-um-Dum," the Dwarf's Yodel Song.

Collectors' items that are avidly sought after include a square and a rectangular

Snow White radio produced by the Emerson Radio and Phonograph Corporation of New York, made in plain, varnished Syroco or colorfully painted Syroco. The rectangular unpainted radio at first seems to have left Dopey out of its lineup of pressed wood figures, but he is soon to be seen hiding in a tree just above and to the left of the speaker. There was an "animated" Snow White music box and a beautiful "animated Snow White Toy Piano" made by the Marks Brothers of Boston. An album of the famous songs from *Snow White* and a ten-note "carefully tuned" dulcimer, which came with a wooden mallet, was pro-

ABOVE LEFT: SHEET MUSIC FOR "HEIGH-HO—IT'S OFF TO WORK WE GO!," FROM *SNOW WHITE AND THE SEVEN DWARFS*, BOURNE CO., NEW YORK, 1939. ABOVE RIGHT: EMERSON RADIO AND PHONOGRAPH COMPANY SOLD THIS PRESSED WOOD (SYROCO) SNOW WHITE AND THE SEVEN DWARFS TABLE-TOP RADIO FOR $14.95 IN 1938.

duced by the J. W. Spear & Sons Company.

Juvenile hand-painted Mode-ware (plastic composition) figural lamps of Snow White, Dopey, and Doc came with colorful Disney illustrated heavy parchment shades. The Snow White lamps were manufactured by La Mode Studios, Inc.; Doris Lampshades Company of New York produced the distinctive Disney lampshades. La Mode Studios also offered figural wall lamps, bookends and night lights. Boxed sets of

Mazda Christmas tree lights with Beetleware shades complete with decal appliqués of scenes from the movie were made by the Thompson-Houston Company Ltd. of London. Storkline Furniture Corporation of Chicago sold a complete line of wood furniture, highchairs, dressers, cribs, and sets of chairs with tables, all made to scale to fit into a child's small room. For outdoor wintertime play, the S. L. Allen Company made a fine wooden 40-inch Snow White and the Seven Dwarfs sled.

George Borgfeldt & Co. offered boxed

porcelain Snow White tea sets: and colorful Beetleware "meal-time" sets came from the Bryant Electric Company. The Ohio Art Company of Bryan, Ohio, produced litho-on-metal Snow White and the Seven Dwarfs boxed children's tea sets, which included a tea-pot, creamer, sugarbowl, cups, saucers,

plates, and a serving tray. Ohio Art also made metal drums and other lithographed tin musical instruments, beach sand pails, shovels and watering cans for Snow White gardens. A tin-litho paint box featuring Snow White and the Dwarfs came from Charles G. Page Ltd. of London. Libbey-Owens Glass Company produced a lithographed metal Snow White tray, a decorated lunch box, and a set of eight Snow White and the Seven Dwarfs glass drinking tumblers. Louis Marx and Company of New York manufactured a wonderful tin-litho "shaking" and "wobbling" Dopey the Dwarf windup toy with rolling eyes. This Dopey toy, with its yellow robe and lavender hat is a very desirable wind-up toy today.

The campaigns for *Snow White and the*

Seven Dwarfs offered a great many incentives to manufacturers of girls' attire and accessories. There was a Snow White handbag from W. Wood Ltd., and a girl's leatherette purse manufactured by King Innovations, Inc., of New York. A Snow White wristwatch was produced by the Ingersoll-Waterbury Clock Company of Connecticut in 1949 and in 1952 one with a red band was sold with a plastic figurine of Snow White by U.S. Time. A wonderful French Bayard Company "nostalgia" alarm clock manufactured in 1969 features Blanche Neige with an "animated" bird second hand with the Seven Dwarfs and five forest creatures on the face numbers.

Cartier of Fifth Avenue in New York might not have been thinking of just "little" girls when they offered their beautiful

Snow White–Seven Dwarfs charm bracelets and pins. Dime-store plastic, enameled metals, and painted composition jewelry were the rage as pins, bracelets, and as buttons for blouses, all featuring Snow White and the Dwarfs. Brier Manufacturing Company of Providence, Rhode Island, produced large quantities of this affordable five-and-dime novelty jewelry. Attractive Snow White plastic barrettes were made by Lapin-Kurley Kew Company of New York. Prized by collectors today and selling in 1939 for only a dime are the multicolored or marbleized Catalin novelty pencil sharpeners and napkin holders that feature decals of Snow White and the Seven Dwarfs. Catalin toothbrushes with decals of the eight characters were also available from the Hughes-Auto Graf Brush

Company of New York, which manufactured hairbrushes for boys as well featuring Grumpy and Dopey together on the box and on the brush itself.

In department stores, sewing centers, and dry goods stores across the country, cotton prints for fabrics depicting *Snow White* scenes and characters were available from Arthur Beir & Company; Colcombet-Werk, Inc., of New York and Paris created similar "pure silk" fabrics. Haircord fast-color textile fabrics, featuring Snow White and the Seven Dwarfs and printed in several different patterns, were offered by the Silko Textiles Company, Ltd. Hand-loomed linen tablecloths, dinner and cocktail napkins, kitchen and guest towels with hand-blocked prints featuring Snow White and the Seven Dwarfs were made by Louis Nessel & Company.

For the younger children there were "Laxteen" baby pants in a pretty Snow White box from American Latex Corporation of New York. To decorate the nursery were framed prints in sets from Aristo, Inc. Celluloid rattles for baby came from the Amloid corporation of Lodi, New Jersey. The British Wool Company in Wembley, Middlesex, manufactured a "Disneyland" nursery yarn featuring Dopey and Snow White. For the older children, Powers Paper Company produced notepads and stationery featuring Snow White and the Seven Dwarfs. Women could choose from ten different Snow White print corsets in the "Smarties" line offered by Miller Corsets, Inc., of Canandaigua, New York. Figural Snow White and the Seven Dwarfs soaps for all came in sets boxed by the Lightfoot Schultz Company to resemble a fairy-tale book.

"BLANCHE NEIGE" ALARM CLOCK HAS AN ANIMATED BLUEBIRD AND TWO RED BIRDS ON THE CLOCK HANDS, MADE BY THE BAYARD CO. OF FRANCE FOR THE NOSTALGIA MARKET, 1969.

You could buy character socks in the children's clothing departments, manufactured by the Herbert Hosiery Mills Company of Jersey City. Herrmann handkerchief Company of New York created boxed gift sets of embroidered hankies of Snow White and all Seven Dwarfs, as well as Snow White kerchiefs. Snow White and the Seven Dwarfs rubber boots and canvas sneakers were packed in shoeboxes with excellent graphics and were manufactured by the Converse Rubber Company of Malden, Massachusetts. Newman and Freedman Ltd. sold "mini tees" in six delightful designs. There were Snow White print pajamas and snowsuits with a Snow White and the Seven Dwarfs print lining from Mayfair Togs, Inc., of New York. Boys' and girls' hats, boys' ties, a tie-rack, belts, mufflers, and gloves were made by D. H. Neumann of New York.

The Odora Company, Inc., of New York manufactured a lithographed cardboard wood and print-fabric-covered Snow White and the Seven Dwarfs Treasure Chest to store all the new Snow White toys and games. These might include Parker Brothers' Walt Disney's Own Game of Snow White and the Seven Dwarfs, complete with a colorful game board. The treasure chest of Snow White collectibles today would include the animated Snow White Valentine cards made by the Paper Novelty Company, the Tap-A-Way Game (with new "electric" tappers) offered by the Naylor Corporation, and the litho-on-metal Snow White Bagatelle and Pinball Game manufactured by Chad Valley Company, Ltd. of Harborne, England. There were target

games from American Toy Works, Snow White and the Seven Dwarfs card games from Pepy's Series Games, London, and jigsaw puzzles from Williams, Ellis Company and the Whitman Publishing Company of Racine, Wisconsin.

The foods product division of Kay Kamen Ltd. went into full gear with many sales promotional gimmicks and giveaways, contests, and prizes. The Mickey Mouse Globetrotting Campaign was brought out again so that bakeries could promote Snow White sliced bread, which came in a colorful waxed-paper wrapper featuring a forest bunny, a bird, all the dwarfs, and Snow White holding a candle. Picture-card inserts and the end-paper stickers were collected and traded by children; these, along with the store window signs, cardboard display boards, streamers,

and pennants issued by Kay Kamen Ltd. for the campaign, are the Disneyana collectibles of today. Snow White and the Seven Dwarfs either appeared on or endorsed in advertisements and store signs Armour Ham, Snow White Ice Cream, Snow White Cake Flour, and Snow White candy packaged in lithographed tins from Belgium.

All-Sweet Margarine was offered by Swift and Company, and Colgate-Palmolive manufactured Super Suds, a soap-powder featuring a scrubbing Snow White who also used Snow White Ammonia in the bathroom. Pepsodent Toothpaste, Johnson and Johnson "Tek" toothbrushes, Kraft Cheese Company, which offered Snow White glass tumblers as a premium, and a Royal Typewriter featured either Snow White, Dopey, or combinations of all the

Seven Dwarf characters. Prominent national advertising campaigns were mounted for National Dairy Products, a popular Dopey Drink, Dietz Gum, and Wrigley's Snow White Doublemint Gum, and a Snow White Soda.

Today all things Snow White and the Seven Dwarfs from the original merchandising period (the late thirties and early forties) are considered the most desirable Snow White collectibles. Original artwork and cels from this Disney masterpiece are now in the category of original Disney Studio art works and sell accordingly as "high art." During the 50th Anniversary celebration of the release of Snow White, the Disney Company, in addition to the commemorative coins and hand-stamped postage cancellations de rigueur on these occasions, licensed over 100 firms to produce "limited edition" merchandise, including a Snow White Golden Anniversary watch, special recordings and albums, a music box, porcelain and bisque figurines, plates and cups, Christmas tree ornaments, T-shirts and slippers, infant wear, sleepwear, and a complete line of greeting cards and holiday and party favors and decorations featuring Snow White and the Seven Dwarfs. These are now regarded by today's new Disneyana collectors as Snow White investibles for the future.

EIGHTEEN

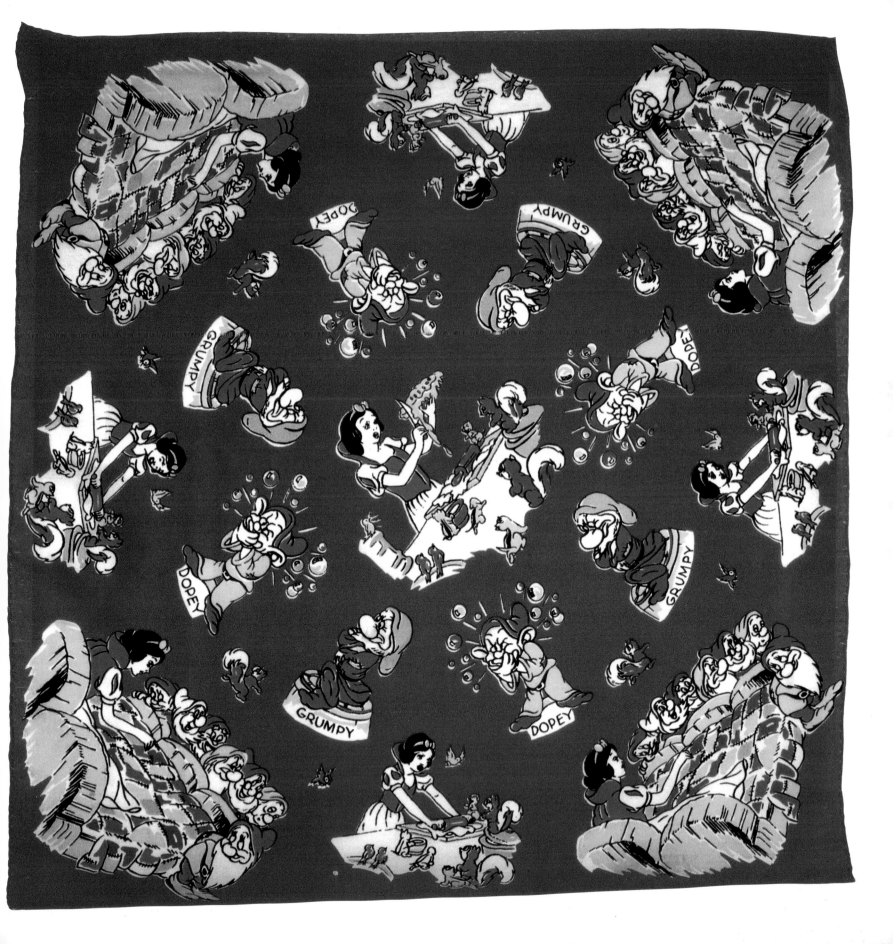

THE FORTIES FEATURE FILMS

PINOCCHIO (February 1940)

The Disney Studio created its second masterful feature-length animated movie with *Pinocchio,* based on the famous children's book *Pinocchio, The Story of a Marionette* by Collodi, the pen name for an Italian writer named Carlo Lorenzini. Collodi was the name of Lorenzini's native village where today a tablet marks the site of the author's birthplace. In *The Art of Walt Disney,* author Christopher Finch heaps critical acclaim upon this second feature, stating that *Snow White and the Seven Dwarfs* may have given Disney his finest moment, but *Pinocchio* is probably his greatest achievement. Finch adds that the movie shared all the qualities that made the first animated feature such a success and that *Pinocchio*'s technical advances have

never been surpassed.

The panoramic opening sequence, which takes the viewer from the white shining star, over the rooftops of the town to Geppetto's lighted window, is only one of the innovations of this delightful and remarkable film. The delineation of character, in particular the development of Pinocchio himself from a wooden toy to a real boy is far more intricate in its scope and detail than that of Snow White. In the same sense, the character of Jiminy Cricket, a tiny insect who is Pinocchio's conscience, comes across as larger than life. Disney artist Ward Kimball struggled a long time in order to come up with just the right image for this charming creature. The Blue Fairy, modeled after dancer Marge Champion, glowing with a golden

ABOVE: PINOCCHIO IS PRESENTED BY MICKEY MOUSE ON THE COVER OF *MICKEY MOUSE MAGAZINE,* DECEMBER 1939. **RIGHT:** AMUSEMENT PARK AND CARNIVAL PRIZES IN 1940 INVARIABLY INCLUDED A PAINTED PLASTER STATUETTE OF PINOCCHIO. **OPPOSITE:** RKO NEWSETTE, APRIL 4, 1940, FEATURES *PINOCCHIO* ON A DOUBLE-BILL WITH *THE SAINT'S DOUBLE TROUBLE,* WITH GEORGE SANDERS AND HELENE WHITNEY.

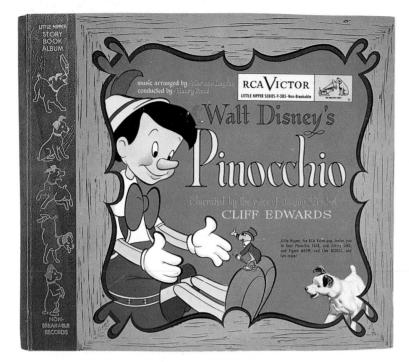

beauty, seems to exceed both Snow White and the Wicked Queen as the "fairest of them all." Only the doddering old Geppetto seems one-dimensional, more a caricature of an old man than a fully developed character. Geppetto's household pets, the cat Figaro and the goldfish Cleo, however, have a real presence and are among the finest creations of the Disney supporting characters.

The insidious sly fox J. Worthington Foulfellow, known as "Honest John"; the pompous Gideon (Giddy) the pussycat; the voracious oversized showman puppeteer Stromboli; not to mention Monstro the Whale with his gigantic jaws are all menacing characters, each imbued with their own unique individuality, commanding our

attention in every frame they appear in. Lampwick, the beer-guzzling, cigar-smoking poolshark bad boy of Pleasure Island, who turns into a braying donkey, is another of Disney's truly frightening characters. *Pinocchio* is not just another fairy tale or children's story but a great fable that examines the conflicts of right and wrong and the choices involved in good over evil and life against death. The story of this happy/sad little marionette becoming a real boy (i.e., a real person) when he is reunited with his father and his home (seen here as the real, intrinsic value of life—care and responsibility to those we love) is a struggle that is easily identifiable to everyone.

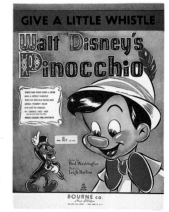

It is unnecessary to compare the musical scores of *Snow White* and *Pinocchio* since they are both excellent. But the ease with which the songs occur in *Pinocchio* should be noted. "When You Wish Upon a Star," the song written by Ned Washington and Leigh Harline and as sung by Cliff Edwards (known on radio and in early recordings as "Ukulele Ike"), who is the voice of Jiminy Cricket, easily won the Academy Award as Best Song of 1940. Big bands of the forties such as the Glenn Miller Orchestra made hit recordings of "Give a Little Whistle" (another Jiminy Cricket song) and "When You Wish Upon a Star." In Great Britain, "When You Wish Upon A Star" and "Give a Little Whistle" were recorded by Joe Loss and His Orchestra. "Little Wooden Head" was recorded by Carroll Gibbons and the Savoy Hotel Orphans and "Turn On the Old Music Box," with a lead vocal by Sam Brown, was recorded by George Scott Wood and the Six Swingers. Other songs such as "Hi-Diddle-Dee-Dee, An Actor's Life for Me" were less well known, but the entire *Pinocchio* score was honored with another Oscar that same year. The voice of Pinocchio was provided by child actor Dickie Jones, and Frankie Darro was the gravel voice of Lampwick.

Pinocchio was completed by the studio in 1939 and premiered on February 7, 1940. On Christmas Day 1939, the Disney version of the story of Pinocchio had a radio preview on the Lux Radio Theater, where it was introduced by Cecil B. de Mille. This enticed children to go to see the film after hearing it on-the-air on Christmas. Since *Pinocchio* was such an on-the-heels followup to *Snow White*, it is often thought of as a 1930s film. It was, of course, made in the 1930s, and retains much of the quaint style of that decade, as well as the detail and artfulness we associate with early Walt Disney.

Pinocchio: The Product

Kay Kamen summed up the Walt Disney film version in the Pinocchio campaign for bakers:

And now Walt Disney has created Pinocchio and you have the opportunity to use it as an advertising medium. So much has been written concerning Walt Disney and his masterpieces that we feel it quite unnecessary to say anything more

here, but all our experience in the developing of successful Campaigns for Bakers has been embodied in this Pinocchio *campaign.*

Baking concerns across the country lined up for the Pinocchio wax-paper wrappers, end stickers and the sixty different picture-card inserts to promote their bread products just as they had for Snow White. Salesmen were instructed to wear *Pinocchio* sales promotion buttons at all times on their routes; and this bread campaign produced a variety of truck and store cardboard display signs, window stickers, streamers, and pennants. National Dairy Products offered giveaway prizes,

including Pinocchio hand puppets, note tablets, paper masks of *Pinocchio* characters, stamp sets, handkerchiefs, and other manufactured character items to children who sent in their *Pinocchio* Dixie Cup ice-cream lids.

Pinocchio and the assortment of characters from the film were licensed to a number of firms, including Calox Antiseptic Mouthwash from McKesson & Robbins, Inc., of New York and Bridgeport, Connecticut. For three empty bottles of this oral hygiene product, which sold for 59¢ and $1.50, you could get a set of six glass

TOP: NATIONAL DAIRY PRODUCTS OFFERED FREE PINOCCHIO MERCHANDISE PRIZES, INCLUDING BELTS, HATS, TOSS TOYS, PAPER MASKS, PENCIL TABLETS, RUBBER STAMPS SETS, HAND PUPPETS, AND HANDKERCHIEFS, TO CHILDREN WHO SAVED THEIR 1940 ICE-CREAM DIXIE-CUP LIDS. LEFT: PINOCCHIO MASK, MADE BY THE EINSON-FREEMAN CO., NEW YORK, A PROMOTIONAL GIVEAWAY FROM GILLETTE BLUE BLADES IN 1939.

tumblers featuring Pinocchio, Jiminy Cricket, Figaro the Cat, Geppetto, the Blue Fairy, and Monstro the Whale—all manufactured by the Libbey-Owens Glass Company. Lampwick, Stromboli, Honest John, Giddy, and Cleo were also available as drinking glasses at various times in association with a number of products. These glasses, decorated in single colors of either yellow, blue, red, or green, would have the character image on the front, while on the reverse would be a poem such as: "The Beautiful Blue Fairy / So Dainty and Coy / Turned Pinocchio the Puppet / Into a Real Boy" or "Geppetto Was Swallowed / by Monstro the Whale, / Who Could Wreck Any Boat / With a Lash of His Tail."

Other product tie-ins were from the Gillette Safety Razor Company, which gave away paper masks from the Einson-Freeman Company of Pinocchio, Geppetto, Figaro, Cleo, a Donkey, and Jiminy Cricket; Jiminy Cricket Bubble Gum; Pinocchio Stick Chewing Gum in a pack, Pinocchio Lollipops and other "gay-wrapped" character candies from the Overland Candy Corporation and Sunlight Butter Company, which offered Pinocchio hats as a premium. Diamond Crystal shaker salt featuring Pinocchio and General Foods' Post Toasties boxes with Pinocchio cutouts on the box sides and back appeared on the kitchen table. Giveaway posters and stamps distributed through Grocers' Alliance were come-ons to promote the film and the products. There was a Pinocchio Ice-Cream-in-a-Cup from National Dairies, a Monstro Soda Pop, and Pinocchio Milkshakes. Disney's *Pinocchio* was used to help sell Dupont house paints, Cocomalt products, Royal Gelatin, Wheaties breakfast cereal (with cut-out masks on the back of the cereal box), and a host of other products.

A good deal of the *Pinocchio* licensed merchandise is marked with a copyright date of 1939, 1940 or 1941. In 1939, W.D.E., or Walt Disney Enterprises, was replaced by W.D.P., or Walt Disney Productions, as the copyright symbol for licensees. The George Borgfeldt Company imported Japanese bisque pieces of Pinocchio, Geppetto, Figaro, Gideon, and Honest John in a number of sizes. These were among the last Made-in-Japan bisques, which were discontinued after the attack on Pearl Harbor and for the duration of World War II. Borgfeldt & Co. also made a toy composition "Walker" Pinocchio toy and a Pinocchio wooden puppet. Louis Marx & Co. of New York produced handsome (in-the-box) litho-on-tin windup toys of a "waddle-shake-walker" Pinocchio and a Pinocchio the acrobat. Louis Marx "roll-over" Figaros, patterned after that company's successful "roll-over" Scottie Dogs and Pluto the Pup "roll-over" toys, were made in 1941. Transogram Company made Pinocchio litho-on-metal paintbox sets.

A Pinocchio painted chalk carnival statue was a game-of-chance prize at Coney Island Amusement Park in New York or at Olympic Park in Irvington, New Jersey, during the years of World War II, as were the Borgfeldt bisque figurines and small molded wood fiber (Syroco) figurines of all the characters. These pressed wood fiber pieces and the chalk statues were sent to stores and carnival supply houses from Multi-Product Company of Chicago. Painted metal figurines from Lincoln Logs, Halsam Company, Chicago, and John Wright, Inc., of Wrightsville, Pennsylvania, were dated as early as 1938. Schoolchildren all wanted the pencil boxes featuring Pinocchio and Jiminy Cricket, as well as the brightly colored Catalin pencil sharpeners and thermometers with decals of the Blue Fairy, Cleo, Figaro, and others made by

Liberty

MAR. 2, 1940

5¢

COPYRIGHT 1939
WALT DISNEY PRODUCTIONS

THE MYSTERY OF UNITY FREEMAN-MITFORD —PATRIOT OR WHAT?

I SAW HELL IN GERMANY AND RUSSIA
THE TRUE WAR STORY OF THE YEAR
BY KENNETH COLLINGS

LEFT: PINOCCHIO, JIMINY CRICKET, CLEO THE GOLDFISH, AND FIGARO THE CAT ON THE COVER OF *LIBERTY* MAGAZINE, VOL. 17, NO. 9, MARCH 2, 1940. MACFADDEN PUBLICATIONS, NEW YORK. **OPPOSITE:** YELLOW CATALIN PENCIL SHARPENER, WITH A DECAL OF CLEO THE GOLDFISH FROM *PINOCCHIO*, PLASTIC NOVELTIES OF NEW YORK SOLD THIS SCHOOL NOVELTY ITEM FOR 10¢ IN THE EARLY 1940S.

Plastic Novelties, Inc., of New York. Girls and boys sent Paper Novelty Manufacturing Company's special animated "Pinocchio or one of his pals" Valentine cards back and forth to one another from 1938 to 1942. The kids could wash with Pinocchio figural soap, which came attractively boxed from the Lightfoot Schultz Company. At bedtime they could read a Better Little Book (1940) from Whitman called *Pinocchio and Jiminy Cricket.* Whitman published various paint books, picture books, coloring books, scrapbooks, and cut-out books. A top collector book is *Pinocchio* published by Grosset & Dunlap and copyrighted W.D. Ent., 1939.

Pinocchio dolls had a great impact on the toy market. Since the character itself was a wooden puppet, all kinds of dolls, marionettes, wood-jointed figurines, and the like were produced. The largest Pinocchio doll, at twenty inches, is from the Ideal Novelty and Toy Company of New York and is made of composition with flexible wood joints. This doll was also available in twelve- and ten-inch sizes.

In 1940, the Knickerbocker Toy Company released Pinocchio composition dolls with wood-jointed "flexy" legs and arms, as well as a Jiminy Cricket and a Figaro, both composition and jointed. A stuffed Donkey doll, a Cleo doll, and a Figaro doll were added to the line. Richard G. Krueger made both wood-jointed and cloth-faced stuffed Pinocchio dolls; and Crown Toy Manufacturing Company of Brooklyn made three composition doll versions of Pinocchio, a hand puppet, and a composition bank with a lock and key. The Seiberling Latex Rubber Products Company made hard rubber figurine dolls of Pinocchio, Jiminy Cricket, Cleo, Figaro, and the Donkey.

The Relaxon Products Company of Chicago produced a line of washable furniture for nursery tots in red, green, and brown leatherette featuring Pinocchio. William Rogers of Meriden, Connecticut, made children's knives, spoons, and forks featuring Jiminy Cricket, the Donkey, and Pinocchio. The Ohio Art Company of Bryan, Ohio, made a play tea set of litho-on-metal featuring a metal serving tray, a teapot, and cups and saucers. The Flexo Corporation of Chicago produced Pinocchio and Jiminy Cricket lamps of thermo-plastic and woodfiber, meant to resemble the hand-carved wood featured in Geppetto's magical toy and clock shop; the parchment shades are decorated with scenes from the movie.

The N. N. Hill Brass Company of East Hampton, Connecticut, and Fisher-Price Toys of East Aurora, New York, made Pinocchio and Jiminy Cricket pull-toys for nursery tots. These pull-toys and the

ABOVE LEFT: PINOCCHIO SOAP FIGURINE WITH THE ORIGINAL BOX, FROM THE LIGHTFOOT SCHULTZ CO., NEW YORK, 1940. BELOW: PORCELAIN PINOCCHIO FIGURINE MADE IN GERMANY BY GOEBEL, C. 1950.

other Pinocchio toys are now regarded as prized pieces. Parker brothers put out a Pinocchio Game set with an attractively designed board, and The Ring-Toss Game—"Toss a ring on Pinocchio's Nose"—from De-Ward Novelty Company, Inc., of Angola, New York, is a game with excellent graphics.

For at-home use there was also the brightly colored plastic Beetleware sets of dishware from Bryant Electric Company of Bridgeport, Connecticut, with two-color imprints of Pinocchio. Pottery companies that produced *Pinocchio* character glass and ceramic knickknack figurines and planters for the home include the National Porcelain Company of Trenton, New Jersey, the Laguna-Brayton Pottery Company, The American Pottery Company, the Evan K. Shaw Company, and even a small firm called Geppetto Pottery. The Goebel sets of Pinocchio and his pals are very desirable collectors' items, though produced in the 1950s. For a child's room or the den you could purchase beautiful framed litho-prints from Courvoisier Galleries or unframed prints that came in character-stamped envelopes. At Halloween the Fishbach Company and Ben Cooper produced boxed sets of masks and costumes of Pinocchio, the Blue Fairy, Jiminy Cricket, and all the other characters from the feature film.

Pinocchio jewelry, manufactured by the Brier Company of Providence, Rhode Island was sold at the dime store in 1940, and never for more than fifty cents. These included plastic pins and charm bracelets, which came on printed cards. More expensive tastes could be satisfied at Cartier, Inc., where Pinocchio pins and charms were made of better materials. At hometown "Pleasure Island" carnivals, at amusement parks, and at the World's Fairs of 1939–1940 in New York and San Francisco, you could win or buy a novelty felt Pinocchio hat with a colored feather stuck in it. Fancy millinery shops in 1939, 1940, and 1941 featured a better-quality hat inspired by *Pinocchio* to be worn by ladies on shopping expeditions downtown or to a ladies' afternoon tea. These "sports fuzzies" were manufactured by the Philbert Hat Company of New York, and came in 23 gay 1940s colors for women. Children's Pinocchio hats were manufactured by the Newark Felt Novelty Company of Newark, New Jersey, or by L. Lewis & Son, New York.

In 1948, separate character wristwatches of Pinocchio and Jiminy Cricket were sold by the Ingersoll-Waterbury Clock Company of Waterbury, Connecticut. The

ABOVE: JIMINY CRICKET HALLOWEEN MASK, MADE OF STIFF MOLDED CHEESECLOTH AND COLOR AIRBRUSHED BY A. S. FISHBACK, NEW YORK, 1940. TOP: KAY KAMEN LTD. PROMOTIONAL PINBACK BUTTON OF PINOCCHIO, GIVEN AWAY AT MOVIE THEATERS IN 1940 AND 1941.

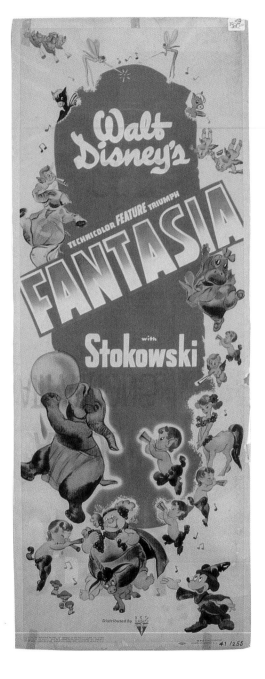

Bayard Company in France manufactured a "nostalgia" windup Pinocchio alarm clock in the 1960s to go along with their Mickey Mouse, Donald Duck, and Snow White clocks.

Walt Disney's Pinocchio character continues to be a favorite in the 1990s, and collectors of Disneyana can't seem to get enough of this puppet who became a real boy nor, for that matter, of the other unique characters from this film.

FANTASIA (November 1940)

*F*antasia is Disney's great experiment in animation. The film initially grew out of a desire on Walt Disney's part to find a suitable vehicle for Mickey Mouse whose popularity by 1940 seemed to be taken over by the feisty Donald Duck. Originally, the plan had been to create a Mickey short based on Goethe's ballad "Der Zauberlehrling," or "The Apprentice Magician." Walt Disney then asked Leopold Stokowski to conduct the Philadelphia Symphony Orchestra in a symphonic musical score for what was to be a fanciful Mickey Mouse cartoon. Never one to miss an opportunity, Disney decided to break new artistic ground, by expanding the concert to an entire "Concert Feature," even though many at the studio were uncertain about the use of cartoonlike characters against rich scenic backgrounds cavorting to symphonic music.

The creative layout established for the series of animated scenes that were to be juxtaposed against the music of Bach's Toccata and Fugue in D Minor, Tchaikovsky's *Nutcracker* Suite, Paul Dukas's *The Sorcerer's Apprentice*, Igor Stravinsky's *The Rite of Spring*, Beethoven's Sixth Symphony, the *Pastoral*, the "Dance of the Hours" from Ponchielli's opera *La Giaconda*, Moussorgsky's *Night on Bald Mountain* and ending with Schubert's "Ave Maria," gave the Disney animators free reign to fully utilize their imaginations. To bring the music and the animation together on the screen, Disney decided to hire the famous narrator Deems Taylor, who was then the music commentator for the radio broadcasts from the Metropolitan Opera.

The production staff and the animators found great enjoyment in the creative process of *Fantasia*. Leopold Stokowski used every available new technological and sonic development in orchestral performance, stereophonic sound, FM radio, and electrical recording. Stokowski's own legend was actually enhanced by his appearance with Mickey Mouse, but when

WALT DISNEY'S *FANTASIA* BY
DEEMS TAYLOR IS A SUMPTUOUS
ART BOOK PUBLISHED IN 1940 BY
SIMON & SCHUSTER, NEW YORK. IT
HAS AN EXCEPTIONALLY FINE ILLUS-
TRATED DUSTJACKET COVER, BLACK-
AND-WHITE STORY SKETCHES AND
TIPPED-IN COLOR PRINTS FROM THE
ANIMATED FEATURE FILM.

ular on the Mickey Mouse "Sorcerer's Apprentice" segment, but the audiences found it "too high brow." The public seemed to feel that Disney was taking too many liberties with classical music by overlaying his own visual interpretations onto it. Commenting on *Fantasia* after its completion, Walt Disney stated, "Perhaps Bach and Beethoven are strange bedfellows for Mickey Mouse, but it's certainly all been a lot of fun!"

Like a bottle of vintage wine, the film garnered more success at the box-office as time went by. *Fantasia* had rereleases in 1944, 1946, 1956, 1963, 1969, 1977, 1982, 1985, and 1990. In the late 1960s, *Fantasia* developed a cult film following with the counterculture who liked to get high on LSD, marijuana, and speed in order to better appreciate and experience the intense visual images. In 1969 a psychedelic poster was issued by the studio, which was happy to capitalize on the viewpoints of the sixties generation. By then stereophonic sound was added to theaters to intensify the experience. Many today think of the film as a work of art unto itself.

The cornucopia of cartoon characters bursting out of *Fantasia* include the Sorcerer Mickey and his "walking brooms"; the Wizard himself; a frightening Tyrannosauras Rex and other dinosaurs; Russian Cossack thistles; sensual fish reminiscent of the coquettish Cleo from *Pinocchio*; Frost Fairies and Fairy Flowers; dancing Chinese mushrooms with faces and a memorable scene-stealing baby mushroom named Hop Low; Diana, Goddess of the Moon; centaurs, centaurettes, unicorns, cupids, and fauns; a Pegasus family; Morpheus, God of Sleep, Zeus, Bacchus, the God of Wine, and Vulcan; hippos and seductive alligators in red capes and feather caps; tutu-clad elephants and dancing ostriches. The many *Fantasia* characters did not inspire a great number of objects in the merchandise market, but the ones that were produced are eagerly sought after by collectors of Disneyana.

In the field of rare antiquarian books there is *Walt Disney's Fantasia* by Deems Taylor, a large-size fine-art book published

a music colleague said, "I'll bet you don't know why I admire you so much. It's because you're the only man I know who shook hands with Mickey Mouse!" Stokowski shook his index finger as if it were a conductor's baton and replied, "No! No! No! No! *He* shook hands with *me*."

Fantasia, in Fantasound and Technicolor, opened on November 13, 1940, just nine months after *Pinocchio*. But it was not to be a box-office success. Newspaper critics lavished praise on the film, in partic-

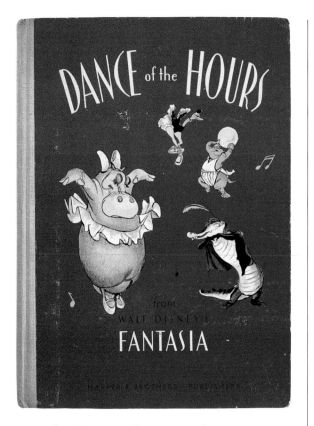

by Simon & Schuster in 1940. Measuring 13 x 9¾ inches in hardback, the book, which originally sold for $3.75, features on the colorful dustjacket a great many of the above characters from the movie, including Mickey Mouse in his wizard's hat and red robe. This book has tipped-in color reproductions from the film and includes a foreword by Leopold Stokowski.

There is an array of coloring and cut-out books and children's storybooks, such as *Dance of the Hours* and *Pastoral* published by Harper and Brothers in New York and London; *The Sorcerer's Apprentice* from Grosset & Dunlap; and

Ave Maria (an interpretation from Walt Disney's *Fantasia* with lyrics by Rachel Field) published by Random House. These hardcover books were all published in 1940. Random House also published *Walt Disney's Fantasia*, a large-format, hardcover children's book. *Fantasia* books are collected with fervor, as are original *Fantasia* movie programs, first-run and subsequent rerelease movie posters and lobby cards. The 1969 psychedelic poster is now sought after by those who collect sixties rock and roll and hippie style posters as well as by enthusiastic Disneyana collectors.

Vernon Potteries, Ltd., of Los Angeles produced some fine ceramic figurines. The company often referred to by collectors as simply Vernon Kilns, was given license to produce their Disney ceramic pieces from October 10, 1940, until July 22, 1942, when they gave over all their rights, molds, and patterns as well as their entire inventory to the American Pottery Company. Vernon Kilns produced 36 different figurines, five bowls, and an

ABOVE: VERNON KILNS CERAMIC FIGURINE OF A "BABY PEGASUS," FEATURED IN *FANTASIA*. LOS ANGELES' VERNON POTTERIES, WHICH MADE 36 DIFFERENT CERAMIC CHARACTER FIGURINES FROM *FANTASIA* FROM 1940 TO 1942, USED MOLDS MADE FROM THE ORIGINAL DISNEY STUDIO ANIMATION MODELS. TOP LEFT: THE BALLET MUSIC FROM THE OPERA *LA GIOCONDA* (THE SMILING ONE) BY AMILCARE PONCHIELLI, WAS USED FOR THE "DANCE OF THE HOURS" SEGMENT IN *FANTASIA*. ILLUSTRATED CHILDREN'S STORYBOOK, HARPER AND BROTHERS, 1940.

assortment of vases using characters from *Fantasia*. These wonderful items are of extremely high quality and are reminiscent of some of the production models that were used in the making of the film itself. Studio production models are scarce and are regarded as art objects by Disneyophiles, when they can be found. Vases, bowls, and figurines are often marked "Disney Copyright 1940—Vernon Kilns." Some of the glazed figurines are studies of the various sprites, centaurs, unicorns, and Pegasus characters including a particularly charming black and white "Baby Pegasus"; dancing elephants, ostriches, and hippos; alluring Nubian centaurettes; and a Hop Low Mushroom salt and pepper shaker set. Among the collectible ceramic bowls are a Hop Low Mushroom bowl, a goldfish bowl, a winged nymph bowl, a satyr bowl, and a sprite bowl. Stunning Art Deco–style vases were produced, one featuring Diana, goddess of the Moon, and the other a muscular Pegasus. Vases and bowls usually came in soft colors like pale blue, baby pink or cream, with hand-painted versions commanding higher prices.

Disney artwork that includes cels and drawings from *Fantasia* are rare, and galleries, collectors, and dealers regard them as among the best in Disney animation art. Characters from *Fantasia* such as the alligators, centaurs, and sprites turn up on World War II Army, Air Corp, Marine, and Navy insignia with great frequency; and certainly these fantasy characters did their part in the war effort to inspire victory.

THE RELUCTANT DRAGON (June 1941)

The *Reluctant Dragon*, filmed in black and white and color, opened on June 20, 1941. It is the inside story of how animated cartoons were produced at Walt Disney Studios. Meant to be both educational and entertaining, the film is narrated by that sophisticated wit Robert Benchley. The two chief characters to come out of this film were the Reluctant Dragon, who was to be the inspiration for the later *Pete's Dragon* and a baby boy in diapers with a high I.Q. named Baby Weems.

The Reluctant Dragon was a four-color Walt Disney Dell Comic Book in 1941, containing two pages of photos from the film. The Dell comic included a two-page foreword to *Fantasia* by Leopold Stokowski and featured Mickey Mouse as the Sorcerer's Apprentice, as well as Goofy, Donald Duck, and Baby Weems. Original children's storybooks of *The Reluctant Dragon* and *Baby Weems* were published by Doubleday. A Special United States Savings Bond issued during World War II featured all the major Disney characters; and right smack in the center is the happy little Baby Weems. The Reluctant Dragon himself was featured during the war years in military insignia.

WALT DISNEY'S
STORY OF
The Reluctant Dragon

INTRODUCED
BY ROBERT
BENCHLEY

FROM KENNETH GRAHAME'S DREAM DAYS

LEFT: WALT DISNEY'S *STORY OF THE RELUCTANT DRAGON*, INTRODUCED BY ROBERT BENCHLEY (WHO IS ALSO IN THE MOVIE), IS ILLUSTRATED BY THE DISNEY STUDIOS WITH WORDS FROM THE CLASSIC CHILDREN'S FABLE *DREAM DAYS*, BY KENNETH GRAHAME (PRINTED IN ITALICS), AND DIALOGUE FROM THE DISNEY MOVIE SCRIPT OF *THE RELUCTANT DRAGON*, GARDEN CITY, NEW YORK, 1941. RIGHT: *BABY WEEMS* HARDCOVER BOOK BY JOE GRANT AND DICK HUEMER, WITH AN INTRODUCTION BY ROBERT BENCHLEY. FROM *THE RELUCTANT DRAGON* (1941), DOUBLEDAY, DORAN, NEW YORK.

Baby Weems
by JOE GRANT
and DICK HUEMER

Introduction by
ROBERT BENCHLEY

DUMBO
(October 1941)

Disney's staff of animators was delighted to get back to work on what they regarded as a more normal feature-length film after *Fantasia*. *Dumbo*, the story of a baby elephant whose ears would not stop growing is thought of today as one of the best of the Disney animated feature films. Bearing some resemblance to Elmer Elephant, the Silly Symphony character of the 1930s, Dumbo, with his oversized ears that eventually enabled him to fly, captivated audiences of the early 1940s.

Both *Fantasia* and *Pinocchio* were considered financially unsuccessful in their

initial release, so it was decided that *Dumbo* would be made to have popular box-office appeal. The production format was kept simple, and expensive effects like multiplane shots were held to a minimum. The cost of the production for *Dumbo* was kept down to $800,000. Critics and audiences alike were moved by the story of *Dumbo* which included a good deal of the slapdash humor used in the animated shorts. With a running time of only 64 minutes this animated feature focused in on sentiment, charm, and humor. *Dumbo* fit easily into the spirit of a time when war was lurking just around every corner and audiences needed to see a movie that could warm their hearts and give them a chuckle. *Dumbo* filled the bill.

Dumbo premiered on October 23, 1941, and was still playing in theaters around the country when America entered World War II after the bombing of Pearl Harbor on December 7, 1941. The musical score includes "Pink Elephants on Parade," "Baby Mine," "Look Out for Mrs. Stork," and "When I See an Elephant Fly." The "Pink Elephants" sequence, in which

ABOVE: DUMBO THE "FLYING ELEPHANT" IN GLAZED MIDNIGHT-BLUE CERAMIC, FROM BRAYTON'S LAGUNA POTTERY, LAGUNA BEACH, CALIF., 1940. BOTTOM LEFT: WALT DISNEY'S *DUMBO* "ONLY HIS EARS GREW!" BETTER LITTLE BOOK WITH "SEE 'EM MOVE FLIP PICTURES," FROM THE WHITMAN PUBLISHING COMPANY, RACINE, WIS., 1941.

Dumbo and Timothy Mouse get plastered drunk and imagine they see hundreds of pink elephants, is regarded as one of the best in the history of Disney animation. After this drunken state, Dumbo, nursing a hangover, encounters four hipster black crows, which were brought to life by Disney animator Ward Kimball. They encourage him to utilize his big-size ears to fly. As a flying elephant Dumbo achieves stardom at the circus.

Dumbo character merchandise became a popular commodity in the marketplace. These included ceramic planters, salt and pepper shakers, and cookie jars of Dumbo from the Leeds China Company of Chicago. Multi-Products of Chicago produced painted plaster and chalk figures of Dumbo to serve as amusement park prizes. Evan K. Shaw Company, the successor to the American Pottery Company, featured Dumbo and his pal Timothy Mouse in their line of Disney figurines, including in their catalog a Mr. Stork and a Black Crow. Vernon Kilns produced Timothy Mouse, the Black Crow, a falling Dumbo, a Dumbo standing, and a Mr. Stork. Knickerbocker produced big-eared Dumbo dolls in the early forties; and Gund produced one in 1949. Walt Disney's *Dumbo* as a "see 'em move" flip page Better Little Book published by Whitman was a popular schoolchildren's treasure in the 1940s. *Dumbo* is also the subject of a great many children's storybooks, such as those from D. C. Heath and Company of Boston and the Little Golden Book series. Dumbo was the star of comic books and an RCA Victor "Little Nipper" Series 78 rpm record album. There are as well colorful Dumbo songbooks and Dumbo sheet music.

The outbreak of war had an instantaneous effect on promotions and products related to *Dumbo*. There would be no more Kay Kamen merchandise catalogs until 1947. Though the production of merchandise continued, there is not the avalanche of merchandise that was produced around *Snow White* and *Pinocchio*. However, promotional campaigns developed by Kamen for the film featured giveaway "Flying Dumbo" pinback buttons, inflatable balloons, and other items; but Dumbo, along with other members of the Disney cartoon gang, was only too happy to get into the fight as Flying Squadron Insignia to help win the war.

BAMBI
(August 1942)

Bambi the fawn has become one of Disney's most appealing and beloved characters; the animated feature based on creatures of the forest is the most touching and lively of the animated feature films. The film is visually rich with a collection of charming forest animal characters that include Bambi, Bambi's Mother, Aunt Ena, Faline, Ronno, Friend Owl, Thumper, the rabbit, Flower, the skunk, and others. The wide-eyed little deer, along with his playmates Thumper and Flower, are the most endearing characters to emerge from the film.

Bambi premiered on August 9, 1942, in London and on August 13 at the Radio City Music Hall, where it attracted record crowds of mothers with their children looking for escape from the pressures of war on the homefront. The smooth, naturalistic style of *Bambi* always evokes a great deal of empathy in audiences, particularly in the terrible scene wherein Bambi's graceful mother is shot after grazing in the meadow by "Man—The Enemy." A tearful, wobbling, frightened Bambi is then forced to confront the real

ABOVE: *BAMBI*, THE AUTHORIZED EDITION BETTER LITTLE BOOK BASED ON *BAMBI: A LIFE IN THE WOODS* BY FELIX SALTEN AND TRANSLATED BY WHITAKER CHAMBERS. THIS BETTER LITTLE "FLIP" BOOK HAS SMALL ILLUSTRATIONS AT THE TOP RIGHTHAND CORNER OF EACH OF THE 424 PAGES SHOWING BAMBI TAKING A PRATFALL IN MOVEMENT. THUMPER AND FLOWER ARE ON THE BOOK'S SPINE. WHITMAN, 1941–42. BELOW LEFT: D-X DUMBO PINBACK BUTTON GIVEAWAY FROM "KAY KAMEN LTD., REPRESENTING WALT DISNEY PRODUCTIONS."

hostilities of the forest alone. Man, the enemy, is also responsible for a forest fire that causes fear, panic, and death among the terrified creatures who run amok in order to escape the flames.

Christopher Finch addresses some contradictions in the film in *The Art of Walt Disney*. For instance, in a real forest would an owl be friendly with a rabbit who is its natural prey? And could we, as audiences, suspend our belief when unlikely creatures talk to one another? In truth, in a woodland fable of this kind anything can happen; and it is not too hard to imbue these creatures with human feelings.

Nevertheless, Finch does regard *Bambi* as an important movie in terms of story development and technique.

There is also wonderful, childlike fun to be had in *Bambi*, even for adults. Thumper and Bambi skidding, twirling, spinning, and falling on an icepond is certainly an enjoyable sequence. The forest

Bambi inhabits is one of those magical, enchanting places where love can truly bloom in springtime. Walt

Disney's legendary love for animals shines through, and in a world at war in the early forties, this must have given audiences some sense of hope. Films of the era like *My Friend Flicka* and *Lassie Come Home* focused in on the love and sentiment with which children regard animals; and a Scottish terrier named Fala who lived in the White House with F.D.R. was beloved by the whole country.

Popular as decoratives in homes of the forties were the fine glazed ceramic figurines of Thumper and Flower from the American Pottery Company of Los Angeles which included in its line at least five Bambis as well as Friend Owl, Bambi's girlfriend Faline, Flower's girlfriend, and Thumper's girlfriend. Bambi dinnerware was made by this same company in 1949. Bambi ceramic planters were always to be found in the kitchen as well as Bambi salt and pepper shakers, all produced by the Leeds China Company of Chicago, which also produced a Thumper cookie jar and salt and pepper sets featuring the popular rabbit. In 1946, Evan K. Shaw Company produced wonderful figurines of Bambi, Thumper, Flower, and other characters from the film. Sometimes these Disney knickknacks are found with an embossed Evan K. Shaw metallic-paper sticker still attached, which is a plus for collectors.

Pinocchio, Snow White, Mickey Mouse, Pluto, and Donald Duck watches had all been produced by the Ingersoll-Waterbury Clock Company and in 1948 they added to their Disney watch line a beautiful Bambi children's wristwatch. Movie posters and movie lobby cards from the original release are good investments today; and certainly the cels or any of the original artwork command higher and higher competitive prices in the art-auction market.

Disney's *Bambi*, from an original story by Felix Salten, was published by Grosset & Dunlap in 1942; this company also published a *Thumper* storybook. Disney's *Bambi* was retold by Idella Purnell in a child's reader published by Heath in 1944 with all-in-color Disney illustrations. Whitman published *The Bambi Story Book, The Bambi Picture Book* and two Better Little Books, *Bambi, The Prince of the Forest* (1942) and *Bambi's Children* (1943), as well as cut-out books, scrapbooks, puzzles, and games. Simon & Schuster published *Bambi* as a Little Golden Book, a Giant Golden Book, a Fuzzy Golden Book, and a Tiny Golden Book.

The "On the Avenue" column in the *New Yorker* magazine of December 7, 1987, reported that the Disney Company claims that one out of every five children's books is based on Disney animated characters.

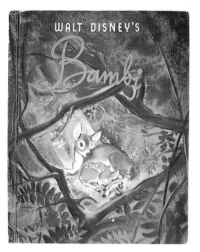

This certainly explains the proliferation of books on *Snow White*, *Pinocchio*, *Dumbo*, and *Bambi* on the marketplace from the 1940s through today. Little Golden Books, for instance, which originated in the forties, are still published in volume. A *Bambi* comic book was published by Kay Kamen with Whitman Publishing Company in 1941 and 1942 as a giveaway for Horlick's Malted Milk and various toy stores across the country who mailed it out with their store stickers on the cover; and this is now a top comic to collect.

Novel merchandise featuring *Bambi* tie-ins include Einson-Freeman Company Bambi and Thumper premium masks from Wheaties; and Donald Duck Rice boxes that feature Bambi and Faline cutouts on the back of the packages. If collectors can

ABOVE LEFT: WALT DISNEY'S *BAMBI*, PUBLISHED IN 1941 BY SIMON & SCHUSTER, NEW YORK, HAS A TEXT ADAPTED FROM FELIX SALTEN WITH DETACHABLE "ART" ILLUSTRATIONS IN COLOR, SUITABLE FOR FRAMING. ABOVE RIGHT: WALT DISNEY'S *THUMPER*, ILLUSTRATED CHILDREN'S BOOK PUBLISHED BY GROSSET & DUNLAP, 1942. BOTTOM RIGHT: GLAZED CERAMIC FIGURES (LEFT TO RIGHT): THUMPER'S GIRLFRIEND, FLOWER THE SKUNK, AND THUMPER. EVAN K. SHAW CO., 1946.

find the whole box intact, so much the better. There was a Sun Rubber Company Thumper squeeze toy and Catalin Bambi pencil sharpeners with character decal appliqués. Framed color prints of *Bambi* from Courvoisier Galleries joined *Snow White* and *Pinocchio* sets that in the war years were already on the walls of the playroom or den.

On the family knickknack shelf you might find fine porcelain Hummel figurines of the characters from Disney's animated features produced by the German Goebel Company, particularly the figurines from *Bambi*, which comprised the majority of the "first series" of 220 pieces pro-

duced in the 1950s and distributed through a Goebel subsidiary, Goebel Art GmbH, West Germany, based in Pennington, New Jersey. Though they were produced through 1967 and are not the so-called golden period, these overglazed pieces are desirable to collect, but for some reason they are difficult to find in the Disneyana marketplace. The ones produced for export to America featured a "Bee" trademark in the shape of a V, with the word "Germany" on the bottom: many Hummels produced for the European marketplace and not featuring the "Bee" trademark were sold as souvenirs to Americans who returned with them in their luggage after visits to the Old Country. This has resulted in some collector confusion, but today all Goebel pieces are seen as choice items. Their scarcity in the current collectors' market also helps to establish these as sought-after items. This is exactly the type of collectible that is often passed on in families from generation to generation and almost never turns up in flea markets or garage sales.

NINETEEN

A DISNEY VICTORY PARADE

During the World War II years, the Walt Disney Studios in Burbank, California, virtually became an extension of the War Department. Mickey Mouse, Donald Duck, Pluto, and the other well-known Disney cartoon characters came to be seen as important icons that symbolized America, and it was deemed that they should be used for propaganda purposes by the military and also on the American homefront. The idea of an angry, writhing duck throwing a ripe tomato at a caricature of Adolf Hitler or the specter of other Disney characters gritting their teeth while riding atop a bomb intended for the enemy somehow helped to inspire servicemen to go happily and bravely to war.

In the January 1943 issue of *Theater Arts* magazine, Thornton Delehanty wrote in a feature article on Walt Disney: "The Government in Washington looks to Disney more than any other studio chief as a factor in building public morale, providing training and instruction to the soldiers and sailors, and utilizing animated graphic art expediting the intelligent mobilization of fighting men and civilians in the cause of the United Nations."

LEFT: "AIRCRAFT WORKER: BUILDING PLANES FOR VICTORY" HOMEFRONT DISNEY POSTER AND WINDOW STICKER, FOR WORLD WAR II FACTORIES. **OPPOSITE:** DONALD DUCK INSIGNIA PATCH FOR 47-3 (AW) BATTALION BATTERY "A," NEW YORK, N.Y.

The U.S. Navy became Disney's biggest customer, and it preempted an entire wing of the studio for the production of a series of films aimed specifically at the instruction of Naval flyers. The Navy requested twenty short subjects using regular photography in conjunction with models, live action, and animated drawing. The Disney training films were geared for pilots, observers, and for those who operated marine craft. Some of them were highly confidential and were restricted by the War Department for military reasons. The Navy maintained a staff at the studio to advise animators, filmmakers, and actors on technical aspects that were important

UNITED STATES TREASURY

WAR FINANCE COMMITTEE

Know All Men By These Presents:

This is to certify that_____
is the owner of a War Bond, thereby becoming an investor in this country's fight for human liberty and a contributor in a world struggle to make life free and forever peaceful for all men.

This Bond presented by:_____

ATTESTED THIS _____ DAY OF _____ 194__

© WALT DISNEY

☆ U.S GOVERNMENT PRINTING OFFICE : 1944—O-620542

parts of training and instruction films.

The Disney Studio devoted over 90 percent of its production during the war years to the output of films made especially for the Navy, the Army, and for government agencies such as the Treasury Department, the Department of Agriculture, and the Office of the Coordinator of Inter-American affairs. At the request of the Department of Agriculture Disney made a one-reeler called *Food Will Win The War* for the purpose of instructing those on the homefront how to grow, preserve, and conserve food. The Office of War Information's bureau of Motion Pictures produced one of the most popular films made by Disney for the government, *The New Spirit*, starring Donald Duck. In 1944, the Treasury Department, under Secretary Morgenthau's order, had the government printing office issue a special all-in-color cartoon-character "War Bond" certificate designed for schoolchildren. The characters seen on this certificate included Practical Pig, Baby Weems, the Seven Dwarfs, Bambi, Pinocchio, Figaro the Cat, José Carioca, Bambi, Donald Duck and his nephews Huey, Dewey, and Louie, Goofy, Pluto, and, of course, Mickey Mouse. Walt Disney himself estimated after the war that his studio had used approximately 300,000 feet of film in the war effort production program.

After the Japanese attack on Pearl Harbor, the intrepid pilots of the A.V.G. (American Volunteer Group, called Flying Tigers) were flying over the Burma Route to China, their planes decorated with Disney insignia. One insignia depicted a venomous mosquito riding atop a Mosquito Fleet PT boat torpedo. The demand for Disney insignia was so intense from America's fighting units that there were long waiting lists which kept the special crew of five Disney artists

busy around the clock filling the demand. Patriotic Disney insignia were created at no charge; and they were used by the R.A.F., the Fighting French, the Flying Tigers, the Women's Ambulance and Defense Corps of America, the U.S. Naval Reserve, as well as all branches of the service including military weather bureaus and the Military Police (MPs).

Donald Duck was used more frequently than Mickey Mouse on insignia as the "Duck" could convey more wrath toward a hostile enemy than could the pink-faced, beatific mouse. Goofy, Horace Horsecollar, Clarabelle Cow, Pluto, the Three Little Pigs, the Big Bad Wolf, José Carioca, Pinocchio, Jiminy Cricket, Snow White and all Seven Dwarfs, together or separately, Peg Leg Pete, Ferdinand the Bull, Dumbo, the Reluctant Dragon, Baby Weems, Bambi, Thumper, Flower, and the many characters from *Fantasia* that included dancing hippos, Chinese mushrooms, alligators, centaurs, centaurettes, dinosaurs, pterodactyls, cupids, unicorns, and ostriches all appeared as insignia patches, as nose-art on planes, in advertisements and posters and on matchbooks. All of these war-

time insignia from the Studio including patches, posters, matchbooks, and instruction booklets have entered the realm of Disneyana ephemera, which is collected by Disneyophiles as well as by collectors of military memorabilia who are legion. In this area, Disneyana and Americana have been interchangeable.

The most popular of all war cartoons, and the one that won an Academy Award in 1943, was *Der Fuehrer's Face*, originally

planned to be called *Donald Duck in Nutziland*. Inspired by the smash hit song with humorous words and music by Oliver Wallace that was recorded by Spike Jones and His City Slickers, the cartoon has Donald Duck striking at the very heart of fascism with ridicule. Donald enters into a nightmare world in Nutziland watching a goose-step ballet. Hitler is the main scapegoat for the Duck's rageful temper. He also hates the overregimentalization and the

"lousy" German food. Eventually, waking up from this "Nutzi" nightmare, Donald clutches a miniature of the Statue of Liberty, and is relieved to find himself "among the free."

In October 1942 WNEW radio's popular disc jockey Martin Block offered listeners to his "Make-Believe Ballroom" show a free recording of "Der Fuehrer's Face" for every War Bond purchased at fifty dollars or more. In one night Block sold $30,000 worth of bonds in this way.

Donald Duck appeared as a character in other war-related cartoons, including *Fall Out—Fall In*, *Sky Trooper*, *The Old Army Game*, and *Home Defense*. Though Donald Duck's stardom during the war ascended over Mickey Mouse's in most quarters, Mickey was to have the last word: During the D-Day landing in France one of the codewords was "M-I-C-K-E-Y M-O-U-S-E," which was a tribute to Disney's work for the war effort.

After the war was won, children in Great Britain put away their Mickey Mouse gas masks; in the latter part of the forties they were occasionally donned for school air-raid drills. During the "fall-out shelter" period in the nuclear 1950s, the ominous masks were discarded and are now rare collectibles, both for Disneyophiles and for military collectors.

South of the Border: Caballeros y Amígos

Nelson Rockefeller, the coordinator of Inter-American Affairs in 1941, asked Walt Disney to go to Brazil, Argentina, Chile, and Peru to make movies that would encourage a better "good neighbor" policy. Rockefeller also wanted Disney to help check the rise of the Nazi propaganda machine that was moving into these Latin American countries. At this time in war-torn Europe there was little market for Hollywood films, with the exception of England, Switzerland and a few neutral countries. Hollywood had already begun to introduce films like *Down Argentine Way* (1940) with Betty Grable, Don Ameche, and Carmen Miranda and *That Night in Rio* (1941) with Alice Faye, Don Ameche, and Carmen Miranda, who was known as "The Brazilian Bombshell," to infiltrate and develop new markets south of the border. The State Department gave Disney a subsidy of $50,000 for each of four animated features to be built around the life and people of Central and South America. More money was raised through private backing to help produce these "good neighbor" films.

OPPOSITE: *THE THREE CABAL-LEROS*, RANDOM HOUSE, 1944, AND GLAZED CERAMIC FIGURINES OF DONALD DUCK AND JOSÉ CARIOCA MADE BY EVAN K. SHAW CO., 1946.

Disney, with his staff of animators, went to work on the first of these pictures, *Saludos Amigos*, which was completed and released in the U.S. in February 1943. The lively film consists of four animated sequences, the first featuring Donald Duck on an expedition in the high Andes to Lake Titicaca; the second depicts a small mail-plane named Pedro that must deliver mail through mountain storms and treacherous wind; the third, "Aquarela do Brasil" introduces José Carioca, the lively South American parrot who teaches Donald Duck to do the samba on Rio's Copacabana beach; the final sequence features Goofy as a vaquero cowpoke in "El Gaucho Goofy." *Saludos Amigos* was such a smash hit at movie theaters that Disney pushed full speed ahead with *The Three Caballeros*, which cost $2 million to produce. For this film, Disney Studio artists went on a special trip to Mexico, a country that had not been utilized in *Saludos Amigos*. The result of their research was a new south-of-the-border caballero character, a wild pistol packin' Mexican Charro rooster named Panchito who joined caballeros José Carioca of Brazil (attired in this film in a Mexican serape) and Donald Duck, the north-of-the-border quacker. It was the perfect trio. Donald

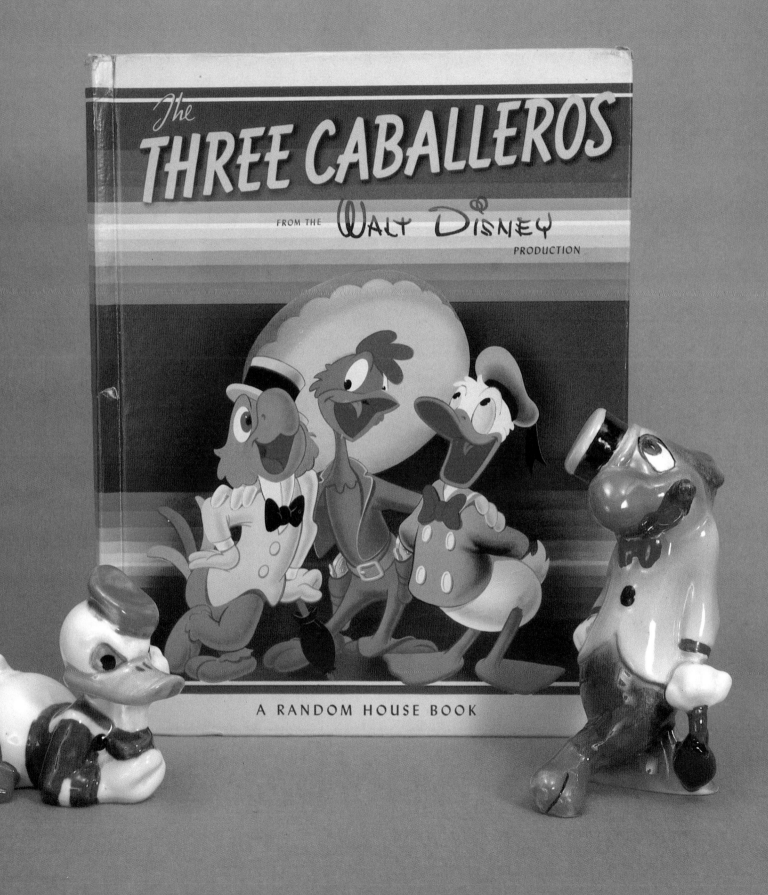

Duck, in colorful live-action animation sequences, dances with Aurora Miranda, the sister of Carmen Miranda, while his peppy pals and another famous Latin actress, Carmen Molina, add to the jubilant fun. The samba music of this dynamic film, along with the brilliant Technicolor, explodes like a panoramic piñata onto the movie screen.

Critic Leonard Maltin in his book *The Disney Films* points out that the animation with live-action sequences in this picture was years ahead of its time in terms of execution and vivid, visual conceptualization. Maltin finds it "right in step" with the present age. Bosley Crowther, the *New York*

Times film critic, called the feature-length live/animated movie "a brilliant hodgepodge of Walt Disney's illustrative art." Unfortunately, when this masterful forties Disney movie is shown in rerelease, it is often cut.

A world premier for *The Three Caballeros* was held in Mexico City on December 21, 1944, with a North American opening at movie theaters across the country on February 3, 1945. Two songs from the picture were popular hits, "Baia—Na Baixa Do Sapateiro" and "You Belong to My Heart—Solamente Una Vez." The title song, which refers to the three "birds of a feather" as "three gay caballeros"—"Ay! Jalisco No Te Rajes!"—was also popular during

ABOVE: PAINTED CERAMIC COOKIE JARS OF MICKEY MOUSE, DONALD DUCK, AND JOSÉ CARIOCA, MADE BY LEEDS CHINA COMPANY, CHICAGO, 1947. BELOW LEFT: DONALD DUCK INTRODUCES JOSÉ CARIOCA OF RIO FROM THE WALT DISNEY PICTURE *SALUDOS AMIGOS* (1943), IN THIS SHEET MUSIC FOR *BRAZIL* (AQUARELA DO BRASIL), FROM THE SOUTHERN MUSIC PUBLISHING COMPANY. COVER ILLUSTRATION COPYRIGHTED BY WALT DISNEY IN 1942.

the last year of the war as sung by Bing Crosby and the Andrews Sisters.

Adding to the list of new wartime Disney characters was the Aracuan, a zany jungle bird who pops up, and in and out of the film—and practically the frame—and who makes a later guest appearance in the film *Melody Time*, and Pablo, the penguin who is unhappy in or out of Antarctica, where he seems to shiver incessantly from the cold. Pablo became a favorite summer character for makers of frozen ice-cream pops. An Andes llama and Pedro, the Mail Plane, both from *Saludos Amigos*, also joined the roster of licensable South American characters with José, the parrot, and Panchito, the rooster, leading the parade.

The green parrot José Carioca appears on one side of a "turn-about" cookie jar produced by the Leeds China Company of Chicago in 1947. When reversed, the other side is his caballero sidekick Donald Duck. In 1946, Donald, Panchito and José were also favorites as glazed ceramic figurines from Evan K. Shaw. Plastic Novelties, Inc., produced Catalin pencil sharpeners with Donald, Panchito and José appliqued on them: and Alladin Color Plastic, Inc., of Los Angeles made charms of Donald, Panchito, and José Carioca for their jewelry line.

Bread campaigns used José Carioca, Panchito, and Pedro, the plane, as end-paper seals, which are collectible Disneyana ephemera today. Attractively packaged 78 rpm record album sets from RCA Victor of songs from both *Saludos Amigos* and *The Three Caballeros* are sought by record collectors and Disneyophiles alike. A Dell four-color comic book by Carl Barks and Jack Hannah entitled *Donald Duck Finds Pirate's Gold,* published in 1942, features a pre–*Three Caballeros* José Carioca–type parrot in the role of a one-legged pirate.

The postwar demand for stories featuring the popular South American parrot was such that Whitman Publishing Company issued the comic book in 1946 as a Better Little Book featuring José on the cover and in the story as a character. Random House published *The Three Caballeros*, told in story form by H. Marion Palmer and illustrated by the Walt Disney Studios. The dustjacket from the 1944 book reads, "Here is a gay new Walt Disney book!" The south of

the border bright and colorful cover and dustjacket of this hardcover book, which sold for one dollar, features Panchito in the center and "Donaldo" and "José" on either side of him. The José Carioca wristwatch, manufactured in 1948 by Ingersoll, sold for $6.95, and this timepiece is now regarded as a hard-to-find but choice item among Disneyana collectors.

ABOVE: WALT DISNEY JIGSAW PUZZLE PRODUCED BY THE JAYMAR SPECIALTY COMPANY, NEW YORK, HAS OVER 300 PIECES WHICH FORM A 14 x 22 INCH PICTURE. FROM THE PEDRO AND GAUCHITO SEGMENTS OF *THE THREE CABALLEROS*, PANCHITO THE ROOSTER TELLS THE STORY OF MEXICAN CHILDREN AT CHRISTMAS, "POSADAS CHILDREN," TO HIS FRIENDS AND COHORTS JOSÉ CARIOCA AND DONALD DUCK, C. 1944. LEFT: PANCHITO, THE GUN-TOTIN' MEXICAN BANDITO CHICKEN FROM *THE THREE CABALLEROS*, GLAZED CERAMIC FIGURINE MADE BY THE EVAN K. SHAW CO., 1946. BELOW: *THE COLD BLOODED PENGUIN* STORYBOOK FROM *THE THREE CABALLEROS*, ADAPTED BY ROBERT EDMUNDS AND ILLUSTRATED BY THE WALT DISNEY STUDIO FOR WALT DISNEY'S LITTLE LIBRARY, SIMON & SCHUSTER, NEW YORK, 1944.

TWENTY

POSTWAR TRAILBLAZERS

SONG OF THE SOUTH

The live-action with animation feature film from Walt Disney that followed in the path established by *The Three Caballeros* was *Song of the South*, Disney's first motion picture in which live actors were used for dramatic impact. Three of the Joel Chandler Harris Uncle Remus tales were brilliantly produced in animation and the wonderful actor James Baskett moved easily into the world of the cartoon characters, playing Uncle Remus and also serving as the voice of Brer Fox. The interrelationships among Brer Fox, Brer Rabbit, and Brer Bear are completely believable, with each character sustaining a uniqueness of character throughout, never turning into parody or becoming overly sentimental as might have happened under a less experienced team. The live-action sequences are combined with the animated characters in a blend skillfully directed by the "cartoon director" Wilfred Jackson and the "photoplay director" Harve Foster. The Disney Studio staff of artists had perfected the animation with live-action players to a new level, far from the days of the Alice comedies. They had made a leap as well in terms of new technique and style from *The Reluctant Dragon* and *The Three Caballeros*.

Luana Patten and Bobby Driscoll are the real-life children who sit on Uncle Remus's lap, entranced by his tall tales of these animal creatures of the Old South. "Zip-a-Dee-Doo-Dah," happily sung by James Baskett, is one of the all-time great

ABOVE: "ZIP-A-DEE-DOO-DAH" SHEET MUSIC FROM *SONG OF THE SOUTH*, SUNG IN THE MOVIE BY JAMES BASKETT AS UNCLE REMUS. MUSIC BY ALLIE WRUBEL AND LYRICS BY RAY GILBERT, SANTLY JOY INC., MUSIC PUBLISHERS, NEW YORK, 1946. OPPOSITE: *SONG OF THE SOUTH* SOUVENIR PROGRAM FROM THE WORLD PREMIERE, NOVEMBER 12, 1946, AT THE FOX THEATER IN ATLANTA, GEORGIA, HOME OF UNCLE REMUS'S CREATOR JOEL CHANDLER HARRIS.

Disney songs, and won an Academy Award for its writers Allie Wrubel and Ray Gilbert. James Baskett won an Oscar as well for his portrayal of Uncle Remus. Other songs from the film are "Sooner or Later," "Everybody Has a Laughing Face," "Uncle Remus Said," and the title song. Toby, the companion to Johnny played by Bobby Driscoll, was played by a young black boy Glenn Leedy, discovered by Disney in a schoolyard in Phoenix, Arizona, and he brings a sense of warmth and good fun to his part. Hattie McDaniel, who won an Oscar for playing Mammy in *Gone With the Wind*, portrays Tempy, the jovial cook in her usual sassy and matter-of-fact manner. The dignified Lucille Watson as Mis' Doshy plays a Southern grande dame.

In an original story by Joel Chandler Harris, Uncle Remus said, ". . . in those days Folks was closer to de Critters . . . and de Critters was closer to de Folks, and if you'll 'scuse me, 'twas better all 'round." This down-on-the-farm with a straight-look-in-the-eye philosophy appealed to Walt Disney, who felt a real kinship with all "critters," whether they be fish or fowl, domesticated or wild. *Song of the South* was a success for Walt Disney on November 12, 1946, when it opened, doing well again at the box office in the 1956 rerelease. Somehow the picture was kept under wraps during the difficult, rage-filled

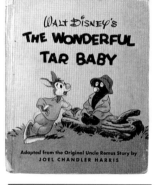

ABOVE: WALT DISNEY'S *THE WONDERFUL TAR BABY*, AS TOLD BY MARION PALMER AND ADAPTED FROM THE ORIGINAL UNCLE REMUS STORY BY JOEL CHANDLER HARRIS. FROM THE DISNEY FILM *SONG OF THE SOUTH*, THIS CHILDREN'S BOOK WAS PUBLISHED BY GROSSET & DUNLAP IN 1946. BELOW: WALT DISNEY'S *BRER RABBIT*, A BETTER LITTLE BOOK PUBLISHED IN 1947 BY WHITMAN PUBLISHING COMPANY. FROM THE FILM *SONG OF THE SOUTH*.

civil rights period of the 1960s, but when it played in theaters again in 1972, it was the most successful rerelease in Disney history at that time. Old Uncle Remus, it seems, as played straight from the heart by James Baskett, could break through the racial barriers.

Products connected to the characters in the film include a Walt Disney's Uncle Remus Game—ZIP from Parker Brothers, school pencil sharpeners of Brer Rabbit, Brer Fox, and Brer Bear, as well as collectible bread paper end seals. Alladin Color Plastic, Inc., of Los Angeles, offered novelty Brer Rabbit jewelry. Ben Cooper, Inc., of New York, offered masquerade costumes of Disney's Brer Rabbit for Halloween. American Pottery Company produced handsome glazed ceramic planter and figurines of Brer Rabbit that are desirable pieces of Disneyana today.

The Wonderful Tar Baby, starring Disney's Brer Rabbit and the Tar Baby, was adapted by Marion Palmer from the original Harris story and published in 1946 by Grosset & Dunlap. *Brer Rabbit* is a Better

Little Book title published in 1947 by Whitman, which reissued the book in 1949, adding an overlay of red ink to the black and white illustrations inside. A giveaway *Brer Rabbit's Secret* premium comic book was issued by K. K Publications and there was an *Uncle Remus Stories* Giant Golden Book as well as an *Uncle Remus* Little Golden Book. The attractive collector album *Song of the South* on 78 rpm records is from RCA Victor. Of course, Brer Bear was perfect as a teddy bear, and there was also Brer Fox and Brer Rabbit stuffed dolls on the marketplace. The handsome, colorful 1946 program from the opening in Atlanta, Georgia, following in the footsteps of that other spectacle, *Gone With the Wind*, is among the prized collectibles from this film.

MAKE MINE MUSIC

Three other Disney films of the postwar era were fundamentally "package" films. Disney had learned from *The Three Caballeros* and *Saludos Amigos* that he could integrate short sequences at a low cost and present them in one feature film. Following World War II, Walt Disney rethought, reorganized, and regrouped the studio. Returning war veterans were put back to work on these new projects. One of the package concepts that resulted was *Make Mine Music* which opened just prior to *Song of the South* on August 15, 1946.

The picture featured a delightful new animated character called Willie the Whale, "the Whale who wanted to sing at the Met," vocalized by Nelson Eddy and included the sounds of the Andrews sisters, Benny Goodman and his orchestra, Dinah Shore, Jerry Colonna, the Pied Pipers, Andy Russell, The King's Men, and the Ken Darby Chorus. The "Blue Bayou" section in this film utilized animation originally to have been included in *Fantasia* with the accompanying music being Debussy's "Claire de Lune." "The Peter and the Wolf" sequence has music by Sergei Prokofiev.

Fun and Fancy Free

Fun and Fancy Free is a live-action and animation picture consisting of *Mickey and the Beanstalk* and *Bongo* that included ventriloquist Edgar Bergen with his dummy cohorts Charlie McCarthy and Mortimer Snerd. It opened September 27, 1947. Cliff Edwards, Dinah Shore, Luana Patten (originally introduced in *Song of the South*), and the

CAMPBELL GRANT ILLUSTRATED *MICKEY AND THE BEANSTALK*, BASED ON THE STORY IN THE DISNEY FILM *FUN AND FANCY FREE* (1947). CHILDREN'S STORYBOOK, GROSSET & DUNLAP, NEW YORK, 1947.

Dinning Sisters add their charm and their various talents to this musical film. "Mickey and the Beanstalk" is a first-rate animated segment with participation from Donald Duck and Goofy.

The character of Bongo, the wonder bear, introduced by Jiminy Cricket, was licensed to a number of manufacturers. Bongo storybooks and paintbooks and an Ingersoll watch manufactured in 1948 were topped off by the amusing Bongo and Lulubelle (his girlfriend) free-standing stuffed dolls from the Gund Manufacturing Company of New York. There was also a *Bongo* Columbia Records 78 rpm album featuring Dinah Shore and an orchestra

conducted by Sonny Burke. *Bongo*, based on a story by Sinclair Lewis, was rereleased in 1971 but failed to garner audiences. "Mickey and the Beanstalk," however, stands on its own as a short subject; and was published as a storybook, with picture illustrations by Campbell Grant, by Grosset & Dunlap in 1947 and by Whitman in their Story Hour series in 1948.

Melody Time

Opening on May 27, 1948, *Melody Time* was a film with seven live-action and/or animated segments. Luana Patten starred again with Bobby Driscoll and Roy Rogers and the Sons of the Pioneers in introducing the "Pecos Bill" segment, and the voices of the Andrews Sisters were heard in

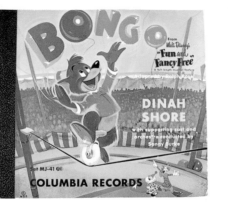

LEFT: 78 RPM THREE-RECORD ALBUM FROM COLUMBIA RECORDS HAS DINAH SHORE NARRATING THE ANIMATED SHORT *BONGO* FROM *FUN AND FANCY FREE*. ADAPTED BY RALPH ROSE, WITH SUPPORTING CAST AND ORCHESTRA CONDUCTED BY SONNY BURKE. RIGHT: *PECOS BILL* (FROM *MELODY TIME*) 78 RPM THREE-RECORD ALBUM FEATURING ROY ROGERS AND THE SONS OF THE PIONEERS, RCA VICTOR, 1948.

La Foire aux Chansons (*Melody Time*) movie poster printed by Les Ateliers, Belgium, in 1948, for RKO Radio Film. Clockwise from left: Donald Duck, Ethel Smith the organist, the Aracuan, José Carioca, Pecos Bill, and Little Toot.

"Little Toot." Dennis Day was the voice of Johnny Appleseed, and the voices and music of Buddy Clark, Frances Langford, Fred Waring and His Pennsylvanians, and Freddy Martin and His Orchestra were heard in other segments. A particularly happy live-action "Blame It on the Samba" has Ethel Smith, the amazing organist, dancing frenetically in her 1940s platform "wedgies" with those two south-of-the-border animated caballeros, José Carioca and Donald Duck.

So Dear to My Heart

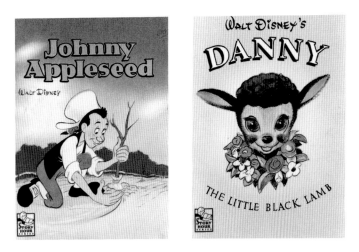

So Dear To My Heart opened on January 19, 1949, starring Burl Ives, Bobby Driscoll, Luana Patten, Beulah Bondi, and Harry Carey. This dramatic and sentimental picture, unlike the previous postwar Disney features, is actually live-action with only a minimum of animation. Walt Disney loved this film, which he said reminded him of his own boyhood years on the farm. Though So Dear to My Heart did not make a lot of money for the Disney Studio, it did have a great deal of nostalgic charm in the manner of a number of other family-style pictures made in the 1940s like State Fair and Meet Me in St. Louis. Musical highlights in the film include Burl Ives singing "Lavender Blue" and "Billy Boy," the latter a duet with Beulah Bondi. Critically well received, So Dear to My Heart helped pave the way for more live-action Disney pictures.

The Adventures of Ichabod and Mr. Toad

The Adventures of Ichabod and Mr. Toad was released on October 5, 1949, and is the last of the 1940s full-feature films done entirely in animation. The two sequences in one movie have the "Mr. Toad" section based on Kenneth Grahame's The Wind in the Willows narrated by Basil Rathbone, and the "Ichabod" section based on Washington Irving's The Legend of Sleepy Hollow narrated by Bing Crosby. The two half-hour segments that comprise this film make for a satisfying full-length animated feature; both have been reissued separately and together to admiring audiences and critical reaction. Character merchandise from this film is scant; but song sheets, storybooks, movie posters, lobby cards, cels, and other ephemera are always desirable to those who seek out oddities in the field of Disneyana.

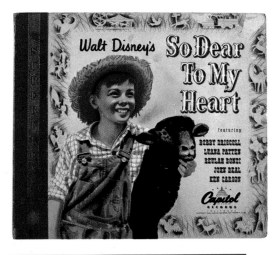

78 rpm four-record album of So Dear To My Heart, narrated by John Beal and featuring members of the original cast, including Bobby Driscoll (pictured on the cover), Luana Patten, Beulah Bondi, John Beal, and Ken Carson. Capitol Records, Hollywood, Calif., 1949.

TWENTY ONE

BABY-BOOMER DISNEYANA
(THE 1950s)

On February 15, 1950, *Cinderella* had its world premiere; it was Walt Disney's first full-length completely animated feature since *Bambi* in 1942, and it was released to great acclaim, earning the studio over $4 million in its first run.

The promotional campaign for character merchandise for *Cinderella* had already been launched by Kay Kamen during 1949. On October 28, 1949, Kamen and his wife were on an Air France Constellation flying from Paris to New York and died along with thirty-seven other passengers and eleven crew members when the plane went off course due to poor weather conditions and visibility. The plane was just ninety miles from its refuel stop in Santa Maria in the Azores when it crashed into the 3,500-foot Mount Algarvia on Sâo Miguel Island.

Kay Kamen was fifty-seven when he died, and his wife Kate was forty-two. He had just signed a new seven-year contract with Walt Disney Productions. He was on his way to New York for a connecting flight to Chicago where he was to attend a Trimfoot Shoe Convention at which a line of Cinderella shoes was being presented. Though Kamen was not to attend the film's premiere, the last of the great Kamen character merchandise catalogs, 1949–1950, helped to sell *Cinderella* and the cast of characters that included two new mice called Gus and Jaq to the merchants. With Kay Kamen no longer at the helm after seventeen years, all licensing matters were given over to a new Character

RIGHT: FOURTEEN-INCH-LONG "MOUSEGETAR JR." WITH WIND-UP MUSICAL BOX THAT PLAYS THE OFFICIAL MOUSKETEER SONG. MADE OF BLACK PLASTIC BY MATTEL IN 1955. OPPOSITE: MATTEL PRODUCED THIS MICKEY MOUSE CLUB NEWSREEL TOY PROJECTOR IN 1956. IT CAME WITH A SOUND RECORD AND SLIDES, AND IS SHOWN WITH ITS ORIGINAL BOX.

Merchandise Division, developed at that strategic point by Walt Disney Productions.

The Character Merchandise Division didn't miss a beat licensing new products for the animated features *Alice In Wonderland*, which premiered on July 28, 1951, and *Peter Pan*, released on February 5, 1953. *20,000 Leagues Under the Sea*, released on December 23, 1954, was a live-action film based on the Jules Verne novel. The 1955 release of the all-in-color feature-length film *Davy Crockett, King of the Wild Frontier*, starring Fess Parker as Davy, sparked Disney's first mass-market character merchandising campaign for live-action films. This film was a result of the popular series that had first appeared on television in late 1954.

In the early 1930s, Roy and Walt Disney had already become aware of the potential of television. Mickey Mouse cartoons were used in early tests of transmitting equipment, and Disney held all television rights

ABOVE: SHEET MUSIC FOR "A DREAM IS A WISH YOUR HEART MAKES," FROM *CINDERELLA*. WALT DISNEY MUSIC COMPANY, BURBANK, CALIF., COPYRIGHT 1948. BELOW: INSPIRED BY WALT DISNEY'S *ALICE IN WONDERLAND*, THIS GREETING CARD HAS THE WHITE RABBIT EXCLAIMING, "I'M LATE! I'M LATE! FORGOT YOUR BIRTHDAY DATE" TO ALICE. MARKED "A VIRA CREATION, MAMARONECK, NEW YORK, 1951." BOTTOM RIGHT: DAVY CROCKETT TOY WATCH ON ORIGINAL CARD.

to his films. This was to his advantage when ABC expressed interest in producing a series called *Disneyland*. Part of the understanding that was reached called for ABC to invest in Disney's theme-park dream, which would have the same name as the series—Disneyland.

The *Disneyland* television series began in 1954, and the phenomenally popular *Davy Crockett* emerged a winner. Originally Walt Disney had thought of developing Daniel Boone or Johnny Appleseed as popular American folk heroes; but when Davy Crockett was chosen, he became an immediate folk hero for children of the Eisenhower era. "The Ballad of Davy Crockett" was a runaway record hit, selling 10 million copies. With 52 million TV viewers, Fess Parker as Davy Crockett joined the ranks of Hopalong Cassidy, Roy Rogers, Gene Autry, and to a lesser extent Guy Madison, as Wild Bill Hickok, all of whom had top Wild West cowboy series. All of

these actors were involved in an avalanche of merchandise connected to their shows. (Included in this was Howdy Doody, the TV "cowboy marionette.")

Fess Parker was paid $50,000 to tour Australia for ten days as Davy in his coonskin hat, and as much as $10,000 for a one-shot appearance in a parade or at a baseball game. Davy Crockett merchandise flooded the fifties marketplace and included toy guns and rifles, fur hats with raccoon tails, suede fringe frontier jackets and pants, litho-on-metal lunch boxes with thermoses (from the Liberty National Corp. of New York), Davy guitars, penknife sets (Imperial Knife Co., Inc.), toys, games, children's night lamps, storybooks. pullwagons, camper tents, schoolbags, cookie jars, cups, mugs, pinback buttons, watches, and clocks.

Another western cowboy character to shine in a Disney television series was *Zorro*, a half-hour, once a week program, which ran from 1957 to 1959. Guy Williams played the dashing Zorro, the masked vaquero in black who had been played on screen by Douglas Fairbanks, Sr., and

Tyrone Power. The series boasted 35 million viewers during its two-year run and like the Davy Crockett merchandise, there were Zorro comics, hats, masks, swords, capes, whip sets, guns, target games, rings, lariats, lunch boxes, and other merchandise associated with this popular character. Davy Crockett and Zorro collectibles are sought after not only by Wild West and cowboyana collectors but by Disney enthusiasts as well.

After three years of work at a cost of $4 million, *Lady and the Tramp*, the first Disney film to be made in Cinemascope, was released on June 16, 1955. Character merchandise for *Lady and the Tramp* was lined up well in advance of this film's release by O. B. Johnston of the Character Merchandising Division, who had learned from Kay Kamen that items already in the stores would help the film itself make more money. Advance advertising campaigns and some merchandise items were being distributed as early as one year prior to the release of *Lady and*

the Tramp. By 1955, the Merchandising Division had developed new sales strategies, including every conceivable kind of tie-in, and even utilizing more established characters like Mickey, Minnie, Donald, and Goofy to help promote the current film on the market, as well as some of the merchandise connected to it.

O. B. Johnston had been with the Disney organization since 1934 and had worked with Kay Kamen. He supervised merchandising in Burbank for Walt Disney Productions in 1955, while in New York the

Merchandising Division was managed by Vincent H. Jefferds, who presided over six sales representatives and a staff of artists. Like Kamen's business headquarters, Jefferds's New York offices were close to the centers of the toy, novelty, and children's clothing industries. As early as 1951, following Kamen's death, there were three merchandising offices in the United States. By 1962, eighteen full-time merchandising representatives covered twenty-three foreign countries. When O. B. Johnston retired, Jefferds took over his position, and William H. G. "Pete" Smith assumed Jefferds's role in New York.

Work on *Sleeping Beauty*, a fairy tale meant to follow in the footsteps of *Cinderella*, had begun in 1952, and the film was released on January 29,

LEFT: DRINKING GLASS TUMBLER IS IMPRINTED WITH SCENES FROM DAVY CROCKETT'S LIFE, C. 1955. RIGHT: FESS PARKER WAS THE MODEL FOR THIS GLAZED CERAMIC DAVY CROCKETT COOKIE JAR, 1955.

1959. By 1958, merchandise for *Sleeping Beauty* was already entering the marketplace. The cost of producing *Sleeping*

Beauty was $6 million—a staggering amount at that time. Though not a financial success in its initial release, appreciation has grown for its artfulness and collectibles from *Sleeping Beauty* are sought after today, but not with the enthusiasm for earlier Disneyana. This would also hold true for the film *101 Dalmatians*, released on January 25, 1961; it also has an appreciable number of collectibles. Three years in the making, and with a release date in the sixties, this animated feature may still be regarded as a fifties-style film. At a cost of $4 million and with 300 animators working on it, it represents to some the

end of the Golden Age.

After *Sleeping Beauty* and *101 Dalmatians*, Disney entered the Mary Poppins era: and to be sure, collectors will easily find a vast array of Mary Poppins merchandise. However, there do not seem to be a great number of Disneyana collectors who focus on—and collect—Mary Poppins memorabilia.

Much of the best merchandise of the 1950s, avidly collected by baby boomers, was connected to and inspired by the second *Mickey Mouse Club*, which had its network television premiere on October 3, 1955, on ABC. During the first three years, the Monday-to-Friday one-hour black and white program was shown to kids after school from 5:00 to 6:00 P.M. Following this three-year period, the show used a half-hour format through 1959, when the popular series came to an end. The show also had great success when it was re-issued from 1962 to 1965

throughout America and in Spain, Italy, France, Japan, Germany, Australia, Finland, Mexico, Switzerland, and Canada, as well as many South American countries, although in these countries sometimes only portions were shown. In 1977 *The New Mickey Mouse Club*, a half-hour program strongly reminiscent of the 1950s program, was videotaped and distributed in fifty-four markets.

Disney issued a quarterly periodical associated with the 1950s television show called *Walt Disney's Mickey Mouse Club Magazine*, in which many of the feature articles focused on the young Mouseketeers stars—Annette Funicello, Doreen Tracey, Jay-Jay Solari, Dennis Day, Sherry Allen, Bobby Burgess, Margene Storey, Lonnie Burr, Eileen Diamond, Larry Larsen, Tommy Cole, Cheryl Holdridge, Darlene Gillespie, Sharon Baird, Karen Pendleton, "Cubby" O'Brien, and, as chief Mouseketeer, Jimmie Dodd. This magazine had a peak circulation of 400,000 the first two years, and in 1957 its title was changed to *Walt Disney Magazine* when it became bimonthly.

Mickey Mouse went from becoming a movie-star mouse to a full-fledged television star on the Mouseketeer TV show. It

was as if this second career gave Mickey and his creator, Walt Disney, a further push into cartoon land immortality. The club show ended with the Mouseketeers leading the kids at home with the song "M-i-c-k-e-y M-o-u-s-e!" spelling Mickey's name out over and over again for millions of viewers. Mickey Mouse Club merchandise abounded in the five-and-dimes, department stores, and gift shops, including T-shirts, Mickey Mouse hats with ears, records, balloons, banners, pinback Mouseketeer buttons, and a number of Little Golden Books dedicated to the *Mickey Mouse Club* and the Mouseketeers. There were several Mickey Mouse Club coloring books, a *Mickey Mouse Club Giant Funtime Coloring Book*, a *Mickey Mouse Club Scrap Book*, a *Mickey Mouse Dot-to-Dot Coloring Book*, a *Mickey Mouse Stamp Book*, a *Mousekartoon Coloring Book*, *Walt Disney's Mickey Mouse Club Annual*, *Walt Disney's Mickey Mouse Club Box of 12 Books to Color*, and *Walt Disney's Big Book*. Recordings included "Songs for the Holidays by the Mouseketeers," "Songs from the Mickey Mouse Club Serials," "27 New Songs from the Mickey Mouse Club TV Show," "Walt

TOP: MICKEY MOUSE SCHOOL LUNCHBOX. COLOR LITHOGRAPHY ON METAL, C. 1958. **ABOVE**: REVERSE SIDE OF THE SAME LUNCHBOX SHOWS DONALD DUCK WITH HIS NEPHEWS.

DISNEYLAND FERRIS WHEEL FEATURES A MECHANICAL BELL THAT RINGS AS THE WHEEL GOES AROUND, AND A WINDUP HANDLE IN MICKEY MOUSE'S NOSE. COLOR-LITHOGRAPHED METAL TOY MANUFACTURED BY J. CHIEN & CO., NEWARK, N.J., C. 1955.

Disney's Song Fest," "Mickey's Big Show starring Donald Duck and Clara Cluck," and "We're The Mouseketeers."

Annette Funicello was the most popular Mouseketeer, receiving as many as 6,000 fan letters a month, and a number of books featured her alone on the cover. These included Annette coloring books, cut-out doll portfolios, comics, and boxed paper dolls, all promoted between 1956 and 1967. Mystery stories like *Annette and the Mystery at Smuggler's Cove*, *Annette: Desert Mystery Inn*, and *Annette: Mystery at Moonstone Bay* had a great success with children.

Some of the multitudinous items that featured the jovial fifties-style Mickey Mouse included the Mousegetar (23 inches) and the Mousegetar Jr. (14 inches) from Mattel, Inc.; Mickey Mouse Club white plastic dinner sets, cups, plates and bowls from Molded Plastics, Inc., of Cleveland, Ohio; a Mouseketeer Western outfit by L. M. Eddy Manufacturing Company, Inc., of Framingham, Massachusetts, which included a hat, tie, badge, belt, two guns, and two holsters; a Mickey Mouse Club Explorer's Club outfit; and a Mickey Mouse bandleader outfit. An attractive Mickey Mouse Club tool chest was manufactured with a variety of tools by the American Toy and Furniture Company of Chicago. The famous black mouse ears

LEFT: MICKEY MOUSE TIN LITHOGRAPH WINDUP TOY WITH FELT EARS AND PLASTIC TUBULAR TAIL. MADE IN JAPAN FOR LINEMAR CO., C. 1950. RIGHT: GOOFY TIN LITHOGRAPH WINDUP ACTION TOY. WHEN WOUND THE TOY WOBBLES AND THE RUBBER TAIL SPINS. LINEMAR CO., C. 1950.

in hard-cotton felt were set on a plastic earmuff-type band called "Mouseketeer Ears" and stamped on each ear "Walt Disney Prod. Mouseketeers." These ears were made by the Empire Plastic Corporation of Tarboro, North Carolina. Hats with ears and ears with plastic bands continue to be manufactured and sold as new collectibles to this day. Many of these Mickey Mouse Club items were offered at and promoted by Disneyland in the 1950s.

Disneyland opened July 17, 1955, consisting of Main Street, Adventure Land, Frontierland, Tomorrowland, and Fantasyland. Toys from Disneyland include a Disneyland Ferris Wheel made by J. Chien Company of Newark, New Jersey, which features a mechanical bell, six gondolas,

and an image of Mickey dead center. A Disneyland Melody Player Music Box with musical wheels is a fine Disneyland collectible. Strombecker Company wooden toys sold at Disneyland include a Casey Jr. train set and a Mickey Mouse bus with Donald Duck. With the advent of television, Davy Crockett, Zorro, the Mickey Mouse Club and the Mouseketeers, and the accompanying merchandising in full swing—and Disneyland opening to resounding success in Anaheim, California— the Disney Studios were on the way to becoming an empire. There would be no limit to their success, and it was all due to M-i-c-k-e-y M-o-u-s-e!

SELECTED BIBLIOGRAPHY

Abrams, Robert, and John Canemaker. *Treasures of Disney Animation Art*. New York: Abbeville Press, 1982.

Bailey, Adrian. *Walt Disney's World of Fantasy*. New York: Everest House, 1982.

Bain, David, and Bruce Harris, eds. *Mickey Mouse, Fifty Happy Years*. New York: Harmony Books, 1978.

Becker, Stephen. *Comic Art in America*. New York: Simon & Schuster, 1959.

Blitz, Marcia. *Donald Duck*. New York: Harmony Books, 1979.

Buxton, Frank, and Bill Owen. *The Big Broadcast— 1920–1950*. New York: Avon Books, 1966.

Culhane, John. *Walt Disney's Fantasia*. New York: Harry N. Abrams, 1983.

Eyles, Allen. *Walt Disney's Three Little Pigs*. New York: Simon & Schuster, 1987.

Feild, Robert D. *The Art of Walt Disney*. London: William Collins, 1947. New York: Macmillan, 1942.

Finch, Christopher. *The Art of Walt Disney*. New York: Harry N. Abrams, 1973.

Geis, Darlene, ed. *Walt Disney's Treasury of Silly Symphonies*. New York: Harry N. Abrams, 1981.

Hake, Ted, and Russ King. *Collectible Pin Back Buttons 1896–1986*. York, PA: Hake's Americana & Collectibles, 1991.

Heide, Robert, and John Gilman. *Cartoon Collectibles*. New York: Doubleday, 1983.

Hollis, Richard, and Brian Sibley. *Snow White and the Seven Dwarfs and the Making of the Classic Film*. New York: Simon & Schuster, 1987.

Kitahara, Teruhisa. *Yesterday's Toys—Celluloid Dolls, Clowns & Animals*. San Francisco: Chronicle Books, 1989.

Kurtz, Bruce D., ed. *Haring, Warhol, Disney*. Munich: Prestel-Verlag and the Phoenix Art Museum, 1992.

Lesser, Robert. *A Celebration of Comic Art & Memorabilia*. New York: Hawthorn Books, 1975.

Maltin, Leonard. *The Disney Films*. New York: Crown, 1973.

Morra-Yoe, Janet, and Craig Yoe. *The Art of Mickey Mouse*. New York: Hyperion, 1991.

Munsey, Cecil. *Disneyana*. New York: Hawthorn Books, 1974.

Neary, Kevin, and Dave Smith. *The Ultimate Disney Trivia Book*. New York: Hyperion, 1992.

O'Brien, Flora, ed. *Donald Duck: 50 Years of Happy Frustration*. Tucson, AZ: HP Books, 1984.

———. *Goofy: The Good Sport*. Tucson, AZ: HP Books, 1985.

Overstreet, Robert M. *The Official Comic Book Price Guide*. Cleveland, TN: Overstreet Productions, 1993.

Peary, Gerald, and Danny Peary, eds. *The American Animated Cartoon—A Critical Anthology*. New York: E.P. Dutton, 1980.

Phillips, Cabell. *From the Crash to the Blitz— 1929–1939. The New York Times Chronicle of American Life*. New York: Macmillan, 1969.

Rawls, Walton. *Disney Dons Dogtags—The Best of Disney Military Insignia from World War II*. New York: Abbeville Publishing Group, 1992.

Shine, Bernard C. *Mickey Mouse Memorabilia—The Vintage Years 1928–1938*. New York: Harry N. Abrams, 1986.

Siegel, Alan A. *Smile—A Picture History of Olympic Park—1887–1964*. Plainfield, NJ: American Impressions, 1987.

Stern, Michael. *Disney Collectibles*. Paducah, KY: Collectors Books, 1989.

Taylor, Deems. *Walt Disney's Fantasia*. New York: Simon & Schuster, 1940.

Thomas, Bob. *Disney's Art of Animation—From Mickey Mouse to Beauty and the Beast*. New York: Hyperion, 1991.

Thomas, Frank, and Ollie Johnston. *Disney Animation, the Illusion of Life*. New York: Abbeville Press, 1981.

———. *Too Funny for Words—Disney's Greatest Sight Gags*. New York: Abbeville Press, 1987.

Tombusch, Tom. *Tomart's Illustrated Disneyana Catalog and Price Guide*, 4 volumes. Dayton, OH: Tomart Publications, 1985.

Waugh, Coulton. *The Comics*. New York: Macmillan, 1947.

The Disney Poster—The Animated Film Classics from Mickey Mouse to Aladdin. New York: Hyperion, 1993.

"In Reiche der Micky Maus—Walt Disney in Deutschland—1927-1945." Potsdam: Filmmuseum, 1991.

SELECTED MAGAZINES

Carr, Harry. "The Only Unpaid Movie Star—Mickey Mouse." *American Magazine*, March 1931.

Disney, Walt. "Merry Christmas, Mickey and Minnie Mouse." *Delineator*, December 1932.

Evans, Delight. "An Open Letter to Walt Disney from Delight Evans." *Screenland*, June 1934.

Jamison, Jack. "Around the World with Mickey Mouse." *The Rotarian*, May 1934.

Johnston, Alva. "Mickey Mouse." *Woman's Home Companion*, July 1934.

McEvoy, J. P. "Mickey Mouse Squeals." *Country Gentleman*, March 1934.

Miller, Diane Disney. "My Dad, Walt Disney." *Saturday Evening Post*, November 17, 1956.

Skolsky, Sidney. "Mickey Mouse." *Cosmopolitan*, February 1934.

Syring, Richard H. "One of the Greats." *Silver Screen*, November 1932.

CATALOG

Mickey Mouse, the First Fifty Years. Department of Film of the Museum of Modern Art, New York, 1978.

INDEX

Hey, Fellers! NEW MICKEY MOUSE and DONALD DUCK TIES!

hurdy-gurdy toys, 13, 14, 53, *54*
Hurter, Albert, 133

I

ice cream, 42, 97, *103*, 159, *159*, 160, 178
Ingersoll-Waterbury Clock Company, 8–9, 10, 42, 62–63, *62*, *63*, 65, *65*, 116, 129, 135–36, *136*, 152, 163, 170, 179, 183
ink blotters, 96, *96*
"It's the Animal in Me," 123
Ivener, Ivy, 26
Ivener, Ruth, 26, *37*, 47
Iwerks, Ub, 29, 30, 38, 105

J

jackets, *70*
jam jars, 93
Jazz Singer, The, 30, *30*
Jefferds, Vincent H., 189
jewelry, 152, 163, 182
   charm, 60, *73*, 152, 163, 179
Jiminy Cricket, 10, 15, 18, 157, 158, *158*, 160, *161*, 162, *163*, 163, 175, 183
Johnny Appleseed, *185*
Johnston, O. B., 189
Johnston, Ollie, 146
Jolson, Al, 30, *30*
José Carioca, 15, 46, 130, 174, 175, 176, *176*, 178–79, *178*, *184*, 185
Julia, James D., 27
Justice, Bill, 24

K

Kamen, George, 42, 118
Kamen, Herman "Kay," 7, 9, 24, 26, *37*, 39–47, *40*, *41*, *44*, *86*, 93, 96–97, *103*, 108, 112, 115, *115*, 116, 126, 130, 134, 141, 147–48, 159, 169, 187, 189
Kay Kamen Ltd., 42–43, *43*, 47, 93, 94, 118, 138, 141, 154
Karp, Bob, 127
Kimball, Ward, 9–10, 12, 13, 53, 157, 168
King Features, 38
"King Neptune," *142*
Kneitel, Kenny, 11
Knickerbocker Toy Company, 11, 13, 14, *20*, 52, *52*, *53*, 128, 134, *134*, 137, *137*, 143, 150, 162, 168–69

L

Lady and the Tramp, 15, 189
lamps, 76, 128, 138–39, 151, 162
Lampwick, 158, 159, 160
Latin America, 176–79
Laurel and Hardy, *27*, 134
lead figurines, *8*
Leaf, Munro, 142, *143*
Leedy, Glenn, 181
Lesser, Robert, 13, 25
Levy, William Banks, 38–39, 42, 53
Liberty, 118, *119*, 126, *161*
Library of Congress, 23
Lichtenstein, Roy, 11, 23
Life, 9, *9*, 13
lighters, 53, *55*
Lincoln Center, 13, *13*
Lindbergh, Charles, 30
linoleum, 77
Lionel Corporation, 9, 10, 19, *20*, 53–57, *54*, *56*, 117, 128–29, *129*
Little Red Hen, The, 127
Little Red Riding Hood, 14, 18, 29, 134, 135, *135*, 139, 141
   dolls and figurines, 137, *137*, 143
London, Gene, 11
Lulubelle, 183
lunch boxes, 152, *192*
"Lunch Box Heroes," 24
lunch kits, 101

M

McCall's Company, 50, 77, 118
McDaniel, Hattie, 181
David McKay Company, 105–7, *106*, *107*, 129, 135, *135*
Macy's, *86*, 87
Mad Doctor, The, 26
magazines, 118, *118*, 119
   Mickey Mouse, *34*, 42, 46, 47, 105, *105*, 115–18, *115*, *116*, *118*, *119*, *125*, 130, *130*, *136*, *157*, 190
Make Mine Music, 182 83
Malce, Michael, 11
Maltin, Leonard, 178
maps, 99–100
marionettes, 150, 162
marmalade, 96
Mary, Queen of England, 35
Mary Poppins, 190
masks, 18, *34*, 90, *90*, *131*, 138, 139, 148, 171

Pinocchio, *159*, 160, 163, *163*
   Snow White and the Seven Dwarfs, 148, *148*, *149*
matchbooks, *174*
Max Hare, 94, *97*, 141
Melody Time, 178, 183–85, *183*, *184*, *185*
Merman, Ethel, 123
merry-go-round figures, *17*, 19
Mickey Mouse, 15, *27*, 37, 67, 134, *141*, *142*, *143*, *157*, 189, 190–91
   in *Fantasia*, *164*, 164–65, 166, 167
   fiftieth birthday of, *9*, 13, *13*, 23, *106*
   image change of, 11–12, 125–26
   movies, 29–31, 33–35, *34*, 37, 38, 39
   origin of, 29–31
   in *Steamboat Willie*, 29, *29*, 30–31
Mickey Mouse and Minnie Mouse merchandise, 7–123, *7*, *9*, *10*, *11*, *12*, *17*, *20*, *23*, *29*, *31*, 37, *44*, *54*, *56*, *59*, *60*, *68*, *69*, *70*, *73*, *74*, *76*, *83*, *84*, *85*, *86*, *87*, *89*, *91*, *102*, 127, 129, *131*, *174*, *178*, *187*, 189, *192*, 193
   auctions of, 24–25, 26–27
   automotive radiator caps, *10*
   for babies and small children, 67–70, *67*, *68*, *69*
   beach toys, 84, *84*, *85*
   books, *86*, 105–13, *105*, *106*, *107*, *108*, *109*, *112*, *113*
   bread, 42, *45*, 94, 118, 154
   buttons, *13*, *33*, *42*, *45*, *75*, *96*, *190*
   circus train, 10, *20*, 53–56, *54*
   clothing and accessories, 12, 70–73, *70*, *72*, *73*, 88, 89, 117
   dolls, 8, 11, 12, 13, *20*, 35, *37*, 39, *39*, 49, *49*, 50–53, *50*, *52*, *53*, 68, 91, 105, *146*
   figurines and toothbrush holders, *4*, 8, 12, 18, *18*, *19*, *25*, 38, 57–59, *57*, *58*, *59*, 76, 127
   food products, 42, 45–46, *45*, 93–97, *93*, *94*, *95*, *96*, *97*, *103*, 117, 118
   games and targets, 79–83, *79*, *80*, *81*, *83*, 89
   Halloween, 90, *90*
   handcars, 9, 10, 19, 56, 128–29
   housewares, 67–69, 73–77, *74*, *75*, *76*, 77
   lead figurines, *8*

magazines, *34*, 42, 46, 47, 105, *105*, 115–18, *115*, *116*, *118*, *119*, *125*, 130, *130*, *136*, *157*, 190
masks, 18, *34*, 90, *90*
museum exhibits of, 23–24, 25–26
music, 117–18, 121–23, *121*, *122*, *123*
radios, *4*, *75*, 76, *76*, 77
school-related, 99–101, *99*, *100*, *101*, *102*, *103*
timepieces, 8–9, 10, 13, 18, *19*, 42, 62–65, *62*, *63*, *65*, 116, 129
toys, 79–91
trains, 10, 19, *20*, 53–57, *54*, *56*, 117
watches and clocks, 62–65, *62*, *63*, 65
windup toys, 12, 13, 14, *55*, *123*, *193*
winter, 88–89, *88*, *89*
World War II and, 173, 174, *174*, 175, 176
Mickey and the Beanstalk, 183, *183*
Mickey & Co., 12, 70
Mickey Mouse, *112*
Mickey Mouse Alphabet Book, A, 109
"Mickey Mouse Book," 105, *105*
Mickey Mouse Book for Coloring, 88
Mickey Mouse Club, 190–93, *290*
Mickey Mouse Clubs, 15, 18, 24, 33–34, *33*, *34*, 37, 42, 118, 121, 138, *187*, 190–93, *290*
Mickey Mouse-eum, 17–20, *17*, *18*, *19*, *20*, 23, 76
"Mickey Mouse" gas masks, 17–18, 176
Mickey Mouse Has a Party, 109
Mickey Mouse Illustrated Movie Stories, 107, *107*

THIS IS MICKEY MOUSE SPEAKING!

AUTHOR ROBERT HEIDE WITH RARE FRENCH 1930S
ART DECO MICKEY MOUSE LAMP.

ROBERT HEIDE was born in Irvington, New Jersey, the town where the Lionel Corporation produced the famous Mickey Mouse Handcar, which saved the company from bankruptcy in the Depression. One of his early childhood memories is of his father, Ludwig, transferring a Mickey Mouse decal onto a handmade wood-shop magazine rack. It was his first encounter with the "Mouse"; and thereafter he became one of Mickey's greatest fans. He recalls that the dime stores of Irvington and downtown Newark, New Jersey, the Woolworth's, McCrory's, and Kresge's were always filled with Mickey Mouse and Donald Duck toys, and these happy five-and-dime memories have led him to seek out and collect Mickey in his adult years.

Educated at Northwestern University, he later studied theater with Stella Adler, Uta Hagen, and Harold Clurman in New York. As a Manhattan-based playwright, his published plays include *Moon, Why Tuesday Never Has a Blue Monday*, and *At War with the Mongols*. His play *The Bed*, which was performed at the world-renowned Caffe Cino in Greenwich Village, was made into a feature-length split-screen film by Andy Warhol. Warhol also filmed the script created by Heide for superstar Edie Sedgwick, *The Death of Lupe Velez* (released as *Lupe*). His recent plays, produced by TNC—Theater for the New City, include *Tropical Fever in Key West* and *Crisis of Identity*. His interest in pop art and American popular culture led him to write numerous articles on a variety of subjects for leading periodicals, including the *Village Voice* and the *Soho News*. He has coauthored eight books with John Gilman. His favorite cartoon character is Mickey Mouse.

AUTHOR JOHN GILMAN GETS A HUG FROM MINNIE
MOUSE AT WALT DISNEY WORLD, FLORIDA.

JOHN GILMAN is a photographer and writer and the author, with Robert Heide, of eight books on popular culture in twentieth-century America. He spent his childhood years in Waikiki, Honolulu, Hawaii. His father, LaSelle Gilman, was the author of several adventure novels and film scripts set in the Far East, and was also a columnist for the *Honolulu Advertiser*, where he covered the bombing of Pearl Harbor. John lived out his youth in San Francisco and Grosse Pointe, Michigan, later settling in New York City. As an actor, he appeared in off-off Broadway productions at the Caffe Cino, the Judson Church, Cafe LaMama, and Theater for the New City. He worked at several publications in New York, and was executive director of the American Society of Magazine Photographers. He has contributed articles and photographs to the *New York Daily News*, the *Village Voice, Antiques World, Portfolio, Collectors' Showcase, Beauty Digest*, and other periodicals. As a collectibles' specialist and a consultant for a number of organizations and museums, his interests run the gamut from 1950s automobiles to movie posters to cowboy heroes to comic characters to Big Little Books and the 1920s, 1930s, and 1940s novels of Edgar Wallace, James M. Cain, Sax Rohmer, and Earl Derr Biggers. Several years ago he was pleased to make a significant trade with a neighborhood antiques dealer—one very large, supposedly decorative and valuable majolica pig in exchange for a very small bisque Mickey Mouse toothbrush holder with a movable arm. He's never regretted it.